*The Communist Tide
in Latin America*

The Communist Tide in Latin America

A Selected Treatment

Edited by DONALD L. HERMAN

THE UNIVERSITY OF TEXAS AT AUSTIN

International Standard Book Number 0–292–71007–0
Library of Congress Catalog Card Number 72–11900
Copyright © 1973 by The University of Texas
All Rights Reserved
Printed in the United States of America
These essays first appeared in *The Texas Quarterly*
XV NO. 1 (1972).

Contents

PREFACE

Martin C. Needler

THIS IS AN APPROPRIATE TIME FOR A NEW APPRAISAL OF THE NATURE OF COM-
munism in Latin America. To a large extent, we have not yet appreciated
that what is true in Eastern Europe is true in Latin America: "Communism"
is no longer a single monolithic movement. To appreciate this fact is also to
see that United States policies in this area are in need of revision.

The death of Stalin and Mao's declaration of independence accelerated
the process of the erosion of the unity of the world Communist movement
foreshadowed by Tito's break with Stalin; but the problem had always necessarily been inherent in a movement whose integrity was based ultimately
on an ideology, that is, on a body of ideas which can be variously interpreted
and which need interpretation in order to adapt to the problems posed by
new situations. The movement's coming to power in Russia had made it possible for previous doctrinal divergences to be submerged; the fact that for
so long the Soviet Union was the only Communist state, and that state was
ruled by an all-powerful dictator, led us to believe that unity of belief and
strategy was an inherent characteristic of the Communist movement. Yet
today there are more varieties of Communism in Eastern Europe than there
are of democratic socialism in Western Europe. The Rumanians, the Yugo-
slavs, and for a time the Czechs showed us quite different versions of state
organization and government policy which were yet recognizably within
the Communist family.

This is all now ancient history and everyone is well aware that a variety
of lines of policy is possible under a Communist label, at least so far as Eastern Europe is concerned. Everyone is also aware that some of the varieties
of Communism are more favorable to the United States than others. Thus it
is clearly preferable to have to deal with a Communist government that takes
the view that "revolution is not exportable" and that peaceful coexistence
with capitalist states is a real possibility, rather than one that believes firmly
in the duty of revolutionaries to make revolution everywhere.

With the erosion of the conception of a unified, implacably hostile Communist bloc, the concept of perpetual cold war also begins to erode, and all
kinds of things become possible. The United States could unofficially encourage the Soviet Union in its attempt to mediate a conflict between
India and Pakistan. The two major powers can follow parallel courses of
action in the attempt to avoid war in the Middle East.

However, there has been a lag in drawing the corollaries for Latin America from what we know about Europe. Traditional anti-Communist rhetoric and attitudes still condition United States policy toward Latin America, the unspoken premise continuing to be that Communist and near-Communist movements are inevitably part of a worldwide conspiracy directed from the Soviet Union and aimed against the United States.

In my view, this is far from the truth. The character of the far left varies greatly from country to country. In Chile, for example, which has one of the largest Communist parties in the area outside of Cuba, the Communists occupy a fairly moderate left-of-center position in the political spectrum, urging caution and action within the established constitutional framework only, while more radical Socialist and splinter Christian Democratic groups countenance the use of violence in order to implement a more radical political program than that of the Communists. Thus it is necessary to examine each situation in detail and with a certain degree of sophistication, rather than reacting in terms of traditional categories that have outlived their validity.

The value of the book the reader holds in his hands consists precisely of deepening and broadening our knowledge of Latin-American Communism in all its complexity, to make possible a more careful and more thoughtful appraisal of Communism's current role in the hemisphere. A variety of approaches to the subject matter is presented here, and a variety of aspects of the subject matter is explored. The book as a whole makes a substantial contribution to our knowledge and understanding, and Professor Herman is to be congratulated in assembling a collection of essays that contain so much of interest and value.

MARTIN C. NEEDLER

CHAPTER I

INTRODUCTION

Donald L. Herman

COMMUNISM IN LATIN AMERICA HAS BECOME INCREASINGLY FRAGMENTED in recent years. Through the immediate post–World War II period, it appeared primarily as an instrument of Soviet foreign policy expressed through local Communist parties. From the late 1950s to the present, Castroism and the effects of the Sino-Soviet split have added new dimensions to the development of Latin-American Communism. These dimensions center upon the tactics which the Communists have had to develop in order to deal with such external stimuli and to cope with longstanding internal developments such as nationalism, non-Communist reform movements, militarism, and dictatorship.

The Latin-American environment offers various opportunities for the Communists to spread their influence: Where there is a wide gap between the haves and the have-nots, the appeal of Communism is enhanced: Where modernization is begun, people suddenly comprehend that improvement in their standard of living is possible. Communists can exploit this too. These socio-economic conditions may well provide some fertile soil for Communist movements. (Taken only this far, however, we could note similar conditions in the U.S. ghetto areas where Communist movements have not been successful, even when attempted). There are more volatile factors which build upon but go well beyond those things already mentioned.

One of the constant themes in Latin America is anti-Americanism, or more explicitly the hostility directed against the United States and its influence in the Western Hemisphere. The degree of intensity varies from country to country, but it influences political development in practically every country. Anti-Americanism may appear in the pronouncements of the government of Venezuela, for example, as it tries to articulate what it considers to be a "Third World" position. Or it may be expressed through part of the rationale for a military take-over as exemplified by the Peruvian coup d' état in 1968. The major social revolutions of twentieth century Latin America have had a strong dosage of anti-Americanism. This was the case with both the Mexican Revolution of 1910 and the Bolivian Revolution of

1952. Certainly the Cuban Revolution was anti-American before Fidel Castro decided to move it in the direction of a Communist framework.

The use of force and violence is central in the political history of the Latin-American states. Revolutions, coups d' état, and assassinations have occurred with distressing regularity. As we shall observe, Communist tactics, as determined by Moscow, called for violent revolution in Latin America during much of the period before World War II. It is true that the policy of "peaceful coexistence" has discouraged such tactics in the post-Stalin era. Furthermore, Chinese "cultural diplomacy" through the early part of 1960 emphasized a relatively less violent method of extending Chinese influence in the area. However, the Chinese have encouraged violent means for the attainment of Communist power since the latter part of 1960.[1] As a result, they find themselves in general agreement with Cuban advocacy of such tactics, although differing significantly with regard to the leadership of a Communist movement. One can anticipate that force and violence will continue to be important ingredients of change in Latin America for the foreseeable future. The form may not appear as blatant as it has in the past. But so long as a significant element of the population does not accept the institutions, i.e., the presidency, courts, and the results of an election as legitimate, the alternatives of force and violence become more serious. And so long as the process of modernization leads to increased political participation which may rise faster than the level of economic development, the newly participant groups may turn to anti-constitutional alternatives which may provoke the military to impose "order" on the society.[2]

And finally the Latin-American environment presents examples of authoritarian rule which closely resemble the political system advocated by the Communists.[3] The dominant role of the state is accepted by most of the political parties. Although many constitutions may indicate otherwise, the political history of Latin America generally has shown the subordination of the individual to the society. The one-party system has been in existence for many years in several of the countries. One can observe the functioning of such systems today, although differing significantly in practice, in Paraguay, Brazil, and Mexico. Added to these factors is the fact that opposition parties or groups often are not tolerated. Not only does this occur under dictatorial regimes, but the relatively nonauthoritarian governments resort to such practices as the state of siege and exiling of political enemies.

Thus the practice of the political systems of many Latin-American states is not far removed from Communism. As a result, many governments have cooperated with Communists within their countries during particular periods, whether they be overt dictatorships or lesser degrees of authoritarianism.

DONALD L. HERMAN

However, during the first several decades of their activities, the Communists found it very difficult to make much headway in the area.

THE INITIAL PERIOD

THE COMMUNIST PARTIES OF LATIN AMERICA WERE ESTABLISHED AFTER THE Russian Revolution of 1917 and the ensuing schism within the world Socialist movement. Lenin and his followers left the Socialist International and formed the Communist International or Comintern. At its second congress in Moscow in 1920, the leaders of the Comintern handed down twenty-one conditions to which all parties had to adhere in order to belong to the international Communist organization.[4] The purpose was to bring the Communist parties under Moscow's control.

The main result in Latin America was to split several Socialist parties and labor organizations. This was followed by the formation of a few small Communist parties which joined the Comintern: in Chile, Uruguay, Argentina, Mexico, Brazil, and Cuba.

By 1923, however, there were only approximately 50,000 Communist party members in all of Latin America. Most of these were students, intellectuals, and a few members of the middle income groups. There also was a small hard core of militant activists. Thus, the workers still had not discovered Communism by this time and the peasants were largely apathetic.

The Communists also were not very successful in the labor movement during this initial period. The Red International of Labor Unions (Profintern) was established during the Second Congress of the Comintern, but the response from Latin America was very limited and the only apparent impact was made in Chile. The principal central body of trade unions of Chile, Federación Obrera de Chile, affiliated with the Profintern in 1921. This was the first central labor body in the hemisphere to go over to the Communists, but the inroads of the Communists went little further at that time. In fact, the Profintern had few Latin-American affiliates in the early 1920s.

For almost the first two years after the formation of the Comintern, the Latin-American Communists seem to have been abandoned to their luck. The twenty-one conditions served as a guide and inspired action. But the Comintern was in need of money. Communications to various Communist movements of the world were difficult, and the Latin-American Communists enjoyed almost absolute independence. However, the situation changed when the Comintern started to direct and control the various Communist parties. In practice this meant sending "political advisers" to different parts of the world. Two of these men, Sen Katayama and Manabentra Nath Roy, played an important role in shaping the early development of Latin-American Communism.

Roy was one of the founders of the Communist Party of India; Katayama was very active in the affairs of the Japanese Communists. The two Comintern agents made their headquarters in Mexico. Because of the revolution then in progress in that country, this seemed in the early 1920s the logical place for a Latin-American headquarters of the Comintern. Roy in particular was influential in arousing Communist sympathizers in Mexico. He followed another Comintern agent in Mexico, Michael Borodin.

Katayama remained in Latin America for approximately eight to nine months. He was influential in causing splits in various Socialist parties and creating Communist parties where they were lacking. In this respect, he set the basis of the monolithic character of the parties. One of his "discoveries" was Victorio Codovilla, one of the future prominent Latin-American Communist leaders.

In general, this early first period of Communism was one of growing pains. The Comintern paid relatively little attention to the activities of the Latin-American Communist parties. Their activities were supervised in a general way by two Swiss Communists, Stirner and Humbert-Droz, whose headquarters were in Moscow. It is true that "political advisers" were sent by the Comintern, but the continued guidance and financial aid which the Communists needed were lacking.

It seems the main problem was a lack of adequate communication. During these early years, one of Moscow's principal sources of information concerning Latin-American affairs was the Russian News Agency, *Tass*, from its correspondent in New York. There was no direct line of communication between the Comintern and the Communist movement in Latin America. However, the relative lack of interest by the Comintern in Latin-America affairs must be viewed in relation to the foreign policy of the Soviet Union during this period. The Soviets were preoccupied with "encirclement" and the areas of Asia and the Middle East which were dominated by the major foes, Britain and France. The United States was a minor foe at the time, and Latin America was considered to be, geographically, the backyard of the United States.

THE EARLY YEARS

DURING THE LATTER PART OF THE 1920S THE INTENSE STRUGGLE BETWEEN THE different factions of the Comintern was reflected in Latin America. Argentina, Chile, Uruguay, and Cuba were particularly affected. Many of the struggles were on personal grounds, but the various Latin-American factions also took the side of one or the other of the Russian groups. However, in no case did a strong dissident Communist party with international connections develop. The "Right Opposition," led in Russia by Bukharin, Rykov, and Tomsky, never had any following of importance in Latin America.

When the Fifth Congress of the Comintern issued the call for Bolshevization in 1924, the Latin-American Communists quickly responded. This was a general slogan, and they were able to justify various tactics within their respective countries under the heading of Bolshevization. The emphasis on following the experiences of the Communist Party of the Soviet Union seemed to be in accord with the aims of the Latin-American Communists at the time. Since this signified a greater degree of centralization, discipline, and control, they were quite willing to follow the new order of the Comintern in order to further the development of their own Communist movements. Furthermore, the Latin-American Communists were competing with the Socialists in their countries in order to gain influence in the labor movement. They believed a hard stand against the Socialist elements would strengthen their position.

Several Latin-American Communists complained they did not receive enough aid from the Comintern. This led to the establishment of a South American Bureau of the Comintern in Moscow. A few years later a large number of Latin-American trade unionists and Communist leaders were invited to Moscow in connection with the celebration of the Tenth Anniversary of the Bolshevik Revolution. They held several conferences with some of the Comintern leaders in April, 1928.

Alexander Losovsky, head of the Profintern, and Humbert-Droz represented the Comintern at the conferences. Preliminary plans were laid for the establishment of the first Communist hemispheric American labor organization, the Confederación Sindical Latino Americano (Latin-American Confederation of Trade Unions or CSLA).

Losovsky's impression of the conferences was that talk of a social revolution was a primitive idea for Latin America. He felt that Latin-American Communists believed that if the Socialist revolution was not produced yesterday, it would arrive tomorrow.... "There were too many small corporative unions in Latin America, too many imagined unions."

Shortly thereafter, the South American Bureau of the Comintern was removed from Moscow to Buenos Aires, and then to Montevideo. The chief of the organization was a Lithuanian Communist named Guralsky. Victorio Codovilla, one of the leaders of the Argentine Communist Party, was in control of the Bureau's finances and became a power in the Latin-American Communist movement.

The Bureau had various activities. The operations and policies of the Communist parties were under its supervision. The Bureau also looked over the activities of all the peripheral organizations established by the Communist parties—branches of the International Red Aid, the Communist Youth International, the Anti-Imperialist League, etc.

About this time also, 1928, *El Trabajador Latino Americano* (The Latin-American Worker) was established in Montevideo, Uruguay. This was the first all–Latin-American Communist periodical. The periodical aided the Comintern in enlisting Latin Americans in their world-wide campaign against "imperialism." The very first issue took up the Comintern campaign— "struggle against English and American imperialists and against reaction from within . . . aid the important struggles of the workers of the distinct countries, whether against capitalism or Capitalist dictators."[5]

However, developments still did not go well for the Communists in the labor movement. Only two Latin-American trade union groups, Chile and Colombia, had joined the Profintern. But decisions had been made which portended better things to come for the Communists. It had already been decided in Moscow to establish a continent-wide trade union organization. There was now a great deal of interest to hold a conference of Latin-American trade unions to put the decision into action.

THE "THIRD PERIOD" OF THE COMINTERN

TWO LATIN-AMERICAN COMMUNIST CONGRESSES WERE HELD IN 1929: IN MONTE-video, Uruguay, and Buenos Aires, Argentina. One dealt with trade union matters and the other with the activities of the various Communist parties. These were the first continent-wide congresses to be held by the Communists.

The Congress of the Latin-American Communist Parties included all the members of the Bureau of Buenos Aires, representatives of the Comintern, delegates from the Communist Party of the United States, and representatives from the Communist parties of fifteen Latin-American countries. All the delegates reported on various topics: persecution of Communists throughout the continent, anti-imperialist struggles, youth movements, problems in individual countries. In general, attempts were made to establish more centralization and organization.

The trade union congress included the delegates from all Communist and pro-Communist trade union groups of the hemisphere. The suggestion of the previous Moscow conference was put into effect, and the Confederación Sindical Latino Americano (CSLA) was established. The Communists were very enthusiastic in their hopes of penetrating the labor movement on a wide scale.

DONALD L. HERMAN

But the desired result was not immediately forthcoming after the Montevideo congress. The mass of the workers was not attracted to the Communist union organizations until the middle 1930s, during the era of the Popular Front. There was fairly good Communist control of some of the unions in Brazil, Mexico, Uruguay, and Ecuador, but the rest of Latin America was not affected very much.

This trade union activity reflected the "Third Period" of the Comintern. It was an era of extreme Communist isolation from other left wing and working class groups. The consequence of the shift in the Comintern aims was known as "dual unionism." In practice it meant that each Communist party set up a trade union movement in its own image and under its direct supervision and control, which affiliated with the Profintern. In Latin America the various labor groups were brought together on a continental basis in the CSLA.

The Third Period of the Comintern was reflected in the doctrine of "social fascism," the resumption of all-out war against Social Democracy. The Latin-American Communists followed Moscow's dictates, and the new slogan was taken up with alacrity—"Social Fascists are the accomplices of capitalism, as always . . . It is evident that the Social Fascist has been and always will be disposed to second the plans of aggression against the country of the proletariat, against the workers and peasants government of the Soviet Union."[6]

During this period, the Soviet Union emphasized that it was threatened by war from the Capitalist countries. It was the period of the Second Five-Year Plan and the Russian people were called upon to make greater sacrifices. Thus, the repeated cry of the coming "Capitalist war" was heard and read throughout Communist circles. The Latin-American Communists once again echoed the call from Moscow—"The imperialist war and in the first instance, the war against the Soviet Union, through which the bourgeoisie and imperialism are going to try, unquestionably, to drag the masses of workers of all the Latin-American countries, is the order of the day. Its first signs have already been understood in the case [sic] of China invaded by Japan . . ."[7]

The Latin-American Communist movement did advance during this period. The Montevideo congresses brought the various parties together, and efforts were made toward better centralization and organization. A continental labor organization was created and a Spanish language periodical was circulated to increase the cohesiveness of the movement. But the Latin-American Communists themselves were aware of problems which had to be overcome if they were to be an important factor in the world Communist movement. The central problems were the agrarian "revolution" and the leadership within the Communist parties.

It was pointed out that not one Communist party in Latin America had a correct agrarian program. The correctness of a program was determined by the degree to which the proletariat established contact with the peasantry under the lead of the Communist party. According to the Latin-American Communist leaders, the peasants were not yet "revolutionary."

In addition, the workers had to be educated to assume the leadership of the Communist movement. Only then could the movement be cleansed of bourgeois influences—". . . leading elements of the Latin-American Communist parties are now composed of intellectuals who are bearers of petty bourgeois psychology. The workers must be brought into the leadership of the parties." The Latin-American Communists are still faced with this problem today.

THE FASCIST DANGER

THE EXTREME ISOLATION OF THE THIRD PERIOD WAS FOLLOWED BY THE ALMOST equally extreme collaborationism of the Popular Front period. This of course reflected the Soviet Union's attempt to establish "collective security" against fascism. The 1935 Seventh Congress of the Comintern called for the widest front on all levels to oppose the Fascist danger.

The Latin-American delegates who went to attend the Seventh Congress held a conference in Moscow. There were several notables who attended—Dimitrov, Manuilsky, Kuusinen, Pieck, Togliatti. Dimitrov and Manuilsky were opposed on tactics. Dimitrov wanted to apply the tactic of the Popular Front in Latin America while Manuilsky maintained that insurrection would be the best course.

The conference ended in a compromise. Manuilsky would be allowed to try his tactic: an insurrectional movement in Brazil. Dimitrov would also be able to try his tactic: a Popular Front in any Latin-American country he might designate. He selected Chile and chose Eudocio Ravines, the Peruvian Communist, to carry it out.

The Popular Front in Chile was very successful for the Communists. It consisted of several political parties and various organizations—Radical Republicans, Socialists, Communists, Democratic Party, Radical Socialists, semi-religious groups, liberal organizations, tenants' leagues, and small shop keepers' guilds. Many foreign Communists came to Chile, and the entire operation was under Ravines.[8]

The Communists allied with the radical political groups by promising to support one of their candidates for President. (Their efforts proved to be fruitful, and Gabriel Gonzales Videla was elected President of Chile.) The movement attracted intellectuals of various shades, lawyers, doctors, and some businessmen. The Communists worked with any politician who might further their aims. They even supported a big landowner for office in order to break the opposition against the Communist party in a local area. Politicians of every shade of opinion, who felt or knew themselves to have been overlooked, were the first to draw close to the Communist successes.

In the labor unions, the Communists supported independent labor leaders rather than trying to put Communists into their positions. They built up an organization which eventually controlled the independent union leader. They compromised with other Socialist labor leaders in order to place Communists in controlling positions.

In the election of March 7, 1937, the Popular Front won a majority in the Senate and Chamber of Deputies of the Chilean legislature. It was a strange mixture which represented the Communist party—"the election definitely showed that the greatest strength of the People's Front is in the industrial regions, and that the petty bourgeois groups are the close collaborators of the proletariat that forms the nucleus of the People's Front. For instance, in the Communist party's representation in Parliament are five workers, two professional people and one small business man."[9]

While the Communists were achieving success in Chile, the Brazilian insurrection proved to be a complete disaster. Many Communists were killed and the Brazilian Communist leader, Luiz Carlos Prestes, was thrown into prison. Thus, the tactics of Dimitrov appeared to be correct for Latin America.

Elsewhere, the Communists made alliances with dictators. This was in accord with the Comintern "line" which was to form the widest possible alliance against fascism. In return the Communist parties had at least limited freedom for agitational and organizational activities. They also were able to build up a trade union movement under their own control. Paradoxical was an article written at that time by a prominent Cuban Communist. His thinking was particularly interesting in view of the present regime in Cuba: "The Communist Party of Cuba, whose profound political understanding of the situation is more responsible than anything else for the changes that have taken place, after considering these recent changes has reached the conclusion that it is necessary to abandon all the out-of-date formulations that are still heard in the party. The situation has changed so that the slogan of the party must be: 'With Batista, Against Reaction,' meaning that we must work openly for the support of the masses to Batista's policies."[10]

The Communists proved to be astute opportunists during this period. In order to avoid antagonizing their political allies of the moment and the governments in the democratic camp, they endeavored to curb labor agitation and strikes. This was the practice in the days of the Popular Front in Chile.

In the labor movement, the Communists moved away from the tactic of "dual unionism" which was prevalent during the Third Period of the Comintern. The CSLA was dissolved in 1936, and the Communist unions in different countries merged with other trade union groups. Shortly thereafter, a conference of Communist and non-Communist union leaders was convened to form a new trade unions federation. The Conference was called by Vicente Lombardo Toledano, secretary general of the Confederación de Trabajadores de México (Confederation of Workers of Mexico or CTM).

The conference met in 1938 and created the hemisphere's first real united front labor body, the Confederación de Trabajadores de América Latina (Confederation of Workers of Latin America or CTAL). Lombardo Toledano was elected president of the executive committee. The organization was not dominated by Communists, but they were a minority with a great deal of influence. The purpose of the new organization was to unify the unions of Latin America.

The Popular Front epoch marked the first period during which the Communist parties of Latin America assumed some political importance in the life of the hemisphere. The Communists sought alliances with groups of all political shades—dictatorial regimes, Socialist and left wing nationalist parties which represented the reformist, moderate left. It seemed the Communists were everybody's friends. Besides increasing their strength in Latin America, they became more important in the plans of the Comintern. The Latin-American Communist movement was now an integral part of world Communism. Although the tactics might have seemed opportunist and at times a paradox, the purpose was quite simple—"United Front of workers of all tendencies for the defense of the Soviet Union . . ."[11]

A PACT WITH HITLER

THE SUCCESS OF THE POPULAR FRONT ERA GAVE WAY TO THE EXTREME ISOLATION of Communists during the period of the Nazi-Soviet Non-Aggression Treaty. There was bitter controversy between the Communists and other elements of the traditional left. With few exceptions, the Latin-American Communist leaders followed the Comintern in its support of the Nazi-Soviet agreements and in the general endorsement of the Soviet's benevolent neutrality toward Germany during the first phase of World War II.

The war was denounced as an "imperialist war." At the thirteenth Congress of the Uruguayan Communist Party, Secretary-General Eugenio Gómez appealed for "a single front of all progressive and peace-loving forces to struggle against the imperialist war, in defense of the Soviet Union, the Socialist fatherland." Lombardo Toledano defended the Soviet desire to stay out of the war as a means to "aid all mankind in the limitation of this terrible destruction."[12] The new formula for Latin America was "Socialist neutrality."

DONALD L. HERMAN

The result of this sudden change in tactics was the isolation of the Communists from the other left wing and working class groups in Latin America. They lost prestige and influence in the labor movement. The Communist parties also lost heavily in membership and prestige. However, the period did not last long, and the Communists were to regain much of their lost strength with the entrance of the Soviet Union into the war.

THE SOVIET UNION ENTERS THE WAR

WHEN GERMANY ATTACKED THE SOVIET UNION IN THE SUMMER OF 1941, THE complexion of the war changed for the Communists. It became a "People's War." Their tactics during the latter part of World War II can best be analyzed by judging the activities in two areas—relations with the dictators and policies in the labor movement.

The Communists desired to preserve the status quo. They viewed revolutionary change as inimical to Soviet interests at the time, and therefore they aligned themselves with the existing regimes whether democratic or dictatorial. In Venezuela, the Communists supported Isaias Medina Angarita 1941–45. The dictator was finally overthrown by a popular uprising supported by the army. The Communists fought to the last to keep him in power.

They continued and strengthened their alliance with Fulgencio Batista of Cuba which dates back to the 1930s. In 1940 they helped elect Batista to the presidency, themselves winning ten parliamentary seats and more than 100 municipal council posts. There was a further cementing of the alliance when the Soviet Union entered World War II. Two Communists were appointed to ministerial posts in March of 1943, and Batista became the first Latin-American chief of state to take Communists into his cabinet. The dictator also turned over a radio station to the party for its own use.

Thus, the Communists reverted to a tactic which had been used in the earlier Popular Front period—an alliance with Latin-American dictators to further the interests of the Soviet Union and the development of Latin-American Communism.

The general Communist position in the labor movement indicated support for the status quo: no agitation for wage increases, no provocation of strikes. The 1944 CTAL Congress held at Cali, Colombia, reflected the Stalinist line. It called for reparations from Germany and Japan at war's end and opposed Trotskyism in Latin America. The Communists obtained control of the CTAL during the Cali Congress. Lombardo Toledano was again elected president of the Executive Committee. Seven out of twelve avowed Communists also were elected to the Committee. Control of the CTAL marked the high point of Communist influence in the Latin-American labor movement. From 1944 through 1946, the Communists continued to be the most powerful political force in the ranks of organized labor in the hemisphere.

Thus, World War II contributed to the growth of Communism in Latin America. The Communist policy was violently pro-Ally and coincided with a majority of the governments of Latin America, democratic and dictatorial. This in turn contributed to the growth of Communist influence in the labor movement. Many of the Latin-American governments subsidized the unions in which the Communists gained important positions. Further successes came to the Communists with Latin America's sympathy for the Allied cause and the Soviets during the war.

THE COLD WAR

WITH THE END OF WORLD WAR II AND THE BEGINNING OF THE COLD WAR, THE Latin-American Communists followed the lead of the Soviet Union by violent opposition to the United States. This mainly has been carried out under the mantle of "nationalism."

The theme has been that the Latin-American countries must not become economically dependent upon the United States. The Communists view trade with the Soviet Union and Eastern Europe as the answer to this "excessive dependence." However, the effects of the Communist efforts have been somewhat limited because of their apparent subservience to the Soviet Union. An outstanding instance was the declaration in 1946 of Luiz Carlos Prestes, leader of the Brazilian Communist Party, that if his country should become involved in war with the Soviet Union, the party would support the Soviet Union. Every other Latin-American Communist party followed suit.

As "nationalists" the Communists oppose foreign investment as an "instrument of imperialism." They oppose the development of petroleum and other natural resources by private foreign capital as exploitation (Brazil, Argentina, Venezuela). They also oppose efforts by the United States and the international financial agencies to stabilize monetary and fiscal affairs as "internal intervention."

Another tactic of the Latin American Communists is to create an attitude of "neutrality" throughout the continent. This maneuver was used during the era of the Nazi-Soviet Pact. It is tied in with the anti-United States theme and campaigns for peace. Thus, there have been the Stockholm "peace" petition and numerous Peace Congresses. An effort is usually made to get signatures of well-known figures on the peace petitions.

Communist influence has declined in the trade union movement since the war. The party of Haya de la Torre in Peru (APRA or American Revolutionary Popular Alliance, currently called the Aprista Party of Peru) is a left wing non-Communist political party. In recent years, it has managed to get

DONALD L. HERMAN

control of the Peruvian labor movement from the Communists. New trade union groups have begun to appear in which Communist influence is at a minimum.

The CTAL has declined in membership. Of the new postwar labor groups, only those in Brazil and Guatemala joined the CTAL. Furthermore, there have been splits in various affiliates of the CTAL which have weakened the position of the Communists in the trade union movement generally. Such splits have occurred in Uruguay, Chile, Colombia, and Mexico. The CTAL is of no real importance today in the trade union movement.

There are two main reasons why Communist strength has declined in the labor movement. Firstly, there is no common Fascist enemy as existed during the war. Many Latin-American governments no longer feel they need the Communists, especially since the need for a major war effort has passed. Secondly, the Cold War has alienated many former sympathizers of the Soviet Union. In turn, the Latin-American Communists are not as popular as they were and their efforts in the labor movement meet a great deal of resistance. In addition, the destruction of Communist power in the trade unions, wherever it has occurred, has fatally undermined the general political position of the party. This is usually in direct proportion to the strength of the non-Communist left wing party within the particular country.

In the latter part of the 1940s and most of the 1950s, the Latin-American Communists used the policy of "dual Communism." This was the tactic of having more than one Communist party in a country. The legally recognized "official" party usually gave "critical support" to the government. The "unofficial" party usually worked underground in opposition to the government. In the case of a dictatorship, one party supported the dictator and the other tried to build up opposition against him. Thus, there were two Communist parties or organizations in Argentina, Peru, Venezuela, Colombia, and Bolivia. At the present time Mexico has two such organizations.

Two conditions are essential for the success of this tactic. First, in the case of dictatorships, the local and international circumstances must favor the use of such a tactic. The condition was propitious during the 1948–58 period. Dictatorships already existed in Nicaragua, Paraguay, and the Dominican Republic. New dictatorial regimes emerged in Argentina, Venezuela, Peru, Cuba, Haiti, and Colombia. Secondly, there must be a means of inducing public forgetfulness of the party's resort to these tactics when the dictator eventually falls, dies, or resigns. This problem is taken care of when the parties divide themselves. There is always a Communist group which opposed the dictator. The group which supported him seems to evaporate into thin air after his demise. The various Communist groups within a country have followed the Soviet line in international matters. The Kremlin doesn't treat the "dissident" group as "heretic."

There are mutual advantages to the dictators and Communists in the use of these tactics. It is favorable to the dictators in order to maintain themselves in power. They can use the Communists to work against their democratic opposition. By allowing a Communist party to exist legally, they have a pretext for saying there is no political persecution in the country. There is also the possibility that the dictator may be a military man without political experience. The Communists are able to provide him with astute political advisers.

The Communists, on the other hand, are able to use the dictator's strength to destroy their own democratic adversaries. They are also able to build up a political and labor organization. When they finally become a strong political factor in the country, they can use the "official" party's support as a bargaining weapon to have the dictator adopt external policies favorable to objectives of the Soviet Union.

The Communists have also used the tactic of "utilization of the inexperienced." This involves taking advantage of the political immaturity of the victorious democratic opposition forces in an effort to bring them under Communist influence and eventual domination. It is really not a new tactic because it was used during the Popular Front era in Chile. However, it has recently proved to be highly successful in Guatemala and Cuba. The pattern is usually the same: maneuver the masses as a political bargaining weapon, organize peripheral mass movements with prominent non-Communists, obtain government subsidization of the movements, use political bargaining power to adopt certain measures, and more recently the exploitation of every opportunity for anti-United States propaganda.

The "international" Communist organizations no longer exist. The Comintern was dissolved in 1943, and the Communist Information Bureau (Cominform) had a life span of nine years, 1947–56. Nevertheless, the Soviet Union maintains a considerable degree of influence with those Latin-American Communist elements oriented toward Moscow.

At present the Foreign Department of the Soviet Central Committee seems to be in charge of communicating with the various Communist parties and governments. It organizes large congresses, small conferences, and "bilateral and multilateral" parleys and receptions. The Soviet Party's Foreign Department has been headed by two members of the Presidium, Mikhail Suslov and Otto Kuusinen; Suslov appears to be in control today. He, of course, is responsible to Brezhnev and Kosygin.

Besides attending the various meetings in Moscow and elsewhere, the Latin-American Communists are trained and given refresher indoctrination courses. One of the principal centers has been described by Daniel James: "In Prague, Czechoslovakia . . . there exists the so-called Institute for the

Study of Latin-American Relations. This Institute, which is part of the Faculty of International Relations of the State College for Political and Economic Sciences, trains agitators, spies, and saboteurs for work in Latin America. The Institute has an enrollment of 750 students, some 15 percent of them enrolled in the School of International Relations . . . The purpose in having Communists from Latin America and Europe study together is to train them as teams. Upon graduation, the Latin Americans return to their native countries and are later joined by European graduates, who may be former classmates . . ."[13] More recently, Latin-American Communists have been trained in North Korea, North Vietnam, Cuba, China, and Algeria. The courses include military instruction, intelligence, and guerrilla warfare.

CASTROISM

THE PICTURE OF COMMUNISM IN LATIN AMERICA HAS CHANGED RADICALLY WITH the advent of Fidel Castro in Cuba. As the Mexican Revolution of 1910 and the Bolivian Revolution of 1952, the Cuban Revolution is a social revolution which has resulted in fundamental changes in the society of the country. These three countries have chosen the means of violent revolution as contrasted with the non-violent revolutionary efforts of the Christian Democrats in Chile and the Democratic Action Party and the Christian Democrats in Venezuela. The Cuban Revolution has also been an important factor in the changes which have occurred in the international developments of the area. These have involved Castro's attempt to export his revolution, Soviet-Cuban relations, the Sino-Soviet dispute: the new challenges which United States policy makers must consider.

There are those who have been sympathetic with the development of the Cuban Revolution while others have been critical.[14] Before Castro came to power, Cuba was not considered to be a peasant country or even a typically "underdeveloped" one. Most of its population lived in the urban areas and the trend was strongly in favor of urbanization. Only Argentina, Chile, and Venezuela rated above Cuba in per capita income. (Of course in Cuba, as in other Latin-American countries, one must consider the distribution of wealth before one generalizes on the standard of living of the people).

The Cuban Revolution, originally based on the support of the middle class, has destroyed the power of that class in favor of the peasantry. Although one can point to statistics which indicate that per capita income has fallen and even that sugar production may fall below pre-revolutionary output, considerable gains have been made by the peasantry. An agrarian reform law has been enacted. State farms have been established similar to the arrangement in the Soviet Union. The peasants do not have title to the land, instead they are paid a wage by the government.[15] In addition, considerable gains have been made in the area of social welfare. An extensive housing program has been undertaken with the goal of providing every Cuban with his own home. Health and medical facilities have been extended to the rural areas. Large-scale school construction has resulted in reducing the level of illiteracy. Recreational facilities are now available to all Cubans; a major effort has been made to eliminate racial discrimination. Allowing for some modifications, these programs have been fairly consistent with the promises made by Castro before his revolution.

Castro failed to restore political freedoms in Cuba, and in this sense he broke the promises he made before coming to power. The Constitution of 1940 and its guarantees of representative government based on democratic procedures are not honored. Power is centralized in the hands of Fidel Castro and the Communist Party of Cuba. Thus the leadership of the Cuban Revolution seems to be attempting to develop the country economically and socially, but at the cost of political freedoms. One can ask the same question about Cuba and other authoritarian but non-Communist governments of Latin America: Is the lack of political freedoms too high a price to pay for social and economic development?

After initial sympathy by the United States government, the relationship between this country and revolutionary Cuba deteriorated and diplomatic relations were broken. Perhaps this was inevitable because of the anti-American nature of the revolution. The United States had supported Fulgencio Batista. Those who opposed the dictator, Communist and non-Communist alike, felt that the struggle against Batista also was a struggle against the influence of the United States in Cuba. The anti-American nature of the movement made it easier for Castro to turn the revolution toward Communism.[16]

Like the Soviet leaders in the early period following the Russian Revolution of 1917, Fidel Castro has maintained his revolution could only be successful if it were followed by other Castro-like revolutions in Latin America. He has tried to identify the revolutionary efforts in the various countries with the Cuban movement: "Cuba was one of the many nations of Latin America placed under the domination of imperialism. One nation of Latin America had to begin the rebellion, and the rebellion against imperialism was begun by Cuba. It is this land of ours which has had the honor and the glory of being the one which initiated the rebellion of Latin America against Yankee imperialism."[17]

The evidence is substantial that the Cuban regime has tried to export its revolution. During the period 1959–60, there were uprisings in Guatemala and Nicaragua. Ships of the United States Navy were sent to the area to

prevent the invasion of the two countries by "Communist-directed elements."
Both the Guatemalan and Nicaraguan governments alleged Cuban complicity
in the uprisings, but the Cuban government denied the charges.

During the same period, there were reported attempted "invasions" of
Haiti. Raúl Roa, the Cuban representative at the August, 1959, Organization
of American States Conference, acknowledged that the "invasion force" (approximately 30 Cubans) had launched its expedition from a Cuban port. He
strongly denied, however, that his government was implicated in any way
and expressed Cuba's readiness to cooperate with the OAS in investigating
the matter.

A few months later, there was another landing of approximately 80–90
Cuban invaders in Panama. Castro denounced the "irresponsible actions" of
the group of Cubans who took part in the landing and called upon them to
desist from the "invasion" immediately.

Although the Cubans have not been successful in exporting their revolution, they have continued in their efforts to foment unrest in Latin America.
The "invasion" attempts have given way to Cuban-sponsored guerrilla
movements. Since the death of Ché Guevara in Bolivia in 1967, there has
been a shift from rural to urban violence. More recently, Latin America has
witnessed urban terrorism, kidnapping, and even assassination of foreign
diplomats and technicians in several of the countries. Although the evidence
is not conclusive, there may well be a link between the terrorists and the
Cuban regime.[18]

At the time of this writing, Castroism has not been emulated in Latin
America. However, it remains a force to be reckoned with which the great
powers cannot ignore, whether it be the tension and danger of a Cuban Missile Crisis or the ideological struggle within the Communist world.

EBBS AND FLOWS OF THE COMMUNIST TIDE

IF ONE IS TO UNDERSTAND THE FULL MEANING OF COMMUNISM IN LATIN AMERICA,
he must view the phenomenon as a dynamic process rather than as a static
entity. It has ebbs and flows depending upon various factors—leading individuals, opportunism, the particular type at a given period (Russian, Chinese, Cuban, Trotskyite, various brands of national Marxism). Communism
is not exclusively or primarily the product of outside influences; in fact, forces
in the hemisphere are probably more important to the development of Communism in the long run. Thus it is necessary to advance beyond our present
knowledge of the subject and analyze the process as we know it today. In
order to accomplish this purpose, we will deal with two major themes: (1)

the influence of outside forces on the Communist movement; (2) left wing democratic regimes and the Communist movement.

In the development of our first theme, we will focus upon (*a*) the effect of the Sino-Soviet split on the Latin-American Communist movement and (*b*) the activities of the Soviet Union in Latin America, particularly in recent years.

Soviet success in influencing the Communist movement in certain areas may be offset by the impact of the Sino-Soviet split. The mere fact that there is such a split indicates that it will have a weakening effect on the Communist movement of Latin America. In the second chapter, however, Professor Alexander broadens current understanding of the conflict by indicating not two but three major participants—Moscow, Peking, and Havana.

It might be said that the position of the Jacobin Left, with leadership in Havana, is a direct result of the outside influence of the Soviet Union. The members of this group feel that Soviet tactics have failed in Latin America, and they spurn the advice of a country which is trying to pursue its national interests rather than the revolution. The Soviet Union finds itself in a difficult position. Its success as a national state makes it less attractive to the more militant elements of the Latin-American Communist movement. In fact present Soviet leaders must try to discourage the tactics of violence which were advocated by their predecessors.

However, as Professor Alexander points out, the Jacobin Left consists of people who are anxious for fundamental social change whatever the cost. They are not traditionally a part of the international Communist movement and, therefore, they are not sympathetic to the needs and desires of the Soviet Union. Although they are ideologically closer to the position of China, the Jacobin Left is too nationalistic and Peking is too far away to assume the leadership of this group.

So we might say that the conflict is really between Moscow and the Havana-led Jacobin Left of Latin America rather than a Sino-Soviet dispute. Nevertheless, its effect has weakened the Communist movement in the hemisphere. The attempt to attain power through violence in Venezuela all but destroyed the Communist movement in that country; conflicts exist within the Communist movements of most of the countries.

Regardless of the effects of this conflict on the Latin-American Communist movement, the Soviet Union continues to develop its relations with the various Latin American countries as it has done in the past. In the third chapter, Professor Oswald traces the development of Soviet relations with several significant countries—Mexico, Uruguay, and Cuba. He points out that the early efforts to foment revolutions through the Comintern have given way to fairly successful trade and normal relations, particularly since 1956. Through his analysis, one can compare the effect of Soviet activities on the Communist movements of revolutionary Cuba and of the social welfare state of Uruguay.

Tension between the Soviet Union and Cuba has increased since the Soviets removed their Cuban rocket sites in 1962. Despite the apparent urgency of internal Cuban disputes concerning such matters as revolutionary strategy and basic patterns of economic development, external pressures are equally significant. Here we speak of Soviet security interests which may not be compatible with the desire of Fidel Castro to lead a continent-wide revolutionary movement in Latin America. Therefore, what are the effects of Soviet pressure on Cuba? On the one hand, the Cuban Communist movement may become less violent and lean toward the Moscow road of "peaceful coexistence." On the other hand, Soviet influence may have the opposite effect of forcing Castro to prove that the violent road to power can be successful in Latin America and, therefore, Cuban leadership of the revolutionary movement will be assured.

Soviet relations with a country that has developed along more democratic lines, such as Uruguay, may raise other questions as far as the Communist movement in the country is concerned. In this example the means of extending Soviet influence can be more subtle, such as visiting professors and cultural exchanges, but perhaps the effects may be more lasting from the Soviet viewpoint. The present economic problems and political instability of the country offer opportunities to the Soviet Union, not only for an increase in Soviet influence, but to make Communism a more acceptable alternative to a larger portion of the population. Professor Oswald defines such refined tactics as "the thin line of distinction between Communist propaganda and politically inspired Soviet academic analysis of contemporary Latin-American problems [which] is an aspect of the ideological assault . . ."

So far we have been discussing primarily the forces external to Latin America and their effect on the Communist movement. However, to develop a more complete analysis, one must consider the internal forces which are also important ingredients.

In the development of our second theme, the left wing democratic regimes and the Communist movement, we find that the Communists have used completely different tactics in their relationships with the governments of the democratic left in Latin America. Throughout most of their history they have opposed such regimes because, as a possible answer to Latin America's needs, such governments appear as a grave threat to the Communist movement. But occasionally they did cooperate with such regimes in the past, and cooperation rather than opposition seems to be the tactic for the present. Although there are Communist-inspired guerrilla movements in opposition to the democratic left today, for the most part, the major elements which make up the Communist movement seem to be cooperating with such governments.

In the cases of Mexico under the Cárdenas government and Brazil under Goulart, we are able to observe the development of Communism in the respective countries during particular periods. In Mexico we raise the question of whether or not a social revolutionary movement, under the guidance of a democratic left wing political party, can offer the strongest resistance to the influence of Communism. For if it does not, then perhaps the generally accepted theory, that the democratic left is the answer to Communism in Latin America, is in need of modification. In order to answer the question, various factors are considered—the Popular Front in Mexico, the attitude of the Communists during the Cárdenas administration, the growth of the Communist movement during that period, the ideological orientation of the government, developments within the labor movement.

In Brazil, as in Mexico, the Communists were able to penetrate the top echelons of labor and student organizations. In fact, they dominated the labor movement as their counterparts had done in Mexico thirty years earlier. Both Goulart of Brazil and Cárdenas of Mexico cooperated with the Moscow-oriented Communist parties, and the parties grew in strength. Some of the leaders of the non-Communist left also were very important to the Communist movement in Brazil. The Communist movement of Brazil was not as unified as that of Mexico during the periods under consideration. The Brazilian Communist movement was divided over theory (violence *vs.* nonviolence) and practice (urban-oriented Communist party *vs.* Peking- and Havana-oriented guerrilla movements). Nevertheless, the Communist movements in both countries flourished under left wing democratic regimes.

The student of Latin-American politics can test the conclusion that Communism in Latin America can develop more rapidly under a left wing democratic regime by analyzing recent developments in other Latin-American countries. Can the same conclusion be reached, for example, in the consideration of the Bolivian Revolution of 1952 and the administration of the Movimiento Nacionalista Revolucionario under Víctor Paz Estenssoro (1952–64)? Did the Communist movement of Chile develop more rapidly under the Christian Democratic regime of Eduardo Frei Montalva and his "revolution in liberty"?

The military of Mexico did not move against the Cárdenas government in order to stop the development of Communism. Perhaps it did not feel threatened to the point where this would be necessary. The military was represented in the government. Furthermore it was the hope of many elements in the country that the Mexican revolution would begin to find solutions to the problems of the country by means other than coup and counter-coup. However, the Brazilian military did feel threatened to the point where it felt compelled to overthrow the Goulart government. The effects on the Communist movement in that country were disastrous.

One can make the observation that the retardation of a Communist movement through direct military involvement in Latin America also retards non-Communist political development within the country. For in addition to resulting in the ebb of the Communist tide, the Brazilian military action of 1964 also caused the ill-treatment of other elements of the left—trials, political rights cancelled, jail sentences. However, it is the effect on the Communist movement which concerns us here.

In the fifth chapter, Professor Dulles has indicated the brief and bloodless 1964 stroke by the military in Brazil met practically no resistance on the part of the Communists. They did not penetrate the ranks of Army officers as they had penetrated to top echelons of labor and student organizations. As a result, the coup had an adverse effect on Brazilian Communism.

The Communist movement was affected in a theoretical and practical sense. Theoretically, there were strong disagreements concerning the relative merits of the violent and non-violent roads to power. Those who advocated violent means were expelled from the Communist party. Nevertheless, various elements continued to adhere to the road of violence—several leaders of the non-Communist left, the Peking-oriented Communist party, the Trotskyites, the pro-Castro guerrilla activists. In a practical sense, the result was a further splintering of the Communist movement. Although these forces were able to agree on a general program in early 1964, they have not been able to reach such agreement since that period. New splinter groups have been formed, and there is no longer cooperation between former allies.

Perhaps more important to the Communists in the long run was the adverse effect the 1964 military action had on Communist influence with organized labor. Several labor organizations under Communist sway were eliminated. Not only does the government no longer aid the Communists in their organizational efforts, but it is actively working to keep Communist effectiveness limited.

At this juncture in the development of Communism in Latin America, the Communist presence in the urban areas is perhaps more important than in the countryside. Communist-led guerrilla activities, as indicated by the diary of Ché Guevara, have been dismal failures.[19] The Moscow position of peaceful coexistence is attractive to certain middle and working class elements in the cities, where most of the Communist strength can be found. Therefore, a substantial decline in Communist strength in the labor movement is a severe setback.

THE 1970s

LATIN AMERICA ENTERED THE 1970S IN AN ERA OF FERMENT AND STRUGGLE among various forces. Panama and Peru experienced coups d' état in 1968, Bolivia had two coups in 1970, and Argentina had one in 1971; Brazil's government placed greater restrictions on political freedoms. In the summer of 1969 President Nixon sent Governor Nelson Rockefeller as his emissary to Latin America. There were violent outbreaks as a result of his trip in almost all of the countries he visited. Even those under authoritarian regimes, such as Argentina, Brazil, and Paraguay, experienced violence. The governments of Chile, Peru, and Venezuela felt it necessary to cancel the governor's visit.

Significant changes took place in 1970 and the early part of 1971 in the Communist movement. Perhaps the event which will have the most far-reaching effects was the Chilean presidential election in September of 1970. Salvador Allende became the first Marxist ever elected president of a Latin-American country. He received approximately 36% of the vote to win by a plurality.[20] The Communist party is an integral part of his Popular Unity coalition, and the party was awarded three of the fifteen members of President Allende's cabinet. Four cabinet positions were given to members of the president's Socialist party. As Professor Needler pointed out in the Preface, the more radical Socialists of Chile support the use of violence to realize a more radical political program than that of the Communists. Will the Chilean Communists prove to be a moderating influence in the cabinet?

Some of the political parties in other countries are trying to create movements on the Allende model, but interesting differences can be observed. In Uruguay, for example, the Broad Front (Frente Amplio) is a development since the 1970 Chilean election. It is attracting dissidents from the traditional Colorado and Blanco parties. The front also includes the Communist party, elements of the Christian Democratic party, the Socialist party, and smaller factions of the left. After some hesitation, the urban guerrilla organization, the Tupamaros, appear to have joined the Broad Front.[21]

In Venezuela, the New Force (Nueva Fuerza) or Popular Front is a recent development in the political history of the country. It consists principally of the Unión Republicana Democrática (URD) and the Movimiento Electoral del Pueblo (MEP). Popular Committees have been formed to attract other political groups. Contrary to the example in Uruguay, the New Force of Venezuela opposes the Christian Democrats as one of the two major political parties of "status."[22] One of the problems, according to Jorge Dager of the Frente Democrática Popular (FDP), is that "everyone wants to be an Allende."[23]

There may be another problem as the New Force develops in Venezuela, in addition to the more immediate needs of agreement to a common program and a presidential candidate for the 1973 election. This is the question of the degree of Marxist influence. According to one spokesman the New Force is left, but it is not Marxist-Leninist. The Marxists comprise only approximately 10%; the leaders of the New Force do not want a Marxist movement. The emphasis in Venezuela will be on nationalism and revolution.[24] According to another spokesman, it is impossible to have the New Force without the Communist party; the Communist party will join the Popular Committees.[25]

Another interesting event occurred in Venezuela: the split of the Communist party. However, rather than a result of the Sino-Soviet split, the immediate cause which led to the break was the Soviet invasion of Czechoslovakia. It is too early to determine whether the second Communist party, the Movimiento al Socialismo (MAS), indicates the development of national Communism of the Yugoslav model or Trotskyism in Venezuela. It is clear, however, that the leaders of the MAS have taken positions independent of the Soviet Union and the Communist Party of Venezuela (PCV).[26]

Due to the difficulties between the PCV and the MAS, the latter is not a member of the New Force at the time of this writing. However, the MAS has joined alliances with other political parties in student elections in some of the states to oppose the "coincidencia" of the two major political parties: Acción Democrática and the Social Cristian–COPEI. One of the leaders of the New Force feels the MAS will become integrated into the movement in time.[27]

In part, the recent strengthening of militarism and reaction to Governor Rockefeller's trip are a manifestation of problems which continue to be of concern to the governments of Latin America and the United States. Some of the tension is caused by the actions (or lack of action) on the part of the United States, and much of this concerns economic policy. For example, there is a need for liberalization of trade between Latin America and the United States. But after all the reports and studies have been analyzed, the basic question remains: Will the United States Congress take the necessary steps to liberalize that trade? The Latin Americans object to United States aid with strings attached. Recently the Nixon Administration eliminated the requirement of "additionality," that loan money be used to purchase goods in the United States often at much higher prices than available elsewhere. The elimination of this requirement is a step in the right direction. However,

United States funds in Latin America are not adequate, and our commitments under the Alliance for Progress have actually decreased.

Part of the Latin-American criticism of the United States also involves political decisions. In a sense, the United States is a victim of its own strength. A superpower in the western hemisphere is bound to have a tremendous political impact in the area. Whatever the United States does or does not do will affect developments within particular Latin-American countries. But given this situation, the United States is still able to make decisions which will be advantageous to itself and Latin America. These involve such questions as the role of the Organization of American States and a policy toward military dictatorships. Except for a short period in the Kennedy Administration, we still have not put Milton Eisenhower's 1958 slogan into practice: "a handshake for dictators and an *abrazo* for democratically elected rulers." We still supply Latin American dictators with expensive military equipment so they can "fight Communism."

The major problems of Latin America are caused by developments within the area. Perhaps one can say that the unrest is related to the dynamics of revolutionary change. Revolutionary in this sense pertains to basic political, social, and economic changes in the society. Such a change can occur through violence as exemplified in Mexico, Bolivia, and Cuba. Or it can come about through non-violent means. I mentioned the example of Chile under the administration of Eduardo Frei Montalva. The government's purchase of 51% of the United States-owned Anaconda Copper Company in the summer of 1969 is an example of such non-violent revolutionary change. Another example occurred a few days later when the military government of Peru decreed a sweeping new agrarian reform. These revolutionary changes, of the non-Communist model, were accomplished by a democratic reform government in the one case and a military junta in the other. They compete for leadership of the Latin-American revolution with the Communist model of Fidel Castro and his followers. And such changes occur within a milieu that is witnessing the problems of a soaring population growth and militant nationalism, both of the left and the right. In the face of these problems, and in the hope of avoiding violent revolutionary change, the policy makers of Latin America and the United States ask themselves a fundamental question: Is there still time?

There are opportunities for the Latin-American Communists in an area which is experiencing these far-reaching and rapid changes. But will the Communists be prepared to take advantage of the frustrations, unrest, and probable upheavals in the years ahead? They can if they are able to unite to bring their maximum influence and pressure to bear. But there are changes

DONALD L. HERMAN

occurring in the Communist world also. The international Communist Congress convened in Moscow in the summer of 1969 under conditions in which it became known that there was fundamental disagreement among the participants. The attempt to paper over the differences was not entirely successful. Indicative of the change in world Communism was the fact that the militant but weak Dominican Communist party dared to refuse to sign the final document.

One of the most basic causes of the change in world Communism is the dispute between the Soviet Union and China. This dispute has affected the Communist movements throughout the world, including Latin America. Its effect will be an important determinant in the development of the Latin-American Communist movement.

NOTES

1. William E. Ratliff, "Chinese Communist Cultural Diplomacy toward Latin America, 1949–1960," *The Hispanic American Historical Review*, Volume XLIX, No. 1 (February, 1969).

2. See Martin C. Needler, "Political Development and Socioeconomic Development: The Case of Latin America," *The American Political Science Review*, Vol. LXII, No. 3 (September, 1968).

3. Rollie Poppino, *International Communism in Latin America: A History of the Movement 1917–1963* (New York: The Free Press of Glencoe, 1964), pp. 41–42.

4. For a complete list of the twenty-one conditions see Jane Degras, *The Communist International 1919–1943—Documents*, Vol. 1, 1919–1922 (Oxford University Press, 1956).

5. *El Trabajador Latino Americano*, Año 1, No. 1, Septiembre, 15, 1928.

6. Ibid., Año 3, No. 36, Diciembre, 1930.

7. Ibid., Año 5, No. 48, Mayo, 1932.

8. Eudocio Ravines, *The Yenan Way* (New York: Charles Scribner's Sons, 1951), pp. 164–181.

9. Hal Clark, "People's Front in Chile," *Inprecorr* (International Press Correspondence), Vol. 17, No. 19, May 1, 1937.

10. R. A. Martinez, "The Latin American Significance of the Cuban Upsurge," Ibid., Vol. 19, No. 18, April 1, 1939.

11. *El Trabajador Latino Americano*, Año 4, No. 43, Octubre, 1931.

12. Vicente Lombardo Toledano, *Nuestra Lucha Por La Libertad* (México, D. F., Universidad Obrera de México, 1941), pp. 22–23.

13. Daniel James, *Red Design for the Americas: Guatemalan Prelude* (New York: John Day Company, 1954), p. 203.

14. See Herbert L. Matthews, *The Cuban Story* (New York: George Braziller, 1961); Theodore Draper, *Castro's Revolution Myths & Realities* (New York: Frederick A. Praeger, 1962); Theodore Draper, *Castroism Theory and Practice* (New York: Frederick A. Praeger, 1965).

15. There are those who argue that the peasants have not gained significantly in Cuba. See Theodore Draper's "Five Years of Castro's Cuba," *Commentary*, 1964.

16. For an interesting study on how and why the Cuban Revolution became Communist see Andrés Suárez, *Cuba: Castroism and Communism, 1959–1966* (Cambridge, Massachusetts: The M.I.T. Press, 1969).

17. *Obra Revolucionaria*, Imprenta Nacional de Cuba (La Habana, Septiembre 9, 1960).

18. *The New York Times*, December 7, 1970.

19. The guerrilla movement of Fidel Castro was not under Communist leadership.

20. In the spring of 1971, when municipal elections were held, the Popular Unity coalition increased its electoral strength to approximately 50%.

21. See the Caracas newspapers *El Nacional*, 24 de Enero de 1971, 8 de Mayo de 1971, and *El Universal*, 25 de Enero de 1971.

22. The Christian Democrats lost the presidential election of Chile in September of 1970. However, the Christian Democrats of Venezuela (COPEI) control the presidency of that country and the government is attempting to institute basic reforms.

23. The Caracas daily *El Nacional*, 21 de Enero de 1971.

24. Interview with Jesús Angel Paz Galarraga, Secretary General of the Movimiento Electoral del Pueblo (MEP), March 5, 1971.

25. Interview with Ramadés Larrazábal, Communist deputy and chief of the parliamentary faction of the Communist Party of Venezuela (PCV), April 16, 1971.

26. See two books by Teodoro Petkoff, *Checoeslovaquia: El Socialismo Como Problema* (Caracas: Editorial Domingo Fuentes, 1969) and *¿Socialismo Para Venezuela?* (Caracas: Editorial Domingo Fuentes, 1970). Petkoff criticizes the occupation of Czechoslovakia by Warsaw Pact troops, rejects the Soviet model as suitable for other countries, and attacks the bureaucracy of the Soviet Union.

27. Interview with Luís Beltrán Prieto Figueroa, President of the Movimiento Electoral del Pueblo (MEP), June 14, 1971.

DONALD L. HERMAN

CHAPTER II

IMPACT OF THE SINO-SOVIET SPLIT ON LATIN-AMERICAN COMMUNISM

Robert J. Alexander

FROM THE BEGINNING, THE COMMUNIST PARTIES OF LATIN AMERICA HAVE been an integral part of the International Communist movement. Hence, in recent years they have been unable to avoid the consequences of the breakup of the Communist International monolith, with the establishment of two main foci of power and doctrine, Moscow and Peking. A number of the Latin-American parties have suffered splits stemming from this worldwide division in the International Communist movement. In addition, however, a third Communist tendency has appeared in Latin-American Communism, finding its inspiration and leadership in the Cuban Revolution, and attracting principally elements which have not belonged to the traditional Communist movement.

LATIN-AMERICAN COMMUNIST ASSOCIATION WITH MOSCOW

THE ASSOCIATION OF THE LATIN-AMERICAN COMMUNIST PARTIES WITH MOSCOW dates from the earliest days of the Communist International. The Russian revolution exerted a powerful attraction in Latin America upon both the Socialists and the Anarchists. Most of the earliest Communist parties of the area came directly out of one or the other of these two older movements.

In Argentina, a dissident Socialist party, the Partido Socialista Internacional, had broken away from the older Partido Socialista Argentino because of opposition to the PSA's friendliness to the Allies during World War I. It was one of the first parties anywhere in the world to join the Communist International, being represented by proxy through the delegation of the Italian Socialist Party at the First Congress of the Comintern in March, 1919.[1]

In 1921 and 1922 respectively the orthodox Uruguayan and Chilean Socialist parties—the Partido Socialista del Uruguay and the Partido Socialista Obrero de Chile—joined the Communist International. In 1922, also, a group of Anarchist trade unionists and intellectuals formed the Partido Comunista do Brasil.

Some of the Latin-American Communist parties were formed through the direct intervention of the Comintern and Moscow. As early as 1919 the Russians sent Michael Borodin—who later became famous as a Comintern agent in China during the middle 1920s—to organize a Communist Party in Mexico, and to use that country, then undergoing the throes of its Revolution, as a base for Communist operations throughout Latin America. His success was only moderate, but by the time he left the country there did exist a Mexican Communist Party. Several Comintern agents, including an American, Joseph Zack, were working in Colombia during the later 1920s, and the ultimate decision to form a Communist party in that country was taken in 1930 by Communist sympathizers upon direct orders from the Comintern to convert their Partido Socialista Revolucionario into an orthodox member of the Communist International.

The case of the Colombian party indicates the degree to which the Latin-American Communists were disciplined members of the Comintern during the period that that group—and its successor, the Cominform—were dominated by Moscow. Another example of this was the decisions of the 1929 Conference of Communist parties of Latin America involving Peru. Delegates to the Conference from that country represented the Partido Socialista del Peru, formed by Communists as a front group to operate legally. They were ordered immediately to form a Communist party. Futhermore, the thesis which they had presented urging the Latin-American Communists to adopt a policy of proselytizing among Indians, and seeking their full integration into the societies of their respective nations was repudiated. The Peruvians were ordered to drop these ideas and adopt instead the Comintern's then current line of self-determination for minority groups, which in this case meant support for the establishment of a separate Peruvian Indian republic.

Upon their return to Peru, the delegates to the Comintern meeting split. Most of them agreed to go along with the orders of the Communist International. A minority refused, and decided to form a new Partido Socialista del Peru.

A number of the Latin-American parties were severely disciplined and even reorganized by Moscow. This occurred in the late 1920s in Chile, when the Comintern Latin-American Bureau in Montevideo refused to recognize the officials chosen by the local members, and named their own. Those comrades who objected were expelled from the party. In 1939 a delegation from the Comintern visited Mexico, and purged virtually the whole leadership of the Communist party, naming in their place local figures who theretofore had played only small roles in the party's national affairs.

ROBERT J. ALEXANDER

Individual Latin Americans participated in the apparatus of the Communist International. For one thing, members of several Latin-American parties helped manage the South American Bureau of the Comintern in Montevideo between 1927 and 1935, although the chief posts in the Bureau were held by East Europeans. Latin Americans also participated in the Latin-American Bureau which operated in the Moscow headquarters of the International. Included among these were Luiz Carlos Prestes (even before he had formally joined the Brazilian Communist Party, of which he subsequently became Secretary General), and the Colombian Ignacio Torres Giraldo.

Other Latin-American Communists played an active role as agents of the Comintern. Thus Victorio Codovilla, founder of the Argentine party and still its head at the time of his death, more than forty years later, served several years in the late 1930s as a Comintern representative in Spain during the Civil War there, being one of the principal engineers of the attempt to seize control of the Spanish Republic for the local Communist party. He was also a leading member of the Comintern delegation which purged the Mexican Communist Party in 1939. Eudosio Ravines, founder of the Peruvian Communist Party, also served the Communist International in Spain and then was assigned as adviser to the Chilean party, in its effort to exploit the local Popular Front.

The Latin-American Communist parties also showed their loyalty to the International Communist movement by passing through all of the phases through which the movement as a whole passed. The early Communist parties of the area first attracted left-wing Social Democrats and Anarchists. By the early 1930s they had become disciplined units of the international organization directed from Moscow, as the result of a series of purges not dissimilar to those which had taken place during the previous years in the Russian and other more important parties. During the Stalinist period, the Latin-American Communist parties became monolithic organizations, with iron-bound discipline, complete lack of internal democracy, "cult of personality," and all of the other attributes of typical Communist parties of that epoch. There was little during this period to sustain the idea that Latin-American Communist parties were somehow "different."

Likewise, the Communist parties of Latin America went through the same process of training and indoctrinating their members, and particularly their leaders, as did similar organizations in other parts of the world. A large number of primary and secondary leaders were taken to Russia for training beginning in the early 1920s and continuing at least as late as the 1950s. The Brazilian, Osvaldo Peralva, has written a fascinating description of his experience in such a training school in the early 1950s, when he was a young and aspiring member of the Brazilian Communist Party hierarchy.[2]

Finally, the devotion of the Latin-American Communist parties to Moscow was openly proclaimed by them throughout the first forty years or more of the existence of the International Communist movement. During the 1920s and early 1930s individual parties as well as international meetings of Communist parties of the area, proclaimed the first duty of Communists everywhere to be "the defence of the Soviet Union." Subsequently, through every change in policy in the USSR, the Latin-American Communists gave their loyal support to "the workers' fatherland." Their publications contained regular eulogistic articles on the Soviet Union. Particularly after World War II, the parties spent considerable time in distributing Soviet periodicals, arranging visits to the USSR and East Europe, and forming Soviet-Argentine, Soviet-Chilean, etc., "friendship" organizations to aid in propagandizing the virtues of the USSR in their respective countries.

Hence, there is a long history of loyalty to the Soviet Union in the Communist parties of Latin America. The most important function of the political careers of their principal and secondary leaders over almost half a century has been to serve the Soviet Union. They have a great deal invested in the USSR emotionally and in terms of time, and are extremely loathe to break with the Mecca of their faith.

ATTRACTIVENESS OF MOSCOW LINE TO COMMUNIST PARTIES

BUT THERE ARE ADDITIONAL REASONS FOR THE INCLINATION OF THE LATIN-American Communist parties to remain loyal to Moscow. Basically, the line of action which Moscow has recommended is much more compatible with the conditions existing in most Latin-American countries, and with the position which the Communists occupy in them, than is that of the Chinese.

Ernst Halperin has pointed out that to an unsophisticated reader the difference in the road to power recommended to the Communists of the underdeveloped countries (and particularly to Latin Americans) by the Russians and the Chinese may appear small. The Chinese do not rule out entirely the peaceful acquisition of power and the use of parliamentary methods, nor do the Russians completely reject the course of violence and guerrilla warfare. However, there is a clear difference of emphasis in the theoretical positions of Moscow and Peking, and an even more obvious split between them in practice.[3]

Herbert Dinerstein has summed up the line of argument generally taken by the Soviet party in the following terms:

In their dispute with the Chinese the Soviets had never taken the position that a peaceful parliamentary transition was the only path to communist revolution. They always insisted that both the violent and the nonviolent paths were possible and that the choice in any given case depended on the circumstances. As a matter of fact, years ago, the South African and the Paraguayan parties were among those who took the position that in their particular countries violent resistance was necessary. But, in general, Soviet discussions since 1960 have allowed that both paths were possible and that the Chinese example of armed struggle is not to be applied automatically to other countries, and have then cited instances of choices that conformed with local circumstances. These examples have invariably happened to be of communist parties that did not consider the armed struggle suitable for their countries.[4]

A typical example of this line of argument of the pro-Soviet forces in Latin America is given by O. Vargas, writing about the situation of the Costa Rican Communist Party (Vanguardia Popular), in the July, 1966, issue of the pro-Soviet international publication *World Marxist Review*. Vargas writes thus:

Thus, the Costa Rican working class and its party, gradually hurdling the catastrophic consequences of the civil war unleashed by reaction in 1948, have successfully forged ahead in recent years in the fight to uphold existing democratic liberties and to broaden the still restricted sphere of their activities. Our working class and its allies have scored big victories in the struggle for democracy and social progress and thus *preserved the perspective of peaceful development of the democratic and national-liberation revolution*. (Italics in the original)

Later in the article Vargas comments:

If the Party were, in these circumstances, to boycott elections, to brush them aside as unimportant, it would inevitably find itself isolated from the masses, from the aspirations of the people, who know from experience that important socioeconomic gains can be won through the election struggle. Such a situation decisively influences the choice of forms of struggle, it lays an imprint on the mass movement. That is why the Communists of Costa Rica are opposed to the attempts to advance a uniform formula for the Latin-American revolution.

Finally, in the penultimate paragraph of his piece, Vargas comments:

The victory of the Cuban revolution is a new landmark in the democratic and national-liberation movement of Latin America. Cuba is building a socialist society. It is the duty of revolutionaries to learn from the experience of the Cuban revolution, and judiciously to follow its example, to show the same vision and decision as that displayed by the men who led the armed struggle. But, of course, not mechanically. Account must be taken of the concrete conditions . . . The question of the conquest of power must be the focal question of all truly revolutionary parties. However, it must be raised in the context of the concrete conditions of the countries concerned. There must be no haste in deciding this question; impatience must not replace historical necessity. The experience of the Peoples

Vanguard Party shows [here it is pertinent to note that in 1948 the Party became, relatively, one of the most influential parties in the country and on the continent, for that matter] that whenever we displayed impatience in the matter of armed action, we paid a very heavy price for this.

However, the Chinese, for their part, have not completely ruled out alternatives to the violent road to power, either, at least in theory. They summed up their position on this issue in the statement of the Central Committee of the Chinese party entitled *Proposal Concerning the General Line of the International Communist Movement* of June 11, 1963, where they quoted Prof. William E. Griffith of the Massachusetts Institute of Technology: "In specific historical conditions, Marx and Lenin did raise the possibility that revolution may develop peacefully, but as Lenin pointed out, the peaceful development of revolution is an opportunity 'very seldom to be met with in the history of revolution.'" The Chinese Central Committee added the comment: "As a matter of fact, there is no historical precedent for peaceful transition from capitalism to socialism."

The generally more pacific road to power favored by the Russians conforms to one fundamental fact about many, if not most, of the Latin-American Communist parties: they have something to lose by abandoning the peaceful approach for the more violent one. In most of the more important Latin-American countries, and in some of the smaller ones, the Communists have achieved a recognized place in the political spectrum of their nations—they are to a certain degree respectable. In many of the countries—Argentina, Chile, Uruguay, Colombia, Peru, Costa Rica, and various others—they have some influence in the labor movement. They also have influence in various national student movements. In Chile and Uruguay as of 1970 (and in several other countries in the recent past) they have members of Congress. Even in some countries where they are technically illegal—such as Peru and Costa Rica, for instance—they have publications and can hold meetings openly. In many countries they have property, held either openly by the party and related institutions, or through fairly well identified dummies.

These advantages the Latin-American Communist parties are loathe to give up. They are naturally hesitant to risk everything on a guerrilla war or a campaign of urban terrorism, which recent events in several Latin American countries have shown is by no means certain of victory, at least in the short and medium run.

Another factor of some significance is the fact that ideologically and practically the Latin-American parties have virtually from the beginning been heavily oriented towards urban labor. We have already noted that various parties have been able to achieve a share of the leadership of the trade union movement.

ROBERT J. ALEXANDER

For the urban worker of Latin America, a guerrilla war in the hills has little attraction, and a campaign of urban terrorism is likely to alienate him from the terrorists at least as much as from the governmental forces trying to put down the terrorism. The reason the Communists have gotten a foothold in the labor movement has been that they have been able to give capable leadership to the day-to-day struggle for more wages, better working conditions, and increased labor legislation. They will be able to continue to have some influence on organized labor to the degree that they can continue to render this service to their worker constituents, and not by the degree to which they can cause armed conflict in the country-side and make life untenable in the cities.

Furthermore, working-class leaders, whether Communists or not, tend to look upon those who are most eager for a resort to violence with a certain class prejudice. The fact is that the insurrectionary road has most appealed to young elements from the middle and even upper classes, and the working-class Communist has tended to look upon these people as bourgeois upstarts with little real interest in the welfare of the workers, however much the insurrectionists may presume to talk in the name of the urban and rural proletariat.

The importance of the labor aspect of this problem is shown by an article in the July 7, 1966, issue of *Voz Proletaria*, organ of the pro-Soviet Colombian Communist Party. In commenting on a proposed meeting of trade unionists called by Jacobin Leftists for the purpose of getting the organized workers involved in the guerrilla campaign, *Voz Proletaria* commented:

To do what has been proposed, the trade unions will have to abandon the economic front and will cease to be trade unions, to become party groups. As is evident, this would have grave consequences . . . in all trade union organizations. The organized workers, deprived of direction for their economic struggles, would fall into the hands of the unions and federations controlled by reactionaries and employers' agents who would not fail to be eager . . . for the perspective of remaining alone, dominant in the field of economic struggle.

There is also a question of age. The leaders of the Communist parties of Latin America tend to be at least middle aged, and in some cases they are old men. To give an extreme case, it is difficult to imagine the extremely corpulent and sendentary septuagenerian Victorio Codovilla, leader of the Argentine Communist Party, taking to the hills for a guerrilla campaign.

Finally, after 1966 the so-called Great Cultural Revolution provided an important new factor to alienate the orthodox Communists of Latin America from the Chinese Communists. The attitude of most Latin-American Communist leaders towards the Chinese developments was characterized by the comment of one of the principal figures of the Costa Rican party to the writer: "No one can take seriously what is going on in China today."

PRO-CHINESE TENDENCIES IN LATIN-AMERICAN
COMMUNIST PARTIES

THESE FACTORS HELP TO EXPLAIN WHY THE LINE OF ACTION RECOMMENDED BY the Russians has tended to be more popular with the Latin-American Communist leadership than has that of the Chinese. However, there have been minority groups in a number of parties which have broken away to form pro-Chinese dissident parties.

The elements which have been pro-Chinese have been of two kinds. They have included some elements from the youth organizations of the Communist parties, and recalcitrant older leaders who for their own personal reasons have broken with the pro-Moscow orientation of the majority of their confreres.

After the collapse of a number of Latin-American dictatorships in the late 1950s, the Communist Youth tended to grow in many of the countries, and began to wield considerable influence in the ranks of the Communist parties, such as those of Venezuela, Colombia, and Peru, for instance. These Young Communists do not share their elders' ingrained loyalty to the Soviet Union, not having gone through the long years of "defending the Soviet Union." They have the impatience of youth of all kinds, are eager for "action" and perhaps in some instances have been contaminated through association with the Jacobin Leftists, and have acquired some of their dislike for discipline and tedious indoctrination.

The rebels from the Young Communist ranks have tended to be more attracted by the "third force" of the Castro-led Cuban Communist Party than by the Chinese party, which like the Russian one was far away and did not have the Cuban advantage of being Latin American. However, some youthful elements have joined the pro-Peking parties.

The pro-Peking Young Communists have been joined by older people who have either found it hard to adapt to the more flexible and "liberal" post-Stalin atmosphere which has begun to permeate even the Latin-American Communist parties; or have been affected by a somewhat Machiavellian attraction to the rising power of the Chinese comrades. Others of the older groups have undoubtedly been drawn to association with the pro-Chinese position because of frustration of their ambitions for leadership in the older parties—clearly a factor in the pro-Chinese split in the Brazilian Communist Party, for instance.

During the last decade, splits along roughly Sino-Soviet lines have taken place in a number of the Latin-American Communist parties. In almost all cases only a relatively small minority broke away from the pro-Russian party to form a pro-Peking group, although in some instances the dissident element

ROBERT J. ALEXANDER

has been large enough to constitute a considerable nuisance to the official party.

One of the earliest splits was that in the Brazilian Communist Party. There a group which had dominated the illegal Communist party from the time it was outlawed in 1947 until it was allowed to come more or less out into the open again about a decade later, resented the return of Luiz Carlos Prestes to the active leadership of the Party. During the eight or nine years in which Prestes had been in hiding, they had been able to speak in his name, but he had apparently not actively determined party policy. Mauricio Grabois and others of the group had shown evidence of a growing association with the Chinese and a disparaging attitude towards the Soviet party even by the middle 1950s. Their personal quarrel with the loyal pro-Russian Prestes confirmed their association with the Chinese in the Sino-Soviet split, and they broke away in 1961 from the Partido Comunista Brasileiro of Prestes to found what they somewhat confusingly called the Partido Comunista do Brasil.[5]

During the administration of President João Goulart (1961–64) the Prestes pro-Russian party sought to infiltrate that somewhat chaotic regime, while the Grabois pro-Chinese party attacked it as "reformist" and, theoretically at least, advocated preparation for a guerrilla campaign, although there is no evidence that they did anything concrete in this regard. When the Goulart regime was overthrown by a military coup on April 1, 1964, neither group was able to react with any vigor, and both were greatly demoralized during the years immediately following the coup.

The two parties continued their separate existence. During the first year after the coup against Goulart, there was considerable discontent in the Prestes party, which early in 1965 adopted resolutions which were much closer to the Chinese line than to the Russian. However, a bit later in the year a Central Committee meeting took the position that the Partido Comunista Brasileiro should work towards formation of a wide front to oppose the government of President Castelo Branco through mass movements and political action.

Since then, the pro-Moscow party has quite clearly been trying to organize a broad political front of those opposed to the military dictatorship, while at the same time seeking contacts with those within the regime who are particularly nationalistic and anti-Yankee. The pro-Chinese party equally has given strong verbal support to the idea of armed resistance to the dictatorship, although there is little evidence that the Partido Comunista do Brasil has actually acquired much influence in those groups which have launched an urban guerrilla campaign since 1968.

The split in the Peruvian Communist Party took place in January, 1964.

The dissident pro-Chinese group claimed representation at its founding convention—which it entitled the Fourth National Conference of the Peruvian Communist Party—from thirteen of the Party's seventeen regional committees. It named an honorary presidium consisting of Marx, Engels, Lenin, Stalin, and Mao Tse-tung. It formally "expelled" the pro-Soviet leaders headed by Raul Acosta, whom it denounced as being "Browderist and revisionist." Saturnino Paredes was elected Secretary General.[6]

The pro-Moscow party gave critical support to the government of President Fernando Belaunde Terry, which had taken office in 1963, and was carrying out a reform program, while the pro-Peking party backed attempts to launch a guerrilla war against the Belaunde government. This insurrection was defeated by the middle of 1966.

The June 7, 1966, issue of *Unidad*, official organ of the pro-Russian Peruvian party gave a clear picture of the position of that group. It contained a page of greetings on the paper's tenth anniversary, including one from *Pravda* and another from the Soviet Peace Committee. It contained a speech given by Raul Acosta, the party's Secretary General, before the 23rd Congress of the Soviet Communist Party, which contained an interesting comment on the split:

In this Congress the Peruvian Communists can inform the successors of Lenin that we have fought with great success against a group of divisionists directed from afar. They, in spite of their insignificant number, attempted to divide our party and even to usurp its glorious name. But today this group has broken into three fractions which attack each other viciously with sobriquets which each deserves ...

Acosta's speech also included a fair example of the position of many of the Latin-American orthodox parties of paying lip service to the possibility of the violent road, but giving most emphasis to other approaches to power. He commented:

In these difficult conditions our party continues the struggle, maintaining close union with the masses and responsibly defending their interests. We consider that, given the reactionary violence, the most viable road for the Peruvian Revolution is the armed road. However, this does not exclude but rather presumes the combined use of all forms of struggle, the strengthening, development, and coordination of all popular organizations and the carrying out of mass action.

This passage came right after a description of the recent defeats of the guerrilla movement in Peru. Elsewhere in the paper there was a resolution of the party's Central Committee calling for formation of a coalition of all

left-wing groups to contest the 1966 municipal elections against the government and the principal opposition parties.

The relatively mild opposition offered by the party to the Belaunde regime
was shown in an article entitled "Concentration Camps in Peru," which ends
with the question, "Are you perhaps not informed of these things, President
Belaunde?" It is also shown by the frequent references to the "capitulation"
of Belaunde in face of alleged opposition of the Aprista Party and the Odria
Union—the two major opposition groups—to the government's program of
reform. The chief enemy, in the eyes of the pro-Moscow party, was obviously
the Aprista Party, not Belaunde.

With the overthrow of President Belaunde in October, 1968, the pro-
Moscow Communist party threw its support behind the nationalistic and
mildly anti–United States military regime of General Juan Velasco. In contrast, the pro-Chinese party was strongly opposed to Velasco, and as it proclaimed in a letter to the Chinese Communist Party, which was published in
the October 24, 1969, issue of the *Peking Review*, believed that "only through
a peoples war can the oppressed people and nations achieve liberation, build
socialism, and march towards communism."

In Ecuador, there was a struggle of younger elements against the pro-
Moscow leadership of party Secretary General Pedro Saad, who for more
than a decade had been a Senator, representing the organized workers of the
coastal regions of the republic. This fight was led by the Central Committee
of the party in the province of Pichincha (Quito).

The struggle between the two factions reached a climax in 1963 when the
Pichincha group sent an envoy to China, to attempt to obtain funds from the
Peking regime. Although the effort was successful, the person who obtained
the $25,000 which the Chinese government provided was arrested upon his
return to Ecuador, and the money was found on his person. The resulting
scandal prompted Pedro Saad to hasten to Quito where he read the Pichincha
Central Committee out of the party, thus formalizing the split in the organization.[7]

The confiscation of the Chinese $25,000 also thwarted an attempt to launch
a large-scale guerrilla operation. This effort had the support of various Jacobin Leftist elements as well as that of the pro-Chinese Communists, while
the Confederacion de Trabajadores del Ecuador, controlled by the Jacobin
Leftist Partido Socialista Revolucionario Ecuadoriano, provided 50,000 su-
cres for the proposed insurrection. Subsequent attempts by Jacobin Leftists
to launch a guerrilla campaign were even less successful than this one of 1963.

In April, 1966, the military dictatorship which had ruled Ecuador for almost three years was overthrown. Thereafter, the Communists were able to

operate once more in the open. The pro-Moscow group began once again to publish their occasional newspaper *El Pueblo*, the first issue of which was dated June 25, 1966.

This newspaper demonstrated the pro-Soviet and pacific line of the Pedro Saad Communist group. It had a eulogistic article on the USSR, commemorating the 25th anniversary of the German invasion of the Soviet Union. It had an appeal to the Partido Socialista Revolucionario to form a united front for the coming elections for a Constitutional Assembly as the core of a new Frente de Liberacion Nacional to rally all "popular and revolutionary forces" and as "an indispensable instrument for obtaining our objectives."

The same issue of *El Pueblo* published resolutions of a recent plenary meeting of the Party's Central Committee. One resolution denounced "the betrayal of a miniscule fractionalist group which attempted to assault the direction of the Party to overcome it and destroy it," and claimed: "The fractionalists didn't struggle against the dictatorship and all their activity was concentrated on attacking the Party, its Directorate, and its policy."

A lead editorial in *El Pueblo* called for unification of all Leftist forces in the country for the coming constitutional assembly elections. But it specified: "In this revolutionary coalition there is no room for anti-Communists and divisionists of the revolutionary movement. There can be no revolutionary coalition with these elements."

In Colombia, elements of the Juventud Comunista (Young Communist League) were long discontented with the relatively pacific policies of the Partido Comunista. The *Peking Review* of May 1, 1964, reported their finally breaking away to form the Union de Jovenes Comunistas. This later became the Partido Comunista Marxista-Leninista, of pro-Chinese orientation. This group gave all of the support within its limited power to guerrilla groups operating in various parts of the country. Although the PCM-L was able to cause some difficulties to the pro-Russian Communist party within the labor movement, its influence was much less than that of the orthodox party.

At the time of the formation of the pro-Chinese Colombian group, there already existed in the country several guerrilla forces, as well as various purely bandit gangs. In addition, the orthodox Communist party controlled several enclaves which for decades had been under their control and had resisted all efforts of the Army to overcome them. As a means of giving an appearance of new militancy to their party, the pro-Russian Communists proclaimed the militia which had been defending these conclaves under their control to be the Fuerzas Armadas Revolucionaries Colombianas. However, this rechristening of the armed forces at the disposal of the orthodox Communists did not signify that they were giving general endorsement to a violent road to power. They still remained loyal to the policy of attempting to build a broad coalition to fight the dominant Liberal-Conservative party combination which controlled the government. They concentrated most of their activity on the labor movement.

An article in the pro-Russian Colombian party "theoretical" journal *Documentos Politicos* of May, 1966, replying to attacks which had been made on the Partido Comunista by other extremist groups for allegedly sabotaging the guerrilla war, outlined the party's official position thus (p. 103):

It is clear that our line maintains the combination of different forms of combat, and we oppose unilateral concepts of the Colombian struggle. In Colombia there are developing violent and non-violent struggles, armed and civic ones, legal and illegal, parliamentary and extraparliamentary. The line forged by the Tenth Congress takes into account this reality.

However, when this same article deals with the armed conflicts issue, it talks only of the defensive actions of militia in its several small enclaves in some of the more remote parts of the country. It comments: "Our armed struggle has frustrated the imperialist plans to convert Colombia into a showcase of the 'invincible' counter-guerrilla struggle. Marquetalia, El Porto, Riochiquito, 26 de Septiembre, and other zones of self defense are not our invention, they are a wall which the Laso plan has found impenetrable."

The reluctance of the pro-Soviet party to participate in violence outside of these enclaves was further shown by an article in the July 7, 1966, issue of its official newspaper *Voz Proletaria*. This piece discusses the problem of workers on a plantation of the Cauca Valley region. It comments that the refusal of peasants on the La Manuelita plantation to join local government-sponsored civil defense units

. . . has been a clear form of self defense of the masses, developed so far within pacific limits, in which the principal weapon has been the formation of a proletarian consciousness. And perhaps one of the lessons best underscored by this experience has been its massive character completely resistant to the shouting and demagoguery of the small extremist groups . . .

It is well known that a correct criterion for self-defense implies the utilization of all the pacific instruments available, so long as the character of the aggression allows them to be operative, but also, collective resistance to aggression by the most adequate means in each circumstance. The workers of Manuelita and all those who are in a similar situation can still find great defensive resources by means of public denunciation, increasing the cohesion of their own forces, of gaining active and belligerent solidarity of the popular masses. . . .

The pro-Soviet stand of this party was clearly shown in the June 30 number of *Voz Proletaria*. It contained an interview with the Colombian Young Communist delegate to the recent congress of the Soviet Konsomols. The delegate,

Manuel Romero, praised the determination of the Konsomols "to cultivate Soviet patriotism, the noble sentiment of friendship of peoples, the readiness to defend with arms in hand the conquests of October, and the sacred frontiers of the Socialist fatherland." The same issue carried a eulogistic review of a recently translated Soviet tome on logic. There was no mention of China in either of these issues of the weekly of the Partido Comunista de Colombia.

In 1970 the Partido Comunista indicated its adherence to the relatively peaceful policies advocated by Moscow by offering candidates in municipal elections, including Gilberto Vieira, the party's secretary.

In Bolivia in the middle of 1965, nine members of the Central Committee of the pro-Moscow Communist party of that country withdrew to form a rival party, of Chinese orientation. It was reported by the pro-Moscow international monthly *World Marxist Review* of July, 1965, to have appreciable influence in three departments and to have small party organizations in three others. However, the bulk of Communist influence in the labor movement continued to be that of the pro-Muscovites.

Some elements of the pro-Chinese Communist party were involved in the guerrilla movement [reportedly] led by Ernesto Ché Guevera in 1967. However, as Richard Gott, writing in *The Nation* of November 20, 1967, commented on that party: "Since the recent mysterious death of the pro-Peking miners' leader, Federico Escobar, the Chinese wing of the Communist movement in Bolivia has all but collapsed, and in fact neither of the two Communist parties now enjoys much support."

The Paraguayan Communist Party, too, has been split in recent years. Herbert Dinerstein comments on this:

The Paraguayan Communist Party, which has suffered under the attentions of the Stroessner regime had for some time been advocating a policy of violence. Recently, the Party split on just how much violence it should employ, and the minority, who followed the more moderate Soviet line, received the blessings of the Argentine Communist Party. . . . The present situation appears to be that the larger section of the Paraguayan Party under the leadership of Creydt, who had been head of the Party for many years, has broken away and that only the remnant is Soviet-oriented.[8]

In addition to the more or less major splits in Latin-American countries which we have noted, there have occurred others of less consequence. In Mexico, Chile, and one or two other countries small groups broke away from the pro-Moscow parties to form miniscule pro-Peking parties, which were no challenge to the influence of the older groups. The January 19, 1968, issue of *Peking Review* claimed ten pro-Peking parties in Latin America.

The Venezuelan Communist Party's attitude has been one worthy of special note. We shall deal with it more amply in our discussion of the Fidelista tendency among Latin-American Communists. Here it is sufficient to note that although the Venezuelan party engaged in guerrilla activities which brought it the approbation of the Chinese Communists, it also succeeded in maintaining close and friendly relations with the CPSU.

THE CHILEAN SITUATION

ERNEST HALPERIN HAS COMMENTED WITH REGARD TO CHILE AND THE SINO-SOVIET conflict that it "is probably the country in which the issues at stake are being debated more extensively and the debate can be followed more easily than anywhere else in Latin America."[9] He might have added that at least until January, 1966, it was the country whose Communist party had been most openly in direct conflict with that of China.

For several years after the Sino-Soviet conflict came to public notice in 1960, the Chilean Communists tried to act publicly as if it didn't exist. However, as early as February 8, 1961, the Chilean party had expressed its concern about the Chinese position in a letter to the Chinese Communist Party. Ernst Halperin quotes a passage of this letter as follows:

In Chile the reactionary press, the Trotskyist groups, and other enemies of the workers' movement wage a sustained campaign of scandal and misinterpretation based on the positions maintained by the Communist Party of China. Furthermore, the position of your party concerning the problem of peaceful coexistence has been joyfully welcomed by the Trotskyists and other renegades of the revolutionary movement.[10]

By January, 1963, public attacks by the Chinese-line Albanian party on the Chilean party's pacific line had sufficiently annoyed the Chileans that they directed another confidential letter to the Chinese party. This letter read in part:

Before terminating this letter we wish to tell the Chinese comrades frankly and openly that we feel preoccupied and justifiably worried by certain situations which affect the normal and fraternal relations between our two parties.

Continually and in increasing quantities, broad mass organizations are receiving a copious correspondence from the Albanian Party of Labor, as well as some Chinese publications, which, instead of furthering the ideological and political unity of the Communist movement, insist on accentuating the divergences to which we have referred above, and what is worse, are threatening to confuse many elements.[11]

In June, 1963, the Chilean party's Central Committee had a long discussion on "the differences of opinion with the Chinese comrades," some of the details of which were made public almost a year later. In this meeting, Luis Corvalan, Secretary General of the party, ridiculed the Chinese as being supported only by the Albanians among all the world's Communist parties. He also attacked Chinese attempts to infiltrate the Chilean party. This part of Corvalan's statement went as follows:

If the Communist Party of China considers our position to be erroneous, it could address itself to the Central Committee of our party, officially presenting to us its point of view of inviting us to a bilateral conversation. This would be the proper procedure. But what has happened is that, disregarding all the norms fixed for interparty relations, it has devoted itself as has been said, to propagating its erroneous concepts in the ranks of our party, to attempting to influence our members, to winning supporters for its line. This is without a doubt an unfriendly attitude, an undermining, splitting, and disrupting activity.

The matter becomes even graver if one takes into account that in order to do this it has sought the collaboration of party members, recruited individually and against the will of our Central Committee, which had been expressly made known to the Chinese comrades. The attitude of the Communist Party of China does not conform to its repeated declarations regarding the equality of all the parties.[12]

In ending his discussion, Corvalan announced that the Chilean party had decided to forbid its members to visit China "until the norms which have been violated by the Chinese comrades are reestablished."[13]

Meanwhile, a small group of Communist party intellectuals had started the so-called Spartacus Group. A publishing house established by the Spartacus Group became the principal vehicle for the publication in Chile of Chinese materials. Members of the group were expelled from the Chilean Communist party in October, 1963.[14] In May, 1966, the Spartacus Group joined with another small faction of dissidents known as the Unión Comunista Rebelde "and other revolutionary people" to form a new party, the Partido Comunista Revolucionario, the establishment of which was hailed in the August 5, 1966, issue of *Peking Review*.

In 1968 the pro-Chinese Communists began publication of what was supposed to be a bi-monthly magazine *Causa Marxista-Leninista*. Its first issue proclaimed that the magazine would have two objectives: "to demonstrate that Scientific Socialism is still valid in all essential aspects," and "to defend and propagate fully the thought of Mao Tse-tung."[15]

Aside from the small number of defectors from the Communist party, the Chinese rallied most of their backing in Chile from Trotskyites and elements of the Socialist party. For some time, their most important ally was Clodomiro Almeyda, leader of the left-wing of the Chilean Socialist Party. Halperin quotes one of Almeyda's statements in favor of the Chinese international thesis thus:

ROBERT J. ALEXANDER

It seems to me that for the semi-colonial and dependent countries, and especially for their revolutionary movement, a policy of peaceful coexistence, systematically implemented in the manner advocated by its most determined partisans, implies a position of subordination and passivity which appears to me to be negative. . . . Furthermore, it seems to me . . . that there is a certain correspondence between the policy of peaceful coexistence between states of different social structure and the internal policy of the peaceful road in the semi-colonial and dependent countries.[16]

Almeyda failed early in 1964 in an attempt to capture control of the Socialist party. Subsequently his influence declined sharply, and by the middle of 1966 the influence of the Chinese point of view had diminished considerably within the Socialist ranks, in considerable degrees as the result of defeats which the Chinese government's foreign policy had suffered in Indonesia and Africa during the preceding year.[17] Thereafter, the more extreme members of the Socialist party were more attracted to the Fidelista version of Marxism-Leninism than to Maoism.

ROLE OF THE JACOBIN LEFT

The Fidelista "Third Force" version of Communism was generally more attractive in Latin America to those elements on the extreme Left who did not come out of the traditional Communist parties, than was the Chinese type of Marxism-Leninism. This current found its inspiration and leadership in Castro's Communist Party of Cuba.

Elsewhere, the writer has defined this group of latter-day Marxist-Leninists as the "Jacobin Left." It consisted until 1959 of small but highly vocal groups in Latin-American politics who, like the French Jacobins of the 1790s, tended to be xenophobically nationalistic, anxious for fundamental social change at whatever cost, and were contemptuous of democracy. These groups developed principally in the 1950s and early 1960s, in many cases as extremist elements within parties of democratic reform. They adopted the philosophical outlook and the slogans of Marxism-Leninism, but in most cases lacked the extensive training and indoctrination of the orthodox Communists. They consisted principally of university (or even high school) students or young professional people, which almost by definition means that they did not come from the socially lower elements of Latin America.

The Jacobin Left was from the beginning rather disparaging towards the orthodox Communists as being too conservative, too little inclined to militant action. They regarded the Soviet Union itself as having become too conservative, with having too little revolutionary fervor, although for a short while after the Russians began helping the Castro regime they were more or less enthusiastic about the possibilities of getting material aid for "the revolution" from the USSR. During this period, the Jacobin Left was willing to work with the orthodox Communists, but after the missile crisis of 1962 and the evident hesitancy of the Soviet Union to get itself involved in any further adventures in Latin America, they tended once again to shy away from their fellow Marxist-Leninists.

At their inception, the Jacobin Left tended to look to the Chinese as being soulmates, particularly as the Sino-Soviet polemics developed. However, the Chinese were a long way from Latin America, and the possibility of their aiding the "revolution" in Latin America was obviously rather limited. As between the Chinese and the Russians, the Jacobin Left certainly favored the former—although this did not necessarily mean that they would have been willing to give the slavish kind of loyalty to China which the orthodox Communists for so long gave to the Soviet Union. Their militant nationalism tended to rule out that possibility; and similarly made the Jacobin Leftists welcome the bid for leadership within the international Communist movement which Fidel Castro clearly began to make in 1966.

The Jacobin Leftists generally have constituted small and relatively isolated groups. Among them might be noted the faction of the Chilean Socialist Party, the element around Ché Guevera in the old Cuban 26th of July Movement, the Movimiento de la Izquierda Revolucionaria in Venezuela, and similarly named groups in Peru and Chile, the Movimiento Popular Dominicano of the Dominican Republic, the Partido Socialista Revolucionario of Ecuador, a small splitaway group of the democratic Leftist National Liberation Party of Costa Rica, and various small groups in Colombia.

THE CUBAN CASE

THE JACOBIN LEFTISTS HAVE SINCE 1959 LOOKED FOR LEADERSHIP IN THE CASTRO government in Cuba. This fact has been a complicating factor in the relations of the Cuban regime with the two factions of the orthodox Communist movement.

The Sino-Soviet controversy was for some years a particularly difficult problem for the Castro government and the Communist movement in Cuba. Although politically and economically very dependent upon the Soviet Union, the Cuban regime for a while showed extensive sympathy for the Chinese side in the international Communist struggle. However, beginning in 1966, the Castro regime provided ample evidence of its intention of staking out its own claim to leadership of a faction in international Communism, independent of both Moscow and Peking; and in this attempt it drew wide support from the Jacobin Leftist Marxist-Leninists.

ROBERT J. ALEXANDER

In some ways at least, Castro might have seemed to be the logical person to be the leader of the pro-Chinese elements in Latin America. He had seized control of Cuba by the guerrilla warfare which Peking tends to recommend as the preferred road to power. His success had inspired many small groups in other Latin American countries to try to copy his example. The success of one or more of these groups with Cuban aid would tend to confirm the position which Castro had arrogated to himself from the beginning as leader of The Revolution throughout the hemisphere. Finally, Castro seemed to be convinced that his own revolution in Cuba would not be secure from American attack until a successful similar uprising had taken place somewhere on the continent, to divert attention of the United States from Cuba.

However, on various occasions Castro made it clear he was not taking sides in the Sino-Soviet fight. Thus as late as January 1, 1965, in a speech commemorating the sixth anniversary of the triumph of his revolution, Fidel Castro commented that "the increases in sugar production will go fundamentally, to the Socialist camp, with prices which are satisfactory for us; because both the USSR and the Popular Republic of China pay us for sugar at more than six cents [a pound] and are the two best consumers that we have."[18]

Several times Castro appealed to the contending factions in the international Communist movement to bury their differences. For instance, as late as March 13, 1965, Fidel commented at some length on "these problems which are concerned with the divisions and discord in the Socialist camp." In this speech, he commented; "Insofar as discord is concerned, unfortunately there has been enough and a bit more than enough, and a bit more than is convenient for the interests of the people, and unfortunately it has been useful to the interests of the enemies of the people."

Castro went on to note that "little countries, like Viet Nam and Cuba, have sufficient instinct to see clearly and to understand that no one more than we in special situations, 90 miles away from the Yankee Empire, is so affected by these divisions and these discords, which weaken the force of the Socialist camp."

In an eloquent denunciation of the split existing in the Communist world, Castro summed up his case thus:

All of us in this revolutionary process have taught ourselves from the beginning the idea that everything which divides weakens, that all that disunites is bad for our people and good for imperialism. And the masses of our people have understood from the first moment the need for unity, and unity has been converted into an essential question for the Revolution, a password for all the people. And we ask ourselves if the imperialists have disappeared, we ask ourselves if the imperialisms are not attacking North Vietnam, we ask ourselves if there they are not killing men and women of the people.[19]

In addition to denouncing divisions in the Communist camp, Castro cautioned both sides against attempting to bring their quarrels to Cuba. In this same March 13, 1965, speech, Fidel proclaimed:

Certainly we have every right, an absolute right, which I think no one can question, to bar from our country and the midst of our people such discord and such Byzantine battles.

And it is necessary that they know that here propaganda is made by our Party! That here orientation is given by our Party! That here this is all something within our jurisdiction! And that we don't want there to come here any apple of discord, because it does us no good. No one can bring here the contraband of an apple of discord! And that our enemies, our enemies, our enemies, are the Yankee imperialists. Our only insuperable contradiction is the Yankee imperialism! The only adversary against which we are disposed to break all of our lances is imperialism.[20]

In spite of Castro's widely proclaimed efforts to remain neutral in the Sino-Soviet dispute, the policies of his party and his government have zig-zagged over the years in response to international pressure and the facts of life within Cuba itself. Between 1964 and 1966 Castro made a serious effort to cement his relations with the USSR; from 1966 to 1969, he was exceedingly provocative in his treatment of both the Soviet Union and China, and was obviously staking out his own claim to independent leadership in the Communist world; starting in 1969 he veered back towards almost ostentatious friendship with Russia, while virtually ignoring the Chinese.

By 1964 the Russians had several reasons to be unhappy with Fidel and the Cuban experiment. For one thing, it was costing them extensive resources which they could as well use elsewhere. Second, Castro and his associates were insisting on the guerrilla war as the only viable road to power in Latin America, and were quarreling with some of the pro-Soviet parties in Latin America which did not agree with this point of view. Finally, his position on the Sino-Soviet dispute was anything but satisfactory to the Russians.

In retrospect, it would appear that the end of Castro's neutrality in the Sino-Soviet feud came in 1964. There may well have been considerable arm twisting of Castro and his friends by the Soviet leaders, to bring them to make such a substantial change in their policies as subsequently took place. However, it also is clear that the Soviet Union made certain concessions, at least in words, that made more explicit than previously had been the case its acceptance of possible alternative roads to power in Latin America.

Herbert Dinerstein cites two articles which appeared in the Soviet theoretical journal *Kommunist* in the middle of 1964 which may well have sig-

nalled the concession which the Soviet Union was willing to make. He quotes
the first of these articles as follows:

A study of the programs of the communist parties of Latin America shows that
the form of struggle has not been absolutized by the Communists and that they
change according to situation in one or another country.
Latin American Communists consistently support the implementation of the
line indicated in the programmatic documents of the international communist
movement and reject the position of the Chinese leaders who are trying to impose
on all the parties the strategy and tactics which they worked out in the specific conditions of their own country.[21]

Dinerstein notes that this article then went on to cite the programs of the
Chilean and Salvadorean parties, both of which opposed the resort to violence. He notes that the second of the *Kommunist* articles, however, made the
following concession to the violence formula:

An analysis of recent events established that in countries where dictators are in
power, dictators who are the henchmen of foreign monopolies, the development
of the struggle on a broad front, including armed struggle, and the creation of
partisan detachments in some areas, is a completely justified course.[22]

Dinerstein adds, "Then follows a warning that this doesn't apply to liberal
reformist regimes."
The meeting of minds between Castro and the Soviet leaders culminated
late in 1964 with a meeting of Latin-American Communist parties in Havana.
Dinerstein notes that this meeting "adopted a resolution which reflected the
policy change which the CPSU had initiated in the summer or, more likely,
had accepted at Castro's urging." He goes on to describe the resolution:

The resolution called for "support in an active form to those who at present are
subjected to severe repressions, such as the Venezuelan, Colombian, Guatemalan,
Honduran, Paraguayan, and Haitian fighters." It took the Soviet side in the Sino-
Soviet conflict and called for the unity of each party. Since none of the Chinese
splinters among the Latin-American Communist parties had been invited to the
meeting, it was obvious that unity within each of the Latin American parties was
to be interpreted as applying to parties which followed the Soviet lead.[23]

Dinerstein comments on the significance of this meeting:

What seems to have happened at Havana is that the Soviet Union on the one
hand secured the support of Cuba and other Latin-American parties against the
Chinese, but on the other hand made support of its position on China easier for
those parties by making explicit that there were several Soviet links in Latin
America. The Havana communique called for a further meeting, or meetings, of
groups of Latin-American communist parties, implying that they should either

concert their activities or agree to pursue different policies in different areas. Unity of the Latin-American parties was restored by the explicit endorsement of diversity of policy.[24]

While negotiations were apparently in progress between the Cuban and Russian leaders, the Cuban Communists were starting a drastic change in two of the issues which had existed between the two groups, internal economic policy in Cuba and alignment of Cuba within the International Communist movement. The net result was that by the middle of 1965 the Cuban Communist Party had moved closer to the Soviet camp in the worldwide dispute—although not necessarily agreeing with all of the CPSU's allies.

Of considerable significance were the changes which had begun by 1964 in Cuban internal economic policy. During the first years of the Castro regime, the government had laid great stress on programs to diversify agriculture and industrialize the country. Castro promised that by 1970 the country would be one of Latin America's major steel producers. It was also to be self-sufficient in agricultural products which the country had previously imported.

Both agricultural diversification and industrialization were failures. The result was that while the land formerly cultivated in sugar had been converted for growing other crops and sugar production declined disastrously, the country did not become more self-sufficient in other agricultural products or manufactured goods. Relatively few new industries were established, but many of those which were equipped with United States machinery were forced to retrench or to close entirely because of lack of replacement parts.

All this added up to a larger financial and material burden for the Soviet Union. By 1964 the leaders of the USSR were skeptical about continuing to spend so much on their Cuban junior partner for an indefinite period of time.

This preoccupation of the Soviet leaders did not apparently go unheeded by the Cubans. By 1964 the Cuban regime had decided to alter fundamentally its economic policy. Castro announced the government's intention of concentrating its efforts on the sugar industry once again. It was his determination, he said, that the country produce 10,000,000 tons by 1970, as compared with about 7,000,000 which was the highest output ever reached by Cuba, and with about 3,800,000 which the country had had in 1963 and 1964. At the same time, the emphasis on immediate industrialization on a large scale was dropped, and the establishment of a steel industry was postponed until the 1970s.

In his speech on the Sixth Anniversary of the Revolution, January 2, 1965, Fidel Castro spoke at some length about this fundamental change in economic policy. First, he admitted the "errors" of the first period when he said:

And there was something which perhaps at the beginning of the Revolution was not seen clearly, and this something was the extraordinary natural conditions of our country, the extraordinary possibilities of our agriculture. What had happened? Sugar monoculture, restrictions of sugar production, the lack of markets, had caused a certain allergy for sugar, had brought about a kind of allergy, a lack of faith in agriculture. The need to develop industry was translated into a kind of subestimation of the possibilities of our agriculture.[25]

Then Castro pointed out that the situation was now going to be different:

Therefore, we have understood that, in the new conditions in which we have a practically unlimited market, in which the needs of the people increase day by day, in which there is practically unlimited internal market, agriculture must be the basis of our development, and the industrialization of the country, industrialization which will not tarry, can be brought about to the degree that we succeed in having an extraordinary agricultural development. Agriculture will be, then, the basis of our economic development, and agriculture will be the basis of our industrial development.[26]

In his earlier speech on January 23, 1964, reporting on his second trip to the Soviet Union, Castro had already indicated the degree to which future economic development of the country was going to have to depend upon the country's ability to export agricultural products, and particularly sugar. Discussing the plans for 10,000,000 ton production by 1970 he noted that "this signifies the possibility, if we work well, that by 1970 our exports, which have been calculated in some 850 million pesos, will reach by this time between 1,200 and 1,500 million pesos." He then adds: "The country can propose the goal of 1,500 million pesos of exports for the year 1970. It can propose it and in consonance with this can propose an economic development in accord with the income which we are going to have."[27]

THE CUBAN INDEPENDENT LINE

ALTHOUGH ACCEPTING SOVIET "ADVICE" ON ITS OWN INTERNAL ECONOMIC POLI-cies, the Castro regime did not adopt the Soviet line on the road to revolution in Latin America and other underdeveloped countries. Some indication of the position of the Cuban Communists on this question was given by the speech of Armando Hart, Organization Secretary of the Partido Comunista de Cuba, to the 23rd Congress of the Communist Party of the Soviet Union early in 1965. Although there was no talk in this speech about the Andes be-coming "the Sierra Maestra of South America," such as Fidel and others had engaged in during earlier years,[28] Hart by no means took a generally pacific line when he commented:

For the unliberated countries of Asia, Africa and Latin America, to accelerate the revolution means to push most decidedly the struggle against the reactionary native classes allied with Yankee imperialism and against imperialism itself. To stimulate the most decided struggle in the conditions of most of the peoples of Asia, Africa and Latin America means to confront the aggression and the violence of the exploiters and imperialists with resolute, combative, audacious and violent action of the revolutionary vanguard and the masses. Conformity and passivity in face of the violence of the oppressors who are attempting to continue the regime of exploitation and blood against the peoples, resorting increasingly to the abuse of force, will never be a revolutionary policy.

While thus diverging from the Soviet line, Hart paid a glowing tribute to the USSR itself. He emphasized the importance of the aid the Castro Revolution had received from "the Soviet Union and the socialist camp in general," and commented, "We wish, in a special way, to recognize the aid which the Soviet Union has given in the defence of our country. The experience of the Cuban Revolution demonstrates, possibly more than any other event, what is the correlation of forces in the contemporary world and the importance which the support and aid of class brothers in the rest of the world has for the struggle and liberation of any people."

The militant position which the Cubans continued to assume on the road to power issue was also demonstrated by its playing host to the so-called Tri-Continental Congress in January, 1966. Although a Soviet delegation took an active part in this meeting, the Chinese were snubbed, and Fidel chose it as his platform from which to announce his open break with China, the resolutions adopted by the Congress were certainly not along the line of the parliamentary, peaceful road to power. It adopted specific resolutions endorsing the guerrilla wars presumed to be in progress in Venezuela, Colombia, Peru, and Guatemala, and called on "all peoples of the world" to support these guerrilla efforts.

Cuba Socialista, the theoretical organ of the Cuban Communist Party, devoted its entire February, 1966, issue to the speeches and resolutions of this Conference, officially known as The First Conference of Solidarity of the Peoples of Africa, Asia, and Latin America.

On Cuban initiative, a special resolution was adopted at the Conference on Peaceful Coexistence. This document read as follows:

Peaceful coexistence refers exclusively to the relations among states of different social and political regimes.

One cannot refer to coexistence between exploited social classes within one country, nor to the struggle of peoples oppressed by imperialism against their oppressors.

Consequently, the argument of peaceful coexistence cannot be used as has been suggested by imperialism and its followers to limit the right of peoples to make their social revolution.

Peaceful coexistence presupposes unlimited respect for the principles of self-determination of nations and sovereignty of all states great and small.

Defence of the Principle of peaceful coexistence carries with it repudiation of imperialist aggression, the criminal use of force against oppressed peoples and decided repudiation of foreign intervention in the internal affairs of other states, which represent violation of the principle of peaceful coexistence. It gives progressive and democratic states the right to repel the aggressor and to give the most decided aid to victims of aggression, and in so doing they are defending the principle of peaceful coexistence.[29]

It is of interest to note that the Latin-American delegations to this meeting were by no means limited to those representing orthodox communist parties. Jacobin Leftist groups and other non-Moscow elements were heavily represented.

The Conference decided to establish both a world-wide Continuing Committee and a similar organization for Latin America. However, the Cubans did not get around to setting up the Latin-American group until May.[30]

A further step towards asserting an independent position of leadership within the international Communist movement was taken by Castro at the Congress in Havana in July, 1967, which established the Organización Latino Americana de Solidaridad (OLAS). The resolutions of this Congress showed sharp divergence from the position of the Soviet Union.[31]

Three resolutions were of particular importance in defining the independent position of the Cuban-led Communist faction. One of these bitterly denounced the Venezuelan Communist party which, with the support of the Soviet Union, has abandoned the guerrilla war in which it had been engaged for several years. A second condemned "a tendency . . . in some states of the socialist camp to grant technical and financial aid" to "puppet governments of Latin America," a direct denunciation of Soviet overtures to the Colombian, Chilean, and other governments.

A third resolution laid down the ideological line, particularly with regard to the road to power, of the Cuban-led revolutionaries. Among other things, this resolution noted the need for "a common strategy," which should be in terms of "a clear, rounded expression of solidarity, the character of which is the struggle itself, extending throughout the continent in the form of guerrilla war and liberation armies."[32]

CASTRO'S BREAK WITH CHINA

WHILE CERTAINLY NOT FULLY ALLYING ITSELF WITH THE SOVIET SIDE IN THE Sino-Soviet dispute, the Castro regime broke spectacularly with China early in 1966. As early as the latter half of 1964 Cuban delegates to International

Communist front organization meetings began to abandon their neutrality and vote and speak for the Russians. Also about this same time, Cuban publications began to play down the importance of events occurring in China and statements of Chinese leaders, while the Chinese commenced to do the same thing with regard to the Cubans.[33] However, no open break between the two Communist leaderships came until January, 1966.

Castro chose the meeting of the Tri-Continental Congress in Havana, on January 2, 1966, to announce his quarrel with the Chinese. He limited this discussion largely to the fact that the Chinese had refused to renew their trade agreement with Cuba to exchange rice for sugar on terms to which the Cubans could agree.

Castro's first anti-Chinese diatribe was answered by a second rank official of the Chinese Ministry of Foreign Trade, a fact which apparently hurt Castro's *amour propre* considerably. Fidel replied to this Chinese statement on February 6, 1966. He started by commenting: "These statements of the Chinese government put in the mouth of a supposed 'functionary' of the Ministry of Foreign Trade of that country, are to a high degree insidious. No one will ever believe that in China an obscure and unknown functionary of the Ministry of Foreign Trade could make a statement in which the Prime Minister of a socialist country, with which formal and diplomatic relations are maintained, is called a liar, statements which involve, because of their political substances and disrespectful manner, the possibility of seriously affecting the relations between two countries like China and Cuba."[34]

Castro first disputed the facts and figures the Chinese gave on trade between the two countries. Then he quoted at great length the speech which he had given on March 13, 1965, which we have previously noted, and in which he warned the larger Communist countries against bringing their quarrels to Cuba. Then he indicated that the Chinese had ignored his warning and had intensified their propaganda in Cuba since he had given his admonition. Part of this section of Castro's speech went as follows:

On September 12th, the Ministry of the Revolutionary Armed Forces reported that a massive distribution of this material was being carried out systematically among the officers of the Revolutionary Armed Forces of Cuba by the representatives of the Chinese government. This propaganda was being sent to the General Staff of the Revolutionary Armed Forces, to the General Staffs of Armies, Army Corps and Divisions, to the General Staffs of the different branches of the Army, to the chiefs of political sections, and in many cases directly to officers of our armed forces at their home addresses. On occasions Chinese representatives tried to make direct contact with Cuban officers and in some cases went so far as to approach officers in an apparent attempt to personally attract them, either to convert them or perhaps to obtain information.

ROBERT J. ALEXANDER

A kind of massive distribution of propaganda, similar to that described in the report of the Ministry of the Armed Forces, was being carried out among numerous civilian state officials, although to a lesser degree.[35]

Castro then noticed that on September 14, 1965, the Cuban government had expressed "our indignation, our protest, and our demand that such activities cease. With complete clarity we told the representative of the Chinese government that these methods and procedures were exactly the same as those used by the U.S. Embassy in our country. . . ."[36]

The seriousness of Castro's break with the Chinese was indicated by the last paragraph of Fidel's speech of February 6. He said:

This pretension of the Chinese government can only be explained as an example of absolute contempt for our country; of total ignorance of the character and sense of dignity of our people. What was involved was no longer the number of tons more or less of rice, or the greater or smaller quantity of cloth, but a much more important and fundamental question for the people: whether, in the world of tomorrow, powerful countries, whether in the world of tomorrow which revolutionaries are fighting to achieve, there will continue to prevail the worst methods of piracy, oppression and filibusterism, which slave and feudal societies, absolute monarchies, bourgeois states, and in the contemporary world, imperialist states, have imposed upon the world ever since class societies existed.[37]

The Chinese responded to Castro's break with them with an apparent attempt to appeal to the Cuban people over the heads of Fidel and his associates. In an article in *Remmin Ribao* of June 2, 1966, which was republished in *Peking Review* and its Spanish-language edition *Pekin Informa* on June 15, 1966, the Chinese indicated that "The Chinese people constantly support the Cuban people in their struggle against Yankee imperialism. Thus it was in the past, thus it is today and thus it will be in the future. The Chinese people will always be the most loyal and trustworthy friends of the Cuban people, and the latter can always count on the full support of the 650 million human beings in China in their just struggle against aggression."

In a somewhat circuitous way, this article attacked Castro and the Russians. It commented:

However, the Krushevist revisionists, in place of exposing the double faced counter-revolutionary tactics of North American imperialism, shout in a loud voice the need for "normalizing" the situation in the Caribbean area. Obviously, with this they mean that the Cuban people should fold their revolutionary anti-Yankee banners of the "Declaration of Havana" and renounce their just five point demands, in the vain effort to have the Cuban people, who continue with their revolution, look for "pacific coexistence" with North American imperialism, aggressive by nature. This is pretended support, and real betrayal, of the Cuban people. We always maintain that it [North American imperialism] is aggressive by nature. There is no other alternative.

However, Castro's polemics with the Chinese did not mean that he was joining the Soviet Bloc. This became clear during the early months of 1966 in an exchange of pleasantries between the Jugoslav Communists (with whom the Soviet leaders maintained friendly relations) and those of Cuba. The Jugoslav press started the controversy by making some comments about some of the Cubans' actions being "adventurous" and otherwise irresponsible.

Granma, the official organ of the Communist Party of Cuba, replied to these Jugoslav observations with a three page blast on May 15, 1966. After dismissing Jugoslav commentaries on the Cuban polemics with the Chinese Communist Party, *Granma's* marathon editorial notes, "We dispute with the leaders of the 'League of Yugoslav Communists' also on matters of principle, but on another plane that has nothing to do with the relationship between Communist Parties, since there is no communist party in Yugoslavia, and the so-called 'League of Yugoslav Communists' is neither a party nor is it Communist."[38] It goes on to accuse the Jugoslav Communists of "coinciding with Yankee imperialism."

Subsequently, Castro became openly critical of the Soviet Union's efforts to establish diplomatic and trade relations with other Latin-American countries. His party openly snubbed the USSR by carrying almost no favorable news from the Soviet Union in its official paper *Granma*. At the time of the celebration of the 50th Anniversary of the Bolshevik Revolution, in November, 1967, the Cuban party sent a very low-level delegation which quite ostentatiously left Moscow in the middle of the festivities.

THE VENEZUELAN EXPERIENCE

THE VENEZUELAN COMMUNIST PARTY IS ONE OF THE TWO ORTHODOX COMMUNIST parties of the area which for some period of time adopted in action the Castro line on the road to power, with the approval of the Chinese, although without declaring itself their ally in the international Communist conflict. It is also a horrible example of the kind of disaster which can overtake a Communist party which does not succeed when its undertakes guerrilla warfare and urban terrorism.

The Venezuelan Communist Party emerged from the period of the Pérez Jiménez dictatorship (1948–58) in a peculiarly fortunate position. Although it had been divided into two parties officially during most of this period, one of which had supported the dictatorship, the other of which had opposed it, it emerged as a united group. Because the dictatorship had wanted to use the Communists against the democratic parties (particularly Acción Democrática) which had the support of most of the country's workers and peasants, it had persecuted the Communists but little, whereas it had decimated the democratic parties, especially Acción Democrática (AD).

As a result of the tolerance of the Pérez Jiménez regime towards the Communists, they had been able to infiltrate very heavily into the newspaper profession, the teaching corps, government employment, from which known members of the democratic groups had been banned. At the same time, however, because during the last months of the dictatorship they had joined in the fight against it, the Communists shared in the credit for the ouster of the Pérez Jiménez regime.

Thus, the Venezuelan Communist Party emerged from the dictatorship as an eminently respectable group, with great influence in the press, and with prestige as fellow fighters, if somewhat tardy ones, in the struggle against the tyranny. Furthermore, because virtually all civilian politicians were convinced that it was necessary for them to present a united front to the military in order to avoid another seizure of power by the army, there was little criticism of the Communists by the leaders of the other political parties.

The Communists participated in the reorganization of the labor movement. Joint slates of all parties were put forward in the first trade union elections, with the result that the Communists controlled about 20–25% of the unions and had a veto power on the actions of the reconstituted Confederación de Trabajadores de Venezuela.

Recognized as a legal political party, the Communists were free to participate in the elections of December, 1958. They supported the candidacy of Admiral Wolfgang Larrazábal for president, and put up their own lists for Congress, getting two senators and half a dozen members of the Chamber of Deputies. The election was also notable for the fact that only one of the three presidential candidates—the victor, Rómulo Betancourt of Acción Democrática—had the political fortitude to attack the Communists and to announce that they would not participate in his administration should he win.

Finally, the Communists had succeeded in making great headway during the last years of the dictatorship and the first year or so of the restored democratic regime in proselytizing among the youth group of Acción Democrática. This was largely due to the fact that during the last few years of Pérez Jiménez, it was virtually impossible for the older Acción Democrática people to provide their youngsters with literature, whereas the Communists had wide freedom to propagandize the Marxist-Leninist philosophy in the jails and outside, with plenty of reading material available to pass on to those among whom they were seeking to win converts.

As a result of this situation, there occurred early in 1960 a serious split in the ranks of Acción Democrática, in the process of which that party—the largest in the country, and a party of the Democratic Left—lost most of its youth group. The dissidents established a rival party, of avowed Marxist-Leninist orientation, the Movimiento de la Izquierda Revolucionaria (MIR).

By 1960, therefore, the Communists occupied a stronger position in the politics of Venezuela than they had ever had before. They had representatives in Congress and in state and municipal legislatures, they had great influence in the labor movement, they had joined with MIR to take control of the student movement away from AD, which had dominated it for several decades. As the Communists were eminently respectable, politicians of most other parties hesitated to publicly attack them, and their prospects for becoming a major factor in the country's politics appeared good.

However, the Venezuelan Communists were under several kinds of pressure. The nearness of Cuba, and the similarity of experience of Venezuela and Cuba under the Pérez Jiménez and Batista dictatorships, had given the Castro phenomenon a peculiar attraction in Venezuela. Although Acción Democrática and Christian Social (COPEI) Party were soon disenchanted with Castro because of the growing brutality of his dictatorship and his increasingly close alliance with the Cuban Communists, these factors didn't reduce his attractiveness to either the MIR or the younger elements in the Communist party.

The importance of the younger elements in the Partido Comunista de Venezuela (PCV) cannot be underestimated in this period. As elsewhere, the national leadership of the Communist party tended to be fairly advanced in age. The Machado brothers, trade union leaders Rodolfo Quintero, Cruz Villegas and Jesús Farías, and other national leaders of the party were men ranging in age from their upper forties to their sixties. But during the last part of the dictatorship and the first year or so thereafter, the Communist party had been flooded by younger people, particularly from the universities, where the party had an influence which it had never enjoyed before.

These younger people were all for militant action. They scoffed at the reform program of the Betancourt Government, which was carrying out land redistribution and industrialization schemes, but at the same time was working closely with the Kennedy Administration and was committed to the maintenance of a democratic regime. It should also be noted that the Betancourt government did little to mobilize youth either in political support of its programs or to participate in them.

At the same time, the Communist Youth were to a degree contaminated by the wildness of their MIR allies. The MIR elements prided themselves on being to the Left of the Communist party, and as ex-AD members were even more bitterly opposed to the Betancourt regime than were the Communists.

The upshot of this was that the older leadership of the Venezuelan Communist Party was forced more and more into a posture of violent opposition to the Betancourt regime. One Communist member of the Chamber of Deputies was captured red-handed by the government at the time of an uprising in Carupano early in 1961. A few weeks later MIR deputy Simón Saez Mérida and several low ranking Communists were caught in Puerto Cabello, when a bloody uprising collapsed there.

As a result of the Carupano and Puerto Cabello rebellions, the Betancourt regime "suspended" legal recognition of the PCV and the MIR, and drove them into a semi-underground position. Some of their headquarters were closed, and although weekly and monthly periodicals of the two parties could still be bought in kiosks and bookstores, the Communist daily newspaper was suppressed.

When the writer was in Venezuela during July and August, 1961, some Communists with whom he talked were predicting an "armed uprising of the people," and that when such a movement took place, the Communists would align themselves "with the people." Early in the following year, incidents of terrorism in the cities of Venezuela began to mount in intensity.

However, it was in December, 1962, that the Venezuelan Communist Party formally endorsed the violent road to power. According to Carlos López, writing in the pro-Soviet *World Marxist Review* of October, 1964 (page 21), a Central Committee meeting of the party in that month "came to the conclusion that in the conditions prevailing in our country, a struggle for power by the democratic and patriotic forces and for the eventual defense of that power made recourse to *armed force* inevitable." (Italics in the original.)

Throughout much of 1962 and the early months of 1963 urban terrorism—assassination of policemen, raids on banks, burning of industiral enterprises, kidnappings—constituted a harassment and a nuisance to the Betancourt government. However, three months before the presidential and congressional election of December, 1963, the urban terrorism reached such proportions that Betancourt took the drastic step of ordering arrest of all Communist and MIR members of Congress, some of whom were known to be intellectual authors of much of the violence. In return, the terrorists' Fuerzas Armadas de Liberación Nacional (FALN) threatened that they would shoot anyone who voted in the December election.

The December, 1963, election proved an almost irreparable blow to the campaign of urban terrorism. People turned out to vote in such numbers that almost 95% of the eligible voters cast their ballots. Furthermore, the victor in the seven-sided contest was Raul Leoni, close friend of Betancourt and candidate of his party, Acción Democrática, while Rafael Caldera, nominee of COPEI, which had been a coalition partner of AD throughout the Betancourt regime, came in second.

After the election there apparently was serious reconsideration of the policy of violence within the Communist party, and perhaps also within MIR. One well-informed Venezuelan reported to the author that early in 1964 a national conference of the PCV broke up in a melee when the more moderate leaders of the party attempted to get it to reverse the violence line.

However, the upshot at that time, as reflected in the April, 1964, meeting of the Central Committee of the PCV was ratification of "the use of force in the revolutionary denouement of the Venezuelan situation and armed struggle as the basic form of the development of the revolution."[39] The only significant shift in the party's line at this time was one away from urban violence and towards guerrilla warfare in the rural areas. The essence of this position was outlined in the previously cited Carlos López article thus:

What forms of struggle will the future people's army use? In the opinion of the C. C. [Central Committee] meeting the main form will be that of the classical "guerrilla" or partisan warfare in the rural localities, with all its attributes. The enemy is particularly vulnerable in the countryside; here his control is less effective, and hence it is here that irregulars can operate with maximum chance of success and with the least losses. The maximum effort will have to be devoted to development of the movement in the mountain areas.

At the same time, of course, we must not neglect the armed struggle in the towns where, as the experience of revolutionary struggle in our country shows, the opportunities are good. Up till now the activity of the so-called combat tactical units in the main cities has introduced a specific character to the revolutionary armed action in Venezuela, distinguishing it from the liberation struggle in other countries. Still, it is clear that this will not be the principal form of struggle.[40]

For some months after this shift in emphasis to guerrilla warfare, the PCV and MIR through the FALN succeeded in causing the government considerable embarrassment. At one time there were guerrilla groups operating in as many as five different states at the same time. One American observer, Norman Gall, writing in the *New Leader* of April 12, 1965, commented thus on the situation:

The fact is, not only in the states of Trujillo and Falcon but elsewhere in key areas of the country, the Venezuelan government is now in a virtual state of war against guerrilla insurgents who are following a prescribed course of violence and economic disruption. This pattern of guerrilla insurgency is a clear reflection of the proliferating Communist literature of violence—a literature deeply indebted to the writings of Mao Tse-tung—and points to the adoption in Venezuela, of the strategy of the "Long War" akin to the conflicts effectively waged in China, Algeria, and Vietnam.

However, the guerrilla campaign was not in fact going as well for the PCV and MIR as this description would have seemed to indicate. There was strong opposition to it within both parties, on the grounds that it was in fact not working, and had only succeeded in isolating the extreme Leftists from the great masses of the Venezuelan people.

Shortly after the Gall article appeared, Domingo Alberto Rangel, leader of the MIR, from his prison cell issued an open letter to his party urging that the guerrilla campaign be called off and that the party return to the path of the democratic struggle for power. At about the same time, important Communist leaders, including former oil workers' union chief Jesús Farías, were reported to be taking the same line of argument.

Obviously, by the middle of 1965 a strong battle was raging in both the Marxist-Leninist parties over the question of violence. This struggle was highlighted when the government released from prison Communist leader Jesús Farías, and MIR chiefs Domingo Alberto Rangel and José Casals. Significantly enough, Farías headed straight for Moscow, where he was received at the airport by high figures in the Soviet regime. The change in the PCV policy shortly thereafter may well reflect his conversations with the Soviet leaders.

By the middle of 1966 the MIR had split into two separate groups, and the Partido Comunista had foresworn its emphasis on the violent road to power. Domingo Alberto Rangel took his faction of the MIR into a merger with another group which had split away from the AD in 1962, the Partido Revolucionario Nacionalista, and with a small left-wing group, the Vanguardia Popular Nacionalista, to form what they called "a single nationalist and anti-imperialist party."[41]

Meanwhile, the Political Buro of the Communist Party had issued a declaration which signified a fundamental revision of its position on the violent road to power. It called upon the party to "abandon our ultraleftist postures," and announced that "there is urgent need for action of the masses." The nature of this action now foreseen by the Buro was indicated by its comment that "intense propaganda, the use of all legal means, in the press, in Parliament, in the street, are the instruments which we must use with agility." Near the end of the declaration was an indication of the basic nature of the change the Buro was now launching in party policy in the comment: "Without renouncing our liberating objectives, secure that this attitude places us on a better road to obtain a government of democratic peace and to strengthen therefore the revolutionary movement, we today extend our hands to all sectors, parties and personalities who ask for this change."[42]

In March, 1967, the PCV went further on the line of abandonment of the insurrectionary line, at least for the time being. At a Central Committee Plenum it decided to attempt to regain legal status and participate in the elections scheduled for December, 1968.

This about-face by the Venezuelan Communists brought them into violent conflict with the Cuban leadership. On March 13, 1967, Castro denounced the Venezuelan Communist leaders as "traitors," and announced his support of those dissident Venezuelan Communist leaders who were continuing the guerrilla war. The Venezuelan leadership countered with a sharp denunciation of Castro for "meddling in the internal affairs of Venezuela." Finally, at the OLAS Conference in Havana in July–August, 1967, to which the Venezuelan Communist Party was not invited, the Cubans pushed through a resolution denouncing the Venezuelan Communist leadership along the lines which Castro had used several months earlier. The few orthodox Communist delegations attending the OLAS Conference opposed this resolution.

The Venezuelan Communists completed their repudiation of guerrilla war by organizing a front party, which gained legal recognition and participated in the 1968 election under the name Unión para Avanzar (Union to Advance). It gained one seat in the senate and six in the Chamber of Deputies. President Rafael Caldera, elected in December, 1968, recognized the Venezuelan Communist Party under its official name, Partido Comunista de Venezuela, soon after taking office in March, 1969.

This flirtation of the Venezuelan Communist Party with the violent road to power did not result in its aligning itself with the Chinese camp in the world Communist dispute. The report of the 1964 Central Committee meeting, which confirmed adherence to the violent line but provided for a switch from urban terrorism to guerrilla warfare, was published in both the pro-Soviet *World Marxist Review* and pro-Chinese publications. Although the Chinese quite obviously approved of the insurrectionary tactics adopted by the Venezuelans, they were unable to prevent the older pro-Moscow leaders of the party from giving up that line once it had failed, or from aligning the party once again firmly with the Moscow camp.

Certainly the use of insurrection had been a disaster for the Venezuelan Communist Party. It had lost virtually all of its former influence in the labor movement, was left without representation in any legislative body and even without any open publications of its own. It had lost significant ground even in the student movement. It was almost completely isolated from the main stream of national politics. Its experience would in all probability remain for some time to come as a horrible example of the dangers of the misfiring of the weapon of insurrection as the Communist means of getting to power in a Latin-American country.[43]

THE GUATEMALAN CASE

LIKE THE VENEZUELAN COMMUNIST PARTY, THAT OF GUATEMALA, THE PARTIDO
Guatemalteco del Trabajo has engaged in guerrilla war against the government of its country. This conflict greatly strained relations between the older
pro-Soviet leadership of the PGT and younger pro-Castro elements which led
the guerrilla effort. An open break took place within the Guatemalan party
early in 1968 similar to that which occurred in the Venezuelan one.

The division in the ranks of the Guatemalan Communist Party was largely
the work of youth elements. Ricardo Ramírez de León, a young Communist
leader who had spent time in both Czechoslovakia and Cuba, returned home
in 1963 and against the wishes of the official Communist party, the Partido
Guatemalteco del Trabajo (PGT), formed a guerrilla group, the Fuerzas Armadas Rebeldes (FAR), with the support of Castro. Although Ramírez officially remained a member of the PGT, the FAR was in sharp conflict with
the official Communist leadership, which was supporting a policy of legal
and semi-legal action, first against the regime of President Idígoras Fuentes
and then against that of Colonel Enrique Peralta.[44]

For some time there were two different guerrilla groups operating in
Guatemala. One was the FAR, of Young Communist origin, the other the so-
called 13th of November Movement, composed principally of young army
officers, led by Marco Antonio Yon Sosa. Although the Communists first expressed support for this group early in 1965, by the end of that year they had
withdrawn their backing.

Fidel Castro also changed his mind with regard to the two competing
guerrilla groups in Guatemala. Herbert Dinerstein has noted Fidel's change
on this issue:

For a long time he favored the MR-13 wing of the Guatemalan movement led by
Sosa, a non-Communist who typically is more strongly committed to extensive
guerrilla warfare than is the Guatemalan Communist Party. In a speech right after
the Havana conference, Castro switched the Cuban position in an attack on Sosa
that was much more prominent than the presence of non-communist Venezuelan
and Peruvian guerrillas at the conference had been. Castro may have attacked the
more militant elements of the Guatemalan guerrilla movement because he disapproved of their policy or, more likely, because he was resentful of their connection
with the Trotskyites. . . .[45]

Subsequently, after Yon Sosa had divested his movement of the Trotskyites, Castro supported the successful effort to unify the two guerrilla forces.
He also backed the break late in 1968 of the FAR with the Partido Guatemalteco del Trabajo, which like its Venezuelan counterpart had turned increas-

ingly against guerrilla activity. Early in 1967 the Guatemalan government of President Julio César Méndez Montenegro largely destroyed the rural guerrilla. As a result, the former guerrilla fighters began to resort to urban terrorism, and their efforts engendered an even more savage terrorist activity by elements of the extreme Right. The continuing urban violence was largely responsible for the defeat of the moderate leftist Partido Revolucionario of President Méndez Montenegro in the 1970 election.[46]

CUBAN QUARRELS WITH PRO-PEKING LATIN-AMERICAN PARTIES

THE FIDELISTA ELEMENT AMONG THE LATIN-AMERICAN MARXIST-LENINISTS HAS not only quarreled with the pro-Soviet parties of the area, but also with the pro-Chinese ones. This split of the Fidelistas and pro-Pekingers is clearly indicated in Chile.

The Revolutionary Communist Party, the pro-Peking group in Chile, published a pamphlet in 1967 entitled ¿Una Linea Pequeño Burgesa en la Revolucion Chilena? (A Petty Burgeois Line in the Chilean Revolution?), which was a polemic against the Fidelist Movimiento de la Izquierda Revolucionaria. The burden of the pro-Peking argument against the Castro line is summed up in the following:

As one would expect, this insurrectionist theory, urged on the whole of America by the Havana leaders, is an obvious expression of the moods, inclinations and thinking of petty-bourgeois elements. Urban terrorism does not involve the masses, is based on isolated actions which can be carried out by a very few individuals, does not need popular support and can cause enemy losses without enlisting the proletarian masses. This is the petty-bourgeoisie's favorite type of struggle, reflecting its individualism and its misgivings about joining the proletariat. Many of these people are capable of throwing a bomb, but very few of them are disposed to go out and share the hardships of the workers and peasants, to learn about class consciousness from the workers and peasants.[47]

After thus denouncing the Castroite line as "petty-bourgeois," the Chilean pro-Peking document denounces the theory developed by Ché Guevara and Regis Debray according to which a small group can engender a guerrilla force out of which will arise a revolutionary party, in the following terms:

The theory of the "guerrilla foco" also has its class roots. It is based on the assumption that a group of petty-bourgeois revolutionaries grafted onto the countryside . . . can carry out armed assaults capable of rallying the peasant masses to its ranks, of arousing the revolutionary conscience of the whole country, and, finally, of taking power. . . . The guerrilla group without the direction of a proletarian party may be able to realize some military successes and even, in some cases, do away with an unpopular government, but if it is not controlled by the proletariat, it inevitably transforms itself into a new oppressor.

CASTRO'S TURN IN 1969–70

AFTER THREE YEARS OF ALMOST UNMITIGATED HOSTILITY TOWARDS THE SOVIET Union, and, after the polemics of the first months of 1966, virtually ignoring of the Chinese, Castro in 1969 swung back once again to a policy of friendliness towards the USSR. This shift was perhaps presaged in his reaction to the Soviet invasion of Czechoslovakia in August, 1968, when after admitting virtually all of the charges made against the Soviet leaders—that they had violated the rights of a small nation, that they had destroyed the autonomy of another nation's Communist party—Castro ended up by saying that this was all necessary, because the Communist rule in Czechoslovakia was in danger.

The extent of this rapprochement in 1969 and 1970 was shown by the treatment of the Soviet Union in the Cuban press, particularly *Granma*. There was once again extensive coverage of Soviet "accomplishments" and "victories." There was very friendly treatment of distinguished visitors from the USSR, including elements of the Soviet fleet; there was very extensive publicity given the small groups of Soviet citizens and people from other pro-Soviet countries of Eastern Europe which came to help in the 10 million ton harvest of 1970.

Most dramatic was the difference between Cuban treatment of the 50th Anniversary of the Bolshevik Revolution in November, 1967, and their treatment of the 100th Anniversary of Lenin's birth in January, 1970. The latter event was the occasion for much lauding of "Lenin's successors" in the Cuban press, and for the presence in Moscow of a large and prestigious Cuban delegation to participate in the ceremonies celebrating the anniversary.

The reasons for this shift of Cuban policy in 1969 and 1970 were probably connected closely with the frantic drive made in those two years to meet the target of 10 million tons of sugar which Castro had set for Cuba in the 1970 harvest. To achieve this, the Cuban regime undoubtedly needed extensive financial and technical help from the Soviet Union, as well as an assured market for the sugar should it be produced. One can surmise that the price for all of this, from the Soviet point of view was that Castro cease his polemics with the USSR and with parties friendly to it elsewhere in Latin America, and that he make his policies conform considerably more closely to those of the Soviet Union.

The shift was probably made easier by the fact that by 1969 it was obvious that the line on the Communist road to power which Castro had been so assiduously peddling between 1966 and 1969 had failed everywhere in Latin America, at least for the time being. Guerrilla wars in Bolivia, Peru, Venezuela, Argentina, and Guatemala had failed, and the efforts in Colombia had been severely curtailed by the Colombian Army. At very least, those who were still anxious to follow the line which Castro had laid down needed time to regroup and reorganize, and this period of recuperation could be used by Castro to improve his relations with the Soviet Union, which was basically opposed to the guerrilla strategy.

However, the Castro government failed in its campaign for the 10 million tons, in spite of efforts which resulted in mobilizing virtually every adult and adolescent Cuban to go out and cut cane. It remains to be seen, as this is being written, whether this failure will mark still another turn in Castro's relations with the two giants of International Communism, the Soviet Union and China.

CONCLUSION

OBVIOUSLY, THE SINO-SOVIET SPLIT HAS HAD ITS IMPACT ON LATIN AMERICA. However, it has been complicated by the emergence of an indigenous Latin-American claimant to hemispheric—and perhaps world—Communist leadership, in the form of Fidel Castro and the Communist Party of Cuba.

All traditional Communist parties have stayed loyal to Moscow. However, small dissident groups have broken away to form pro-Peking parties in a number of countries. Much more significant than these pro-Peking splitaways has been the emergence of a group of Havana-oriented parties and groups, advocating and frequently practicing urban terrorism and rural guerrilla activity as virtually the only legitimate Communist road to power. These Fidelista parties have drawn some support from younger elements within the old Communist parties, but have found their principal source of support in the Jacobin Left, consisting of Marxist-Leninists who have never previously belonged to a Communist party.

NOTES

1. For information on the early history of the Latin American Communist parties see Robert J. Alexander, *Communism in Latin America*, Rutgers University Press, New Brunswick, 1957.

2. See Osvaldo Peralva, *O Retrato*, Edicões O Globo, Porto Alegre and Rio de Janeiro, 1962.

3. See Ernst Halperin, *The Peaceful and the Violent Road, A Latin American Debate*, MIT Center for International Studies, September, 1965.

4. Herbert Dinerstein, *Soviet Policy in Latin America*, The Rand Corporation, May, 1966, p. 29.

5. Peralva, op. cit., pp. 273–75.

6. *Peking Review*, February 14, 1964.

7. This information on the Ecuadorean split was supplied to the author by a well informed foreign resident of Ecuador, who shall remain anonymous.

8. Dinerstein, op. cit., pp. 35–36.

9. Ernst Halperin, *Sino-Cuban Trends—The Case of Chile*, MIT Center for International Studies, March, 1964.

10. Ibid., p. 56.

11. Ibid., p. 71.

12. Ibid., p. 79.

13. Ibid., p. 80.

14. Ibid., p. 147.

15. *Causa Marxista-Leninista*, Volume I, Number 1, undated, but mid-1968.

16. Halperin, op. cit., p. 141. For an ample study of conflicting trends on the Chilean Left also see Ernst Halperin, *Nationalism and Communism in Chile*, MIT Press, Cambridge, 1965.

17. Interview of the writer with Federico Klein, former International Secretary of Partido Socialista de Chile, in Santiago, Chile, June 25, 1966.

18. *Obra Revolucionaria*, Havana, No. 1 of 1965, p. 26.

19. *Obra Revolucionaria*, Havana, No. 6 of 1965, p. 10.

20. Ibid., p. 13.

21. Dinerstein, op. cit., pp. 29–30.

22. Ibid., p. 30.

23. Ibid., pp. 30–31.

24. Ibid., p. 31.

25. *Obra Revolucionaria*, Havana, No. 1 of 1965, pp. 11–12.

26. Ibid., p. 12.

27. *Obra Revolucionaria*, Havana, No. 3 of 1964, p. 16.

28. *Problemas de la Paz y del Socialismo*, Bogota, Colombia, May, 1966, p. 20.

29. *Cuba Socialista*, theoretical organ of Partido Comunista de Cuba, February, 1966, pp. 151–52.

30. English language version of *Granma*, official newspaper of Partido Comunista de Cuba, May 15, 1966, p. 5.

31. For an extensive treatment of the Tri Contental and OLAS Conferences, see D. Bruce Jackson, *Castro, The Kremlin and Communism*, Johns Hopkins Press, Baltimore, 1967.

32. *World Outlook*, New York Trotskyite publication, September 22, 1967, p. 780.

33. Dinerstein, op. cit., p. 30.

34. Fidel Castro, *Betrayal by Chinese Government of Cuban Peoples Good Faith*, Havana, 1966, p. 5.

35. Ibid., p. 25.

36. Ibid., p. 26.

37. Ibid., pp. 27–28.

38. English version of *Granma*, Havana, May 15, 1966, p. 2.

39. *World Marxist Review*, monthly publication of pro-Soviet Communist parties, October 1964, p. 22.

40. Ibid., p. 23.

41. *Nuestra Palabra*, organ of Partido Comunista Argentino, Buenos Aires, June 22, 1966.

42. Ibid.

43. For a fuller discussion of the Venezuelan Communists' experience with guerrilla war, see Robert J. Alexander, *The Communist Party of Venezuela*, The Hoover Institution Press, Stanford, 1969.

44. Letter to the writer from Carlos Manuel Pellecer, former leader of Guatemalan Communist Party, dated June 23, 1965.

45. For an extensive treatment of the Guatemalan guerrilla war, see Eduardo Galeano, *Guatemala: Occupied Country*, Monthly Review Press, New York, 1969.

46. Dinerstein, op. cit., p. 40.

47. *World Revolution*, organ of Progressive Labor Party of United States, Winter, 1967, p. 32.

CHAPTER III

AN INTRODUCTION TO USSR RELATIONS WITH MEXICO, URUGUAY, AND CUBA

J. Gregory Oswald

THE HISTORY OF USSR RELATIONS WITH COUNTRIES OF LATIN AMERICA SINCE 1917 is very uneven. In diplomacy, it is anomalous, in trade relations almost insignificant. But in the realm of ideological impact and international political and military role playing, USSR ties with certain states and political parties of Latin America have become increasingly important. A combination of Slavic soul and Soviet scheming, the USSR presence in Latin America is there to stay. And it will grow stronger in time as it has in Europe, Asia, Middle East, and Africa. Assuming that this generalization is acceptable, we might first proceed to a basic historical periodization of Soviet–Latin-American relations and then examine more closely Soviet ties with Mexico, Uruguay, and Cuba.

The contemporary preeminence of the USSR in Cuba is paradoxical in the history of Soviet–Latin-American diplomatic relations. From 1924 until 1960, Soviet efforts to broaden political and economic ties with the countries of that region were largely frustrated. But in the decade since the Cuban Revolution the Soviets have renewed and expanded their political and economic relations with most of the countries of Latin America.

There are seven discernible stages in USSR–Latin-American relations: 1) the period from 1924 to 1935, during which time the Soviets established trade and diplomatic relations with Mexico and Uruguay, while at the same time they alienated these and other Latin-American countries by their financial and subversive support of Latin-American Communist parties adhering to the Third Communist International (Comintern). The Comintern was dedicated to serving the political and foreign policies of the USSR, and was extensively directed and financed by the Communist Party of the Soviet Union (CPSU); 2) the period from 1936 to 1941, in which time USSR reached the nadir of its relations with the countries of Latin America; 3) the period 1942 to 1946, when the governments of most Latin-American countries and the United States, encouraged the USSR's heroic war effort against Hitler Germany, and toward the close of the war encouraged the integration of the

Soviet Union into the United Nations organization, with the result that fifteen Latin-American nations extended varying degrees of official recognition to the USSR; 4) the early Cold War period, 1947 to 1952, when the governments of Brazil, Chile, Colombia, Cuba, and Venezuela broke diplomatic relations with the USSR; 5) the post-Stalin period from 1953 to 1960, when the USSR set out to carve a niche for itself in the markets and minds of Latin America. At the Twentieth Congress of the CPSU in Moscow in 1956, the Soviets opened a political and ideological campaign against the patterns of domestic government in Latin America, and against United States economic relations with most of the Latin-American states; the expansion of trade and cultural relations with Argentina, Uruguay, Mexico, and Chile was undertaken in visits to Latin America by leading USSR government officials. Soviet diplomatic recognition and economic support of Cuba in 1960 opened a decade of unexpected Soviet successes in Latin America. 6) the period 1961 to 1964, during which the USSR succeeded in reestablishing diplomatic and trade relations with Brazil, gained a monopoly in Cuba's economic life and won a guarantee of non-military intervention by the United States in Cuba. The period witnessed the expansion of trade relations of the USSR with Mexico after a visit to Moscow by the director of the Foreign Trade Bank of Mexico; and the renewal of Soviet-Chilean diplomatic relations. 7) the post-Khrushchev period, 1964 to 1970, during which the Kosygin-Brezhnev regime has sought and gained extended normalization of Soviet–Latin-American relations. It was also the period of USSR rejection of Castro revolutions and guerrilla warfare as the only means to achieve socialism. Soviet awareness of the evolving weaknesses of ultra-conservative governments and the growing demand for socio-economic reforms explains Soviet emphasis on the wisdom of winning Latin-American Communists to support popular front tactics among urban working class groups even to the extent of cooperating with the Catholic Church and other conservative forces willing to adopt progressive reforms, as in 1970 Chile. Revolutionary and guerrilla activity in Latin America are approved only in principle by Soviet political leaders, as these developments are disruptive of Latin-American Communist party unity and continued Soviet economic penetration of the area. The economic emphasis in Soviet diplomacy in Brazil, Chile, Peru, and Bolivia is prompted by Soviet ambitions to be included in Latin-American trade relations.

SOVIET RELATIONS WITH MEXICO

THE HANDFUL OF PROFESSIONAL BOLSHEVIK REVOLUTIONARIES WHO DIRECTED the seizure of power and the reorganization of the Russian Empire in November, 1917, had little respect for and, in fact, despised the accepted canons of diplomatic and economic concourse practiced by most of the nations of the civilized world. Not for long, however, as politico-economic reality at home and abroad forced the continual reevaluation of the situation and resultant compromises of Marxist theory and Leninist practice. From the compromise with the German armed forces at Brest-Litovsk in March, 1918, to the USSR-German diplomatic and trade agreement at Rapallo in April, 1922, the new Soviet state moved toward normalization of relations with non-Communist states. To save the revolution, Lenin introduced the New Economic Policy in March, 1921, an amalgam of socialist and capitalist economic principles, thereby making it possible to legitimize USSR trade and diplomatic ambitions abroad.

The willingness of the Soviets to trade with as many nations as possible became the harbinger of economic and diplomatic rapprochement with the nations of the Western Hemisphere. Yet, despite trade feelers from Argentina, Uruguay, Venezuela, and Panama, no formal trade or diplomatic relations developed between the USSR and Latin-American countries until Mexico initiated the possibility of trade with the Soviets. In the summer of 1923, talks between the Mexican ambassador to Germany and Soviet representatives in Berlin turned on the possibility of Soviet purchases of Mexican cotton. In September, 1923, Telles, the Mexican representative in Washington, D. C., informed B. E. Skvirsky, the Soviet representative there, that he was in favor of suggesting to his government the normalization of Mexican-Soviet relations. The Soviets quickly responded and urged that official discussions be held between the representatives of both nations in Berlin, where the USSR and Mexico had official diplomatic status. In June, 1924, the Soviet Commissar for Foreign Affairs, George V. Chicherin, stated in an interview with a correspondent of the Argentine newspaper La Nación: "We would be very pleased to renew relations with Argentina and with all the countries of South America. A display of initiative by any South American country in this regard would be met with support and mutual understanding."[1] On August 4, 1924, Mexico and USSR established diplomatic relations with each other. The two countries conducted official trade and diplomatic relations from 1924 to 1930, but after continual Mexican complaints of Soviet support of the revolutionary and subversive activities of the Mexican Communist Party, Mexico ousted the Soviet diplomatic mission and severed relations with the USSR in February, 1930.

In December, 1924, Stanislav S. Pestkovsky, arrived in Mexico as Minister Plenipotentiary to the Calles regime. An active participant of the Bolshevik Revolution, Pestkovsy had been a friend of Lenin, former assistant commissar in the Council of Nationalities, ex-manager of the Soviet State Bank and chairman of the civil war Revolutionary Committee of Kirghizia. Pestkovsky was a superb choice as Soviet Minister of Mexico. Dark-eyed, goateed, and soft-spoken, he made a distinct bourgeois impression as, in top hat and morning coat, he presented his credentials to the Mexican Foreign Minister. In fact, the Soviets cherished this diplomatic breakthrough in the Western Hemisphere almost as much, perhaps, as they pride themselves in their role as tutors of the Communist revolution in Cuba.

In the first months after his arrival, Pestkovsky was introduced to the domestic scene in Mexico by Bertram D. Wolfe, Comintern agent-provocateur and acquaintance of G. V. Chicherin, the Soviet Commissar of Foreign Affairs. Late one night, in June of 1924, during sessions of the 5th Congress of the Comintern in Moscow, which Wolfe attended as a delegate of the Mexican Communist Party, he was called by Chicherin to discuss the wisdom of Soviet diplomatic recognition of Mexico. Wolfe, in an interview with the author, said Chicherin admitted to him that he knew practically nothing about Mexico, and he sought Wolfe's opinion regarding Mexican domestic politics and trade possibilities with that country. The latter enthusiastically urged Soviet diplomatic relations with Mexico, and pointed out the usefulness of such an arrangement insofar as USSR support of the Mexican Communist Party was concerned. Chicherin then appointed Wolfe to be the secret political adviser to Pestkovsky in Mexico. Wolfe returned to Mexico City and for many months lectured and published his views on "How to Destroy the Capitalist State" in the Mexican Communist Party newspaper *El Machéte*. Wolfe was much more openly involved than the Soviet Minister in attempting to organize the Mexican labor movement against labor leaders and the Mexican government, and in July, 1925, he was deemed persona non grata and had to leave the country. But it was Pestkovsky who paid the penalty for his relations with Wolfe and members of the Mexican Communist Party. By December, 1924, he was already seriously suspected of involvement in fomenting revolution among the Mexican working class—a charge levelled by Mexican President Plutarco Elías Calles himself.[2] Meanwhile, trade relations between the USSR and Mexico grew from almost nothing to about two million rubles in exports to the Soviet Union between 1925 and 1926. As pressures mounted against Pestkovsky, who was again (in May, 1925) considered to be indirectly involved in an alleged plot to overthrow the Calles government,[3] Chicherin decided to recall his Minister to Mexico in December, 1925. It is doubtful that Pestkovsky was involved in any such plot, but the existing political situation in Mexico was volatile, to say the least, and the Soviets replaced Pestkovsky with the appointment of Madame Alexandra M. Kollontai, internationally famous for her advocacy of free love in the USSR.

Kollontai arrived in Vera Cruz in December, 1926, a veritable heroine of naturalness in humanity, and she was lionized by the Mexican press. Trade between the USSR and Mexico advanced apace, with the Soviets importing 2.75 million rubles of Mexican goods; between 1926 and 1929, the USSR exported over two million rubles worth of products to Mexico. Kollontai left Mexico in June, 1927, alleged victim of bad health, but likely sensitive to Mexican press suspicions that she was also involved in propagandizing the proletariat. She was replaced as Minister to Mexico by Dr. A. Makar, who was the official representative to that country until February, 1930, when he and his wife were brusquely, and quite literally, thrown out of Mexico for their alleged links with revolutionary elements of the Mexican Communist Party. This diplomatic rupture between the two nations lasted until 1942, when the former ambassador to the United States, Konstantin A. Oumansky, was accepted as ambassador to Mexico.

The Soviet-Mexican economic relationship was not significantly productive during or immediately after World War II. Total Mexican trade with the USSR from the war period until 1958 was less than one million dollars, but a definite upswing begins when from 1959 to 1967 the total trade between the two nations amounted to more than 17 million dollars. Even so, this is an insignificant amount compared with trade figures between the USSR and Argentina and Brazil. An interesting statistic is evident in the fact that annual trade between the USSR and Latin America increased from $30 million in 1956 to $182.9 million in 1966. However, by the following year the figure fell sharply to $45.8 million and only partially recovered to reach an estimated $97 million in 1968.[4]

The Soviet Union established an expansionist policy in economic, diplomatic, and cultural relations with various states of Latin America after the 1956 Congress of the Communist Party of the Soviet Union. Communist propaganda thereafter stressed the advantages of trade with the USSR and its bloc, claiming Mexico could sell them its surpluses, remedy foreign exchange shortages, and gain long-term, low interest credits and technical assistance. USSR-Mexican trade and exchanges jumped from 1.2 million rubles in 1958 to 4.4 million rubles in 1960. The rise is directly related to the visit of Soviet First Deputy Premier Anastas I. Mikoyan to Mexico in November, 1959, when he inaugurated a three-week Soviet industrial exposition in Mexico City. Exchange agreements reached a peak of 6.7 million rubles between the two nations in 1962, and dropped to 2.2 million rubles in 1964. The USSR has in reality made only a minor contribution to Mexican economic development. Trade has been erratic and on a low comparative scale. But the USSR is committed to a program of participation in the Mexican economy, and the Mexicans could well benefit if the USSR followed through with aid and extensive development loans.

The cultural and diplomatic offensive of the USSR in Mexico has brought mixed results. In January, 1959, the Soviets established the Society for Friendship and Cultural Cooperation with Latin-American countries. USSR scientists, scholars, artists, and members of collective farms are enjoined to cooperate and exchange visits with their Latin-American counterparts. The Mexican Charge d'Affaires in Moscow, attending the organizational meeting of the group, pledged his country's support of its activities. "Anything which brings people closer together and leads to mutual understanding," he said, "deserves our full support."[5] Soon after this meeting, the Soviets suffered a diplomatic set-back in Mexico City.

In March, 1959, the Mexican government demanded the withdrawal of the Soviet military attaché, Nikolai M. Remisov, and the USSR Embassy's second secretary, Nikolai Aksenov, for conspiring with the Mexican Communist Party in planning revolutionary agitation among Mexican railroad workers. On April 6, 1959, Mexican secret service police discovered a cache of communist propaganda literature designed to incite uprisings among railwaymen, and a loud cry from several nationalist groups demanded severing diplomatic relations with the USSR.[6] In April, an editorial in the Mexico City newspaper *Excelsior* questioned the activities of the large Soviet embassy staff of 34 official representatives. In comparing that number with the 44 official representatives of the U.S. embassy, whose work was related to a giant economic and cultural affairs relationship with the people and government of Mexico, *Excelsior* suggested that "the Soviet embassy was serving as an educational center and gateway into the many Latin-American countries which did not accept diplomatic representatives from the USSR."[7]

Nikita S. Khrushchev was not only refused a visit to Disneyland, U.S.A., but his request to visit Mexico during celebrations marking the 150th anniversary of Mexican independence was also declined. The Mexican Foreign Office explained that it believed it would be improper to have two high ranking Soviet officials visit their country before the Mexican President had had an opportunity to return the visit of Deputy Prime Minister Mikoyan.[8]

The flow of Communist propaganda from Mexico to Central America was interrupted in late June, 1961, when Soviet diplomatic pouch shipments were seized by Mexican authorities at the International airport in Mexico City. Four tons of Soviet, Chinese, and Cuban Communist propaganda literature were confiscated by the Mexican government in an attempt to curb the passage of such materials through their country.[9] One would be mistaken to presume, however, that such an action by the Mexicans is aimed at aggravating Mexican-Soviet relations, which have been and remain formally correct if not always cordial.

Mexico has succeeded in maintaining an independent foreign policy throughout the "cold war" era, and it so happens that this policy likewise tends to serve the interests of the USSR in Latin America. Mexico's refusal to adopt OAS sanctions against Castro's Cuba, for example, was greatly appreciated by Soviet leaders and propagandists who encourage such neutrality in the current ideological struggle between East and West. Soviet government officials have cultivated this relationship by inviting mutual exchanges of parliamentary representatives, official and academic delegations. Former President López Mateos, in visiting Europe in May, 1963, made it abundantly clear to the world that his government was determined to maintain an independent foreign policy and to expand its world trade agreements. In a speech in Belgrade, he compared Mexico to Yugoslavia in that both refused to be dominated by either bloc in the Cold War.[10] In Poland, he restated his faith in the possibility of coexistence among nations which, though they subscribed to different political institutions, could cooperate if the people and governments of these nations respected each other's national sovereignty.[11] In his welcoming speech to President Tito, who visited Mexico in October, 1963, López Mateos called for increased economic and cultural ties with Yugoslavia, and once again proclaimed Mexico's policy of non-intervention in international affairs.[12]

In an effort to broaden Mexican-Soviet trade relations, an official Mexican Economic Commission led by Ricardo Zevada toured Soviet cities in June, 1964. After discussions and observations of the USSR economy, Zevada is quoted by the Soviets as saying, "There is nothing to prevent broader trade with the socialist countries. . . . We can offer cotton, coffee, metals, and a wide assortment of fibres. The socialist countries can sell us heavy and light industry equipment."[13] Despite this, economic exchange between the two countries did not exceed two million dollars in 1966.

An important center of communication between the government and peoples of the USSR and those of Mexico is the Mexican-Russian Institute of Cultural Exchange. Established in 1944, the Institute became and remains a vibrant center of Soviet propaganda in Mexico. It also facilitates USSR-Mexican visitors' exchanges, and aids as a bridge between Soviet embassy personnel, Mexican Communists, and Communist sympathizers. In recent years the Institute has acted as an agent for the People's Friendship University in Moscow. The Institute distributes information on admission requirements and has received applications of students seeking admission. The Institute publishes a number of periodicals, the most successful of which is *Cultura Soviética* (1944–55), changed to *Intercambio Cultural* since the mid-fifties. Officials of the Soviet embassy in Mexico City have participated in activities of the Institute, but the extent of their moral, material, or political assistance is not easy to ascertain.

Contemporary Soviet diplomacy in Mexico is infinitely more mature and sophisticated than it was before World War II. Kremlin leaders and their appointees do their utmost to separate the interests of Mexican Communists and the international Communist movement from those of the USSR. Selfish, as it obviously is, in terms of the Soviet commitment to the success of international Communism, USSR relations with Mexico have proved highly successful. The fact that a Soviet intelligence agent such as KGB official Georgii S. Visko, ostensibly a member of the Commerce Section of the USSR embassy in Mexico City, is identified, or that Colonel Sviatoslav F. Kuznetsov is a known Soviet military intelligence officer posing as cultural attache is no serious matter to the Mexicans.[14] Recognition of these facts of political life by the latter suggest that they are willing to condone them if the Soviets do not direct their covert activities in a way which would embarrass Mexican international relations or encroach upon Mexican national sovereignty. Surely, the questionable political tactics of former USSR diplomatic missions to Latin America, as in Uruguay, might have taught the Soviets to distinguish between legitimate commercial and cultural relations and obvious meddling in the internal affairs of Latin-American states.

SOVIET-URUGUAYAN RELATIONS

FORMAL DIPLOMATIC RELATIONS BETWEEN THE USSR AND URUGUAY WERE ESTABlished when the latter granted the USSR de jure recognition on August 21, 1926.[15] Occurring later than the Mexican recognition of the USSR, Uruguayan-Soviet diplomatic relations are nevertheless the most sustained, and in many ways, the most significant of USSR–Latin-American diplomatic relations, discounting—for reasons to be discussed hereafter—the dramatic ties of the USSR with Communist Cuba. Prior to diplomatic recognition, the Uruguayans disclosed an interest in establishing economic relations with the USSR, with the result that in 1925 the Soviets responded with the formation of Iuzhamtorg (South American Trading Corporation) in Montevideo, the Latin-American equivalent of Amtorg (American Trading Corporation), with offices in New York. The Iuzhamtorg office was directed by Boris Kraevsky, agent extraordinaire, who was granted the official right to represent the New York Amtorg before South American secretaries of state and national and provincial authorities. He traveled to several South American capitals, seeking to win diplomatic recognition of the USSR, and during each visit he made heavy purchases of local goods and raw materials for shipment to the Soviet Union. In Montevideo, on August 9, 1926, Kraevsky succeeded in his basic purpose, gaining Uruguayan diplomatic recognition of the USSR. In a forward-looking observation, the official USSR government newspaper

Izvestiia reported: "The act of Uruguay will undoubtedly have an influence on Argentina and other countries of South America [in recognizing the USSR], and it will be of great importance to the Soviet market."[16] The *New York Times* reported a conversation with Kraevsky, in which he claimed that between January and August, 1926, the USSR purchased goods from South American countries valued at more than seven million dollars.[17]

Considering the near absence of USSR–Latin-American trade and the emergent state of the Soviet economy of the mid-1920s, Iuzhamtorg was an unqualified success. A prominent official of Iuzhamtorg commenting on the significance of this trade is quoted by *Izvestiia* as follows: "South America is a tremendous market for the distribution of various manufactured and semi-manufactured goods and raw materials and is beyond doubt of interest to the USSR . . . Our imports from South America in 1925–26 amounted to $5,976,461; in 1926–27: $14,759,194, and in 1927–28: $18,000,000 . . . and our exports to South America increased to one million dollars in 1927–28."[18] Assuming that these are quite reliable statistics, it is difficult to explain the naïveté and political cupidity of representatives of the USSR in Uruguay in subsequent years. Wherever they served in Latin America, Soviet functionaries could not refrain from mixing business with politics. Kraevsky, for example, was very much suspect of serving as a link between the Comintern and the Communist parties of Brazil, Argentina, Uruguay, and Paraguay for whom he supplied propaganda materials and funds from Moscow. "Authorities of several South American republics," notes Professor Rollie Poppino, "were convinced that the Iuzhamtorg director and his associate were engaged in subversive activities, inciting riots in Uruguay and Argentina and attempting to foment violence in southern Brazil and Paraguay."[19] The Comintern had established a South American Bureau in Buenos Aires shortly after the Sixth Congress of the Comintern in Moscow in 1928 and it remained there until it was ousted in 1930, moving then to Montevideo. The major purpose of the bureau was to assist the existing Communist parties of South America, encourage the creation of new parties where they did not already exist, and to coordinate the policies and propaganda activities of member groups. Meanwhile, Kraevsky was replaced as director of Iuzhamtorg in 1930 by Alexander Minkin. Kraevsky was denied entrance to Brazil in 1930, and he was deported from Chile in June, 1932. He made his way back to the Soviet Union in 1935.[20]

The Uruguayan Foreign Minister in 1932 was confident that "Communism cannot prosper in Uruguay because the laws of the country guarantee the rights of the workers and offer them a great measure of well-being."[21] Furthermore, the Uruguayan economy was largely dependent on foreign trade, so that allowing Iuzhamtorg to remain active in Montevideo, despite the fact that the Iuzhamtorg office in Buenos Aires had been shut down by police who suspected that Argentine Communist activities were too closely linked with Soviet business activities, was merely common sense to the Uruguayans. Consequently, the USSR was invited by the Uruguayan Foreign Minister, Alberto Manet, to exchange permanent diplomatic representatives and to conclude a trade treaty between the two nations. The Soviets swiftly concurred, and diplomatic missions were exchanged in the spring of 1934.[22] A major trade treaty was signed between the two states in May, 1935. The commercial exchange would be not less than £100,000 nor more than £300,000 although the amount could be increased by mutual consent.[23] The treaty agreement was hardly in effect when Soviet political machinations in Brazil caused a rupture in diplomatic relations between the USSR and Uruguay.

On December 27, 1935, the Brazilian government charged that the Soviet legation in Montevideo had been dispatching revolutionary instructions to Luis Carlos Prestes, who had been leading a major revolt against the Getulio Vargas government. Furthermore, Alexander Minkin, the director of Iuzhamtorg in Montevideo, was allegedly in direct contact with Prestes and supplied him with Soviet gold.[24] Consequently, Minkin was ordered out of Uruguay the next day, and the USSR was informed that "the Soviet government instigated and supported the Communist elements in Brazil through the agency of the Soviet mission to our government."[25] Diplomatic relations between Uruguay and the USSR were severed by the former on December 28, 1935.

In breaking relations, President Gabriel Terra cited the Brazilian revolt as being led by a graduate of the Comintern. And there is absolutely no doubt that Prestes, "the Cavalier of Hope," was inspired and trained by the Comintern, that he was loyal to Moscow, that he had embraced Marxism-Leninism, and that his visits to the USSR were clearly linked to developing a Soviet-style revolution in Brazil.[26] Terra added, "The Soviet government cannot disclaim connection with the Comintern and its revolutionary program in South America, for Joseph Stalin opened and closed the last congress of the Comintern— and," concluded the President, "we have proof that Minkin was organizing a revolution in Uruguay for next February or March."[27] Minkin, of course, denied the charges, declaring there was no dependency whatever between the Soviet government and the Comintern. José Espalter, Uruguay's Foreign Minister, handed back Minkin's denial note saying Minkin no longer had diplomatic status in Uruguay. Minkin demanded proof of the Uruguayan charges, but the Uruguayans considered the case closed.

The Soviet rhubarb was further exacerbated when *Izvestiia* soon after published a demand that the Uruguayan government must prove its charges and implications of Comintern propaganda before the League of Nations.[28] It claimed the Uruguayan government made its decision under pressure of the Vatican and Brazil, and implied that the real reason for the rupture was the USSR's refusal to purchase 200 tons of Uruguayan cheese! Maxim Litvinoff, Soviet Foreign Minister, declared before the League of Nations that Uruguay had insisted on deporting one Simon Radovitsky, an anarchist-terrorist jailed in Montevideo, to the USSR, on the grounds that he was born in Russia. The Soviets denied his entry, and "in a fit of pique," the Uruguayans demanded that the denial be compensated by the Soviet purchase of 200 tons of cheese. Bordering on the absurd, it seems likely that if cheese were the major difference between the two nations, the USSR might well have purchased the cheese and restored a potential million dollars in business and political ties with Uruguay. Iuzhamtorg in South America was closed with Minkin's departure, and the two nations were to be estranged diplomatically until January, 1943.[29]

Soviet writers are quick to point out that the USSR enjoyed de facto recognition from at least nine Latin American countries before World War II, and engaged in commercial relations with Argentina, Brazil, Venezuela, Cuba, Mexico, Paraguay, Uruguay, and Chile, "despite the animosity of the U.S.A. and other imperialistic powers."[30] But none of these countries were sympathetic to the tactics and performance of the Soviets in Latin America. The remarkable performance of the USSR in the war with Nazi Germany, however, turned Latin-American popular and political sympathies toward the restoration of relations with the Soviets.

Uruguay announced its readiness to renew diplomatic relations with the USSR in 1942 if the United States would negotiate between the two. Secretary of State Cordell Hull and President Franklin D. Roosevelt looked favorably on the support of Latin-American states of the Allied war effort and, consequently, the Uruguayan Foreign Minister, Alberto Guani, met in Washington with Maxim Litvinoff, the Soviet ambassador to the U.S. Enroute to the United States, Guani stopped in Rio de Janeiro where he stated, "Uruguay broke diplomatic and commercial relations with the Soviet Union in 1936. Now, however, the situation is completely different. The Soviet Union is playing a preponderant role in the battle against Nazi Germany . . . I cannot see any inconvenience in the re-establishment of relations with the Soviet Union."[31]

Guani, who became Vice President of Uruguay on March 1st, 1943, met with Litvinoff on January 27, and the two exchanged notes re-establishing diplomatic and commercial relations between their countries.[32] The Uruguayans joined in the war against Germany in February, 1945, and later that year supported the entrance of the USSR into membership in the United

Nations organization. Amicable relations between the two nations led to a three year most-favored-nation treaty of friendship, trade, and navigation, signed in Moscow by the Uruguayan ambassador, Emilio Frugoni, and the Soviet Minister of Trade, Anastas Mikoyan, on August 9, 1946. The Soviets were now entitled to send a twenty-three man trade mission to Montevideo; the Uruguayans were also entitled to estabish a trade mission in Moscow.

Brazil and Chile broke diplomatic relations with the USSR in October, 1947, as the Cold War alienated the USSR in Western Hemisphere diplomatic circles. Uruguay did not sever official relations, but her legation in Moscow was closed. The USSR mission to Montevideo remained open. The crux of the matter lay with a renewed indictment of the USSR by Brazil which charged that Moscow instructions were being relayed to Luis Carlos Prestes and the Brazilian Communist Party via Uruguay; also, Prestes was accused of crossing the Brazilian-Uruguayan border to evade Brazilian police and receive instructions from Moscow. Uruguay later refused to grant asylum to Prestes.[33]

After the death of Stalin in 1953, the USSR embarked on efforts to increase trade relations with Uruguay, and in 1954 a mutually attractive trade pact was signed between the Bank of the Republic and the State Bank of the USSR, good for two years with automatic renewal unless disapproved by either country.[34] Uruguay gained, in effect, a barter agreement with the USSR, whereby a clearing account for the USSR must exist in the Uruguayan National Bank, while the Uruguayans at no time owed money to the Soviets but, rather, exported in goods what they owed them.[35] In the period 1952–58, Uruguay, Argentina, and Brazil were the prime Latin-American trading partners of the USSR and the East European bloc, providing between 63% and 98% of all exports from Latin America to the Soviets and their allies. In 1956, Uruguay signed a new three-year most-favored-nation trade, commerce, payments, and navigation pact with the USSR, and by 1958 Uruguay had six separate trade agreements with the Soviet Union.[36]

Oil has become an increasingly important factor in Soviet commercial and political relations with Uruguay since the latter has increased demands and less ability to pay in cash. In return for oil, Uruguay has bartered wool and beef products.[37] The USSR has taken advantage of Uruguay's cash shortage predicament as in 1960 when the Soviets tried to force Uruguay to agree to exchange more wool for petroleum, but the latter resisted as more than one-fourth of her direct and indirect exports were being purchased by the USSR and domestic opposition pressures of the ruling Blancos government began to mount. A change in United States tariff regulations relieved the situation, and after 1960 direct Soviet trade with Uruguay began to decline.[38] Yet, a $15,000,000 barter agreement was signed between the two in 1963, thus making Uruguay the only Latin-American country whose trade with the USSR and its bloc has amounted to more than ten percent of the total trade with the exception of Cuba. However, in 1963, the United States was still Uruguay's chief trading partner, followed by Western Europe and the United Kingdom with the USSR close behind.[39]

The Soviet-Uruguayan trade pact of 1954 led to an exchange of full-fledged ministers and the re-opening of the Uruguayan diplomatic mission in Moscow in late 1955. Juan A. Lorenzi was sent as ambassador to Moscow, while Soviet ambassador Sergei S. Mikhailov arrived in Montevideo on January 2, 1956. The presence of Mikhailov generated much more than trade activities between the two countries. As though he were answering the unspoken doubts of those greeting his arrival, Mikhailov offered the assurance that "there is no danger of political infiltration with (Soviet) trade. Revolutions are not exported."[40] With the advantage of historical hindsight, however, one can hardly not observe that these were strange words coming from a man who, five years later, took leave from his foreign service post to launch and become director of the Latin-American Institute of the USSR Academy of Sciences in Moscow (1961–66). The publications and philosophy of this Institute, which Mikhailov programmed and elucidated, constitute the hard core views of official USSR opposition to and disparagement of the fundamental way of domestic and international life of Latin America's peoples. In an early directive he made it clear that the Institute would study two primary problem areas, namely, "the economic competition of two systems in the underdeveloped countries," and "the history of the workers' and national liberation movements of Latin America."[41] He describes Latin America as "a continent of struggle . . . against United States imperialism . . . and the forces of internal reaction."[42] The often thin line of distinction between subversive Communist propaganda and politically inspired Soviet academic analyses of contemporary Latin-American problems is an aspect of the ideological assault waged, since 1956, against the United States and Latin-American opponents of Communism. At every level of USSR political, economic, and intellectual activity related to Latin America, the new doctrine of "peaceful co-existence" was expounded.

Ambassador Mikhailov's presence in Montevideo (1956–61) coincided with the newly enunciated doctrine which was introduced by Nikita S. Khrushchev when Lenin's doctrine on "the inevitability of war" was invalidated by the realities of the nuclear age. It was Mikhailov's duty, therefore, to implement as much as possible the theses of this new doctrine which required that Soviet Communists and their confréres pursue "an ideological, political, and economic struggle" against the world of capitalism, "for the triumph of Socialist and Communist ideas."[43] This official doctrine of the

Communist Party of the Soviet Union was, naturally, implemented by USSR diplomatic representatives wherever possible. It is not incongruous therefore, that Mikhailov's official relations with the Uruguayan government were marred by numerous charges that the Soviet embassy was a center of espionage in South America, and that the unnecessarily large Soviet staff contained too many probable spies involved in activities which were prejudicial to the national security and internal political stability of Uruguay.[44] Benito Nardone, member of the National Council and, in 1960, president of Uruguay, demanded that the government sever diplomatic relations with the USSR in April, 1959. Nardone was joined in his demands by fellow Council member César Batlle Pacheco and the newspaper *El Día*. The Soviet Embassy apparently believed a diplomatic break was imminent and tons of printed materials were loaded on a Soviet fishing vessel.[45] The threat was enough to cause the Soviets to pay heed to a second warning when, as President of Uruguay, Nardone said he wished the Soviet Embassy to cut its diplomatic personnel from 80 to 6. By September the Embassy complied and the matter was dropped.

Diplomatic ties between the two countries have been further strained by such developments as the Soviet explosion of a massive nuclear bomb in October, 1961, with its resultant fallout hazard; charges by the Uruguayan government that the Soviet Embassy was involved in labor agitation by its leadership and very active participation in the newspaper strike of late 1965; and most seriously that the USSR condoned resolutions approved by members of the Tri-Continental Conference in Havana in January, 1966.[46] The Soviet ambassador to Uruguay, Igor Kolosovsky, was asked to explain statements made at the Conference since the USSR had sent one of the largest delegations to the meeting, headed by Sharaf R. Rashidov, a candidate member of the Presidium of the Central Committee of the CPSU and First Secretary of the CP Central Committee of Uzbekistan. Kolosovsky had the diplomat's aplomb to say that the Soviet delegate did not represent the opinion of the Soviet government, and he insisted that the USSR strictly observed the sovereignty and independence of nations and would not export revolution— but it would assist victims of imperialist aggression.[47]

The clearest Soviet statement on the matter of USSR "export of revolution" to Latin America was made by Dr. Victor V. Vol'sky, present Director of the USSR Academy of Sciences Latin-American Institute. "The Soviet people," he said, "are of course, in deep sympathy with the revolutionary forces operating in the capitalist world, and they express a class solidarity with them and support their cause. Such support, however, is not equivalent to the 'export of revolution.' It is, rather, opposition to the involvement of imperialist powers in the internal affairs of nations. It is opposition to the 'export of counter-revolution.' "[48] He concluded, "Ideas require no visas, borders cannot restrain them, and they cannot be stopped."[49]

The ambivalence reflected in the remarks of Vol'sky and Kolosovsky is typical of the ambivalence evident in the pronouncements of the academic and diplomatic communities of the USSR. The Soviet scholar maintains "the Soviet people" are committed to the struggle against the "export of revolution" by the import of their own revolutionary views, while the behaviour of a CPSU official, such as Rashidov, is presumably beyond the control of Soviet diplomats. Little wonder that Soviet-Uruguayan diplomatic relations have been in a state of flux since their inception.

SOVIET-CUBAN RELATIONS, 1959–70

USSR DIPLOMATIC RECOGNITION OF CUBA ON MAY 8, 1960, MARKED THE FORMAL emergence of the Soviet Union as a decisive political and economic power in the Western Hemisphere. Seizing upon historic circumstances, Kremlin leaders gained indirect control of the domestic and international affairs of the semi-captive regime of Premier Fidel Castro. For the first time in history the USSR achieved the ability to influence the course of development of a Latin-American country. This continuing influence has been at once a political plum, an economic drain, and an ideological challenge to Soviet leaders.

Soviet-Cuban political relations have waxed and waned since 1962 when a "credibility gap" emerged with the USSR withdrawal of offensive intermediate ballistic missiles from the Caribbean island. Dependence on Soviet economic assistance and its tendency to be erratic in time of political disagreement with the USSR is painfully clear to Premier Castro. By 1970, however, the "maximum leader" had apparently learned to live with Kremlin dictates and their effect on Cuban national sovereignty. His earlier revolutionary dreams of industrialization of the Cuban economy were shattered in 1964 by USSR insistence that Cuba remain a sugar producer in the Soviet ruble bloc. USSR literature on the achievements of the Cuban revolution implies that when Castro's economy is in order, he might be encouraged to develop a more industrialized and technological economy. But if Cuba is to warrant continued Soviet economic support, without which the revolution cannot survive, she must pay her way largely by exporting sugar to the Soviet camp, and importing from them the basic essentials for her economic existence.

Another area of tension in the "equal partnership," as the Soviets describe Cuba's dependency, is created by the fact that USSR leaders have proved to be more concerned at all times with their own national security than with becoming a shield for the emergence of the latent "caudillo messianism" of Castro or the martyred Ernesto Ché Guevara. The March 13, 1967, Anniversary speech of Castro and the December 17, 1967, *Pravda* rebuttal of his criticism of the foreign policy of the USSR in Latin America are a basic example of Soviet refusal to support Cuban-style revolutionary adventurism in other nations of Latin America. Castro's respondent purge of scores of high-ranking pro-Soviet members of the Communist Party of Cuba was more an expression of chagrin than a solution to the widened ideological breach between the CPSU and the Castro controlled party. Basic differences between them exist in the application of the principles of Marxism-Leninism to the realities of politico-economic and social life in contemporary Latin America. Castro, fundamentally in support of Mao Tse-tung's philosophy of aggressive guerrilla warfare in the rural countryside and, adding his own unorthodox concepts of urban guerrilla war as expressed in Régis Debray's *Revolution in the Revolution,* clashes head-on with the Soviet demands for a policy of "evolution toward revolution." This USSR policy has been repeatedly stated in a myriad series of academic and political comments about the "real significance" of the Cuban Revolution to the peoples of Latin America.

The USSR has spent between two and three billion dollars bolstering the Cuban economy and military establishment since 1960. Cuba is the Soviet sponsored experiment in the Western Hemisphere which dare not fail as that would cause the Soviet camp and Latin-American Communist parties much embarrassment. Heavy military involvement and financial ties with the ruble bloc countries make it clear that Soviet influence in Cuba is a matter of vital importance to the USSR. Ultimately the progress or failure of Cuba as the Soviet sponsored Marxist-Leninist model in the Western Hemisphere is certain to influence the broader course of USSR–Latin-American diplomatic and economic relations.

The path of Cuban-Soviet relations since 1959 has been strewn with more political discord than agreement. Castro's sensitivity toward economic dependence on the USSR has brought angry accusations of Soviet exploitation of Cuba's predicament.[1] Yet since Vice Premier Anastas Mikoyan's February, 1960, visit to Havana the military needs of Communist Cuba were assured. And from that moment, one might say the nature of the Cuban revolution would be decided by Soviet foreign policy.[2]

Alienated from the U.S., Castro was forced to turn to the USSR to insure his existence. The most expedient manner of receiving the kind of economic and military aid he needed from the Soviet Union was to make his revolution a socialist one, thus obligating the Soviet Union to aid and protect him. But the Soviets seemed less than eager to accept Castro and his revolution into the Communist community. Theodore Draper in his *Castroism: Theory and Practice* shows that the Soviets and the Cuban Communist Party did not view Castro as an ally until rather late in the game. Instead they seemed to

J. GREGORY OSWALD

regard him as another petit-bourgeois leader who might possibly make his peace with the U.S. and continue the social structure essentially unchanged. Even if he became radical in his internal policies, they expected the U.S. to topple his regime as it had toppled the one in Guatemala in 1954. The Soviets viewed Latin America in general and the Caribbean in particular as an area where American power limited Communist activities severely.

As 1959 wore on Castro became more radical in his internal policies, and his relations with the U.S. worsened. It seemed to the Soviets that a genuine social revolution in Latin America had occurred. Moscow supported him verbally and then economically. On July 9, 1960, Soviet Premier Nikita Khrushchev stated that Soviet artillerymen could, if necessary, back up the Cuban people with rocket fire.[3] When Castro tried to make this vague statement more specific, Khrushchev replied that his promise of missile support had been only figurative. But Castro could not be stopped in his pursuit of the reluctant Soviets and insisted that he had always been a Marxist-Leninist. Now that Castro was a declared Communist, it became increasingly awkward for the Soviet Union to evade helping him politically and economically especially since the Communist Party of Cuba came under his discipline.[4] Two weeks later Castro issued a call for anti-imperialistic revolutions in Latin America. Immediately afterwards he introduced a series of measures designed to transform Cuba's market economy into a state-operated, centralized command economy of the Soviet type. In August, 1960, he began to nationalize Cuban sugar and oil. On April 16, 1961, he announced the Cuban Revolution to be a socialist one.[5] The next day the Bay of Pigs invasion occurred. The Soviets were overjoyed at this most recent development. Obviously the U.S. was losing her grip on Latin America and possibly the Cuban Revolution could be exported.[6] But the Soviets and the Chinese would still not recognize the socialist nature of Castro's regime because his dictatorship was that of the individual and not of the party and therefore depended on one man for its survival. To overcome this, Castro announced on July 26, 1961, the merger of the PSP (Cuban Communist Party) and two Castroite groups, but he did not hesitate to alter the Cuban Communist Party to his own needs and to establish his dominance by eliminating many of the old Communist Party members from positions of power. So by mid-1962 Castro was still not firmly established, but he was offered the alternative of medium and intermediate range Soviet missiles instead.[7] The Soviets had fallen far behind the U.S. in ICBMs and it seemed an easy solution to move their short range missiles closer to the target and use Cuba as a military base. For Castro this was desirable because it would bind the Soviets irrevocably to his defense and would deter the U.S. from another invasion venture.[8]

The Soviet Union and Castro suffered a great defeat in the outcome of the missile crisis. It became a turning point in their relations and the origin of the present conflict.[9] Soviet handling of the crisis was a definite blow to Castro's prestige and regional revolutionary stature. Since Castro's appeal lay in his presumed independence of great powers, the Soviet removal of the missiles without consulting him highlighted the reality of his dependence on one great power and a second-rate one at that. Khrushchev's retreat confirmed the position of the "Guevarists" who believed that in the long run the Castro regime's survival could not be secured through military and economic dependence on the Soviet Union but only by carrying the revolution to the continent.[10] The Soviet Union on the other hand had lowered her sights, accepted the status quo, and seemed to be waiting for a better day. As a result of this reassessment, Soviet efforts were concentrated more on immediate objectives, such as encouraging existing Latin-American governments to counteract U.S. economic influence, and to oppose U.S. policies in general rather than on the ultimate goals of assisting revolutionary movements to establish democratic or socialist regimes.[11] The Soviet Union obviously did not find it an expedient policy to encourage yet other Cubas which demanded Soviet aid and protection. This underlies the basic contradiction evident in the Soviet-Cuban conflict. While the export of the revolution to the continent was absolutely indispensable in Castro's eyes to secure the survival of his regime, the Soviets were unwilling to risk additional permanent commitments in the Third World, least of all in Latin America. Moreover, in contrast to the Cuban position, the survival of the Castro regime did not figure on the Soviet list of priorities as the most important problem of all, but rather as a minor, albeit explosive third-rate question.

In spite of this conflict Castro was still dependent upon the Soviets for his survival and the Soviets could not ignore him because of the growing rift with China and the adverse propaganda they would receive from the Communist world if the U.S. toppled Castro. Much of Castro's rage at the Soviet missile pull-out was vented upon the Latin-American Communist parties. As Castro continued to accuse the Latin-American Communists of being bureaucrats and satellites rather than revolutionaries, the Communist parties feared Castro might drag them into a quagmire of guerrilla warfare. Soon thereafter, perhaps at their behest, Castro was invited to Moscow for serious talks.[12] The outcome was a joint Castro-Khrushchev communique, published May 23, 1963, which contained a carefully worked out compromise formula on Latin-American revolutions. Castro was to cease his attempts to dictate the policies of Latin-American Communists—the communique stated that the question of the peaceful or nonpeaceful way toward socialism in one country or another would be decided by the struggling peoples themselves. Castro was finally accepted into the socialist camp the same day although he was not admitted to Comecon or the Warsaw Pact and his treaties with the Soviets would have to be renegotiated each year.[13] Castro perhaps pulled the wool over the Soviets' eyes by inventing the phantom party PURS (United Party of the Socialist Revolution) and appointing himself Secretary-General of this shadow organization when the requirements for admittance to the socialist camp came up.[14] In return for the reformist concessions he made, the flow of Soviet and Eastern-European aid increased once more and important medium term commercial agreements were signed with the Soviet Union and other socialist countries in 1963 and 1964.[15] He was also awarded the Lenin Peace Prize in May, 1963. Although this reconciliation was a result of political and economic exigencies, Moscow welcomed it because it came at a time when her conflict with Peking had already produced a worldwide division in the international Communist movement.

It became apparent soon enough that Cuba had not renounced any of her basic positions and refused to join the traditional Communist leadership in moves against Chinese splinter groups. Castro refused to sign the Nuclear Test Ban Treaty and rejected the proposition sponsored by Brazil, Chile, and Mexico in the U.N. to create an atom-free zone in Latin America.[16] He also continued accusing Latin-American leaders of neglecting their duty in guiding their people to the revolution. As the months passed in 1964, it seemed apparent that Castro felt bound to the communique only to the degree that it remained expedient. With the victory of Eduardo Frei over the Communist-backed Allende in Chile, the "peaceful way" had failed the test in Cuban eyes. A rise in world sugar prices also gave Castro a heady feeling of independence from the strings of the Soviet dole. Thus in September, 1964, Castro once again spoke out openly on the inevitability of armed struggle almost everywhere in Latin America.[17]

With the fall of Khrushchev, Soviet leadership exerted itself in dealing with what it apparently perceived as some particularly irksome blunders, most notably the disarray in the Latin-American Communist movement. Castroism was exerting a disruptive influence on the Communist movement which was becoming increasingly out of proportion to his declining prestige in Latin-American society as a whole and the old Communist parties were in serious straits after three setbacks. In Venezuela a new president had been elected in a massive voter turn out despite the efforts of the Communists to disrupt the elections; in Brazil, the leftist president Goulart was overthrown with little opposition from the Communists and leftists; in Chile Frei won over the Communist-backed Allende. The publication of two articles on Latin America in consecutive issues of the Soviet Communist Party theoretical journal *Kommunist* which usually emphasized internal Soviet affairs signified the new Soviet involvement. Herbert Dinerstein concluded that the articles indicated an important Soviet policy shift because *Kommunist*'s rare articles on foreign affairs express the official view of the Communist Party of the Soviet Union.[18] The policy shift was supposedly the approval of armed struggle and guerrilla activity in some Latin-American countries.[19] In fact the second article stated this, but it also added that in a country where dictatorship had been overthrown and a liberal reformist regime established the tactics of partisan warfare should not be used.[20] So, although the Soviets endorsed the use of armed struggle when necessary, they excluded the one place in which guerrilla tactics had been used by a Communist party—Venezuela. Ironically, Venezuela was the one place Castro was most concerned about. The articles really conceded nothing of importance except their willingness to confront the problem of armed versus mass struggle and this new attitude had little relation to the Soviet estimate of the prospects for revolution in Latin America. Rather, this was a deliberate calculation leading towards the eventual handling of the Chinese problem. Italian Communist leader Palmiro Togliatti upon his death bed left a memorandum advising the Soviets on the Chinese question. Togliatti's evaluation was that Chinese vulnerability was most obvious when challenged on concrete problems rather than on theoretical generalities; therefore, China should not be confronted in an international conference. Instead, the Soviets should proceed by groups of parties to a series of meetings for a profound examination and a better definition of the tasks presenting themselves today in the different regions of the Communist movement. After these regional conferences the Chinese would be isolated enough to make an international conference safe if it were still necessary.[21] Therefore, by seeming to be sincere about revitalizing the Latin-American Communist movement along more militant lines the Soviets manipulated Castro and the Latin-American Communist parties to agree to convoking a regional meeting to discuss concrete situations.

The conference was convened in Havana in late September, 1964, with twenty-two Latin-American Communist parties attending. Although the Soviets announced that the conference had been called at the behest of the Cubans, the evidence indicates it involved primarily a Soviet initiative designed to drive a permanent wedge between Castro and the Chinese, isolating Latin-American Communism from Chinese influence.[22] The conference brought Castro face-to-face with Soviet-line Communist leaders from most of the Latin-American countries with no competing Castroite or pro-Chinese factions present as alternatives. In those countries where the party was split into pro-Soviet and Chinese groups as in the case of Brazil, Peru, and Chile only the pro-Soviet faction was represented.[23] As long as the pro-Soviet Communists seemed willing to make concessions to Castro's views, he acted in

J. GREGORY OSWALD

concert with them and concessions were made. The Cuban Revolution was praised and supported. The Communist parties of Latin America were called upon to publicize the successes of her revolution, to demand that their governments officially recognize the Castro regime, and to systematically oppose the U.S. sponsored blockade of Cuba. In return for Castro's agreement to deal only with the established Latin-American Communist parties, the Soviets and their followers conceded, although they did not specifically support, the necessity of encouraging armed struggle in the controversial Venezuelan case, Guatemala, Honduras, Colombia, Paraguay, and Haiti. If the Communist parties wanted to maintain their opportunism in some areas, Castro at least would have some countries following Fidelista lines. Despite these reconciliatory measures, the Soviets arranged the conference so that Castro would not be the undisputed leader of the Latin-American Communist parties. They skillfully preempted Castro from this possible role by having the Chilean and Italian Communist parties conduct bilateral negotiations with the Cubans. These negotiations enhanced Cuba's prestige within the Communist movement, but they also made Castro aware that his views on Latin-American Communism were subject to constant discussion and approval.[24] The most important event of the conference, however, was the development of a schism between Havana and Peking, the rejection of Chinese positions, and a commitment to ban all factional activity. Thus the conference worked predictably well for the Soviets just as the Italian Togliatti had foreseen.

In early 1965 guerrilla action in Venezuela was stepped up, Colombian Communists made new sounds of support for the guerrillas in the hills, and a new guerrilla organization, the FAR (Rebel Armed Forces) made its appearance in Guatemala with the approval of the local Communist party. The pro-Soviet parties were also trying to fulfill the solidarity with Cuba agreement of the Havana Conference. Castro, for his part, avoided pronouncements on the inevitability of armed struggle in Latin America. He even switched support from a dissident Castroite group in Guatemala to the Communist approved FAR later in the year.[25] A year of truce seemed to have set in. The Soviets started maneuvering Castro toward another Soviet-sponsored meeting in March, preparatory to an eventual world Communist conference. Although Castro was not present at this meeting, he arranged for his brother Raul and other revolutionaries of the 26th of July Movement to represent Cuba. Ernesto Ché Guevara had dropped out of sight apparently because his continued criticism of various aspects of the Cuban Revolution and his distaste towards the Soviet pressure that was partly responsible for Castro's continued concessions, displeased Fidel. The Soviets must have made it clear to Castro that the price of their economic support was the adoption of rational economic practices. Castro shelved Guevara's rapid industrialization plans, gave top priority to the development of agriculture, and reformed the state bureaucracy. He also introduced material and industrial incentives, a policy irksome to Ché.[26] Latin-American Trotskyists have stated that Castro liquidated Ché on Soviet instructions in return for continued financial aid.[27] Later events have shown this to be unlikely. Nevertheless, Ché's disappearance definitely facilitated Soviet-Cuban rapprochement.

This harmony began to dissolve when the U.S. invaded the Dominican Republic to put down a left-of-center revolution. The Soviets used the temporary successes of the rebels in resisting the imperialistic intervention as proof that Communists in Latin America could best advance their interests by being part of authentic bourgeois-democratic movements. After the crisis they began peddling the old "popular front" theme as the requirement of the moment. Since the main Soviet interest in the 1964 Havana conference compromise had been the isolation of the Chinese, and the pro-Chinese groups were declining rapidly, they must have been seeking means of conveniently retiring from the more expensive aspects of the compromise. The conference had been only a tactical step forward, and the Soviets could easily afford to take two steps backward in the future to a more realistic position. The major point of the Havana agreement was that each Communist party would determine its own correct line and implement it without competition from externally supported splinter groups. If one party decided circumstances no longer required armed struggle, Castro was restrained from supporting factional groups by the agreement. For the Soviets the Dominican crisis signified the change of circumstances:

If the Cuban revolution ushered in an age of people's democratic, socialist revolutions in the Western Hemisphere, the present developments in Dominica are the beginning of a new period, in which the conditions are being created for broad national anti-imperialist fronts to resist North American imperialism.[28]

The Soviets insisted that this revival of imperialism would drive reformers into the Communists' arms as long as the Communists remained cool. The *World Marxist Review* devoted its August issue to Latin-American problems, the main thesis being that armed struggle would come soon enough. The main objective it maintained was to form national fronts opposed to imperialism and play down partisan slogans and actions that might repulse moderates. The *Review* also emphasized that the most important factor in Castro's victory in Cuba had been the broad united front which supported him, not the guerrilla tactics which the Cubans espoused throughout the continent.[29] Moscow also resurrected Seventh Comintern Congress themes of increased world-wide use of united or popular front tactics.[30] The themes

PRECEDING PAGE:

ABOVE: Raúl Roa, Cuban Foreign Minister (left), attending the United Nations, was uncommunative when snapped at a lunch counter September 1, 1960. *See* p. 25. *A New York Journal-American* photo by courtesy of the Photography Collections, Humanities Research Center, the University of Texas.

BELOW: Ernesto (Ché) Guevara at the airport, returning to Cuba, December 17, 1964, after addressing the Assembly of the United Nations. *See* pp. 25, 29, 48, 52, 70, 95, 100, 174. *A New York Journal-American* photo by courtesy of the Photography Collections, Humanities Research Center, the University of Texas.

RIGHT: Fulgencio Batista, Cuban dictator driven into exile by Fidel Castro, attends a bull fight in Cascais, Portugal. He is the man at lower center in dark-rimmed glasses. *See* pp. 17, 19. Wide World photo.

RIGHT: Vicente Lombardo Toledano drowsing immediately behind former Mexican President Lazaro Cárdenas who is reading a speech to the Regional Communist Peace Conference in Mexico City, March 5, 1961. *See* pp. 18, 19, 125–28, 132 n 8. Wide World photo.

ABOVE: Victorio Codovilla, one of the top Argentine Communist leaders (July, 1958). *See* pp. 12, 13, 37, 41. Wide World photo.

LEFT: Eudocio Ravines, a Peruvian Communist (February, 1964). *See* pp. 16, 37. Wide World photo.

ABOVE LEFT: Following a threat by Communist terrorists to kill anyone who attempted to vote in the Venezuelan general election December 1, 1963, ninety-five percent of the electorate turned out. The above scene is at one of the voting places in Caracas. *See* p. 65. Wide World photo.

BELOW LEFT: Marco Antonio Yon Sosa, third from right, in cap, organizer of MR-13, the second guerrilla group in Guatemala, at first made up mainly of young army officers. *See* p. 69. Wide World photo.

ABOVE: Gov. Nelson Rockefeller shakes hands with members of the crowd after wreath-laying ceremony in the main square of Asuncion, Paraguay, June 20, 1969, while on a trip through South America for President Nixon. *See* p. 30. Wide World photo.

ABOVE: Fidel Castro and Salvadore Allende in cavalcade through Santiago, Chile, upon Castro's arrival from Cuba for a visit, November, 1971. *See* pp. 10, 24, 30, 31, 70, 107. Keystone Press photo.

RIGHT: Osvaldo Pacheco participates in the debate in the House of Deputies on a Senate passed bill to exclude Communists from elected offices, January 8, 1948. Wide World photo.

ABOVE: Luis Carlos Prestes (across the desk
from Khrushchev) in the Kremlin February
7, 1964. *See* pp. 136–37; also pp. 43, 84,
86, and throughout Chap. V. Wide World
photo.

ABOVE: Vladimir Palmeira, at top, dressed in black, head of UME, at a rally after the death of a student in a formidable demonstration. *See* pp. 169–70, 175. Keystone Press photo.

ABOVE RIGHT: Some of the students arrested at the Thirtieth National Congress of the UNE in São Paulo in October, 1968. *See* p. 170. Keystone Press photo.

BELOW RIGHT: Leonel Brizola, former governor of the Brazilian state of Rio Grande do Sul and PTB leader, November, 1969. *See* pp. 138–39, 158–60. Keystone Press photo.

BELOW FAR RIGHT: Carlos Marighella killed in a police ambush in São Paulo, Brazil, November 4, 1969. *See* pp. 175–76; also pp. 139–40, 147–48, 155, 169, 171. Wide World photo.

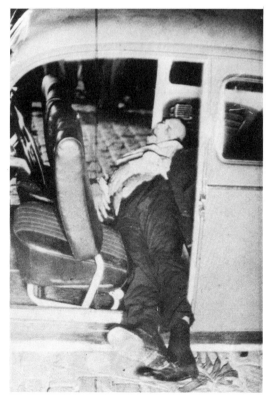

O caminho já foi apontado:

GREVE GERAL CONTRA o ARROCHO

A classe operária começou a passar das palavras à ação na luta contra o arrocho salarial. A greve deflagrada em Minas — que uniu 15 mil operários das empêsas mais importantes da Cidade Industrial de Belo Horizonte — apontou concretamente o caminho da luta. Já dizíamos em nosso número anterior que a única forma de enfrentar de fato a política patronal era lançando mão da arma da greve. Os operários mineiros mostraram como estão dispostos ao combate: sem contar com o sindicato, tendo contra si a repressão policial e as ameaças de Passarinho, realizaram uma greve que só não foi vitoriosa por faltar uma organização de base. Coragem e fôrça tiveram em dose suficiente para

POLITICA OPERARIA

Orgão Central do Partido Operário Comunista

Maio 68   NCR$ 0,50   No. 17

A fundação do Partido Operário Comunista

A partir dêste número, como se vê, POLITICA OPERARIA aparece como órgão oficial do PARTIDO OPERARIO COMUNISTA. É que do desenvolvimento da luta interna na esquerda —dentro e fora do velho partido comunista— chegamos à unificação da Organização Revolucionária Marxista POLITICA OPERARIA com a DISSIDENCIA LENINISTA, que já rompera com o partido reformista no processo da discussão interna. Nêste número transcreveremos a Resolução Política aprovada no Congresso que deu nascimento ao PARTIDO OPERARIO COMUNISTA.

Defendendo a linha da revolução proletária e socialista, o P.O.C. se empenha em levar já à prática os princípios que a POLITICA OPERARIA sempre defendeu no combate ideológico ao reformismo e que a Dissidência LENINISTA levantou nos debates internos que a distinguiram no velho partido.

A disposição de luta manifestada pelo proletariado agora, após 4 anos de dura repressão, mostra que há hoje um campo fértil para as idéias revolucionárias. Organizá-lo a partir das fábricas, preparar a classe para seus instrumentos de luta com a perspectiva da greve geral, preparar as formas armadas da luta de classe a começar pela guerrilha que estabelecerá a aliança com os trabalhadores do campo, é a tarefa para um partido revolucionário hoje no Brasil. Esse partido não nasce acabado; sua construção se dá ao lado das tarefas que cumpre. E é para essas tarefas revolucionárias que o P.O.C. convoca hoje tôdas as fôrças combatentes e revolucionárias do proletariado, que já despontam por todas as partes do país.

apavorar o ministro e os patrões. As experiências da greve estão hoje não só nas cabeças dos operários mineiros mas também nas dos seus companheiros do país inteiro, que agora se preparrão para a levar avante a luta. E, mais do que tudo, o exemplo vindo de Minas animou o movimento operário de forma extraordinária e tôdas as parcelas combativas da classe apontarão êsse exemplo para a massa.

Em São Paulo os trabalhadores fizeram do 1º de Maio uma data de luta. Impedindo a comemoração dos pelegos com seu governador e realizando uma passeata e um comício com as bandeiras legítimas da classe, os operários em São Paulo deram outra colaboração para o prosseguimento da luta. A greve geral, a organização dos operários nas emprêsas, foram os objetivos principais levados às ruas ao lado do brado de "operários no poder".

Em Minas e no Rio Grande do Sul a polícia enfrentou violentamente as manifestações operárias enquanto que na Guanabara, prevalecendo as diretrizes reformistas, a burguesia pôde permitir comemoração, reprimindo apenas os setores mais consequentes.

Assim, começou o proletariado a se mover por todo o país. E não nos iludamos: será um longo e duro caminho. Até aqui vimos ações isoladas que provam a fôrça da classe mas que não são suficientes para dobrar o poder dos exploradores.

A greve em Minas mostrou onde ainda estamos fracos: na organização pelas bases. Esse é lo trabalho mais imediato de suas lideranças.

Mas a greve e as manifestações do 1º de Maio nas principais cidades do país mostraram outra coisa: que é preciso uma liderança autêntica da classe, pois as direções reformistas e pelegas fogem da luta onde ela estoura e só sabem andar nas salas dos ministérios e políticos burguêses.

Da própria luta vai se formando uma nova vanguarda da classe, ainda dispersa nas fábricas e bairros proletários. O que os identifica é a disposição de organizar a classe nas emprêsas para travar a luta contra o regime, com seus próprios métodos e objetivos. A constituição duma Frente Unica Proletária será no momento um grande passo para a mobilização geral da classe.

PELA GREVE GERAL CONTRA TARIA!

PELA FORMACAO DOS COMITES DE EMPRESA!

PELA REVE GERAL CONTRA O ARROCHO E A DITADURA!

ESTAMOS REPETINDO...

Por que pegar em armas?

Quando se defende a coexistência pacífica entre o socialismo e o capitalismo, e se anuncia, ao mesmo tempo, a necessidade de pegar em armas pela causa da libertação dos povos subjugados ao imperialismo, parece que se está caindo em contradição.

Tal, porém, não acontece.

A competição pacífica vem demonstrando ao mundo as vantagens da economia socialista, que não se baseia no lucro e na exploração; e onde os fantasmas da fome, do analfabetismo e do terror policial já não atormentam os homens. Em contraposição, mostra as debilidades do sistema capitalista que não pode prescindir das guerras, e ressalta a farsa da democracia burguesa, na verdade uma ditadura de classe, onde os grandes proprietários e os agentes imperialistas têm direito a tudo e a imensa massa assalariada não tem direito a nada.

Êsse é o quadro real, que os comunistas têm o dever de mostrar e explicar detalhadamente às massas populares, nos países dependentes, para que, conscientizadas, sintam necessidade de lutar, de tôdas as formas, pela sua libertação.

É importante compreender-se que, no plano internacional, é possível coexistirem pacificamente os dois sistemas antagônicos. Mas, dentro da realidade nacional de cada país subjugado, não é possível conciliação entre os opressores imperialistas, cujos testas de ferro estão enquistados nas administrações públicas e empresariais, e a imensa massa oprimida e explorada, desejosa de arrancar o País do jugo estrangeiro e de encontrar melhores condições de existência.

Para lograr êsse intento é necessário, porém, que assumam as rédeas de govêrno, contribuindo assim, como bem ficou assinalado na Conferência Tricontinental de Havana, para enxotar o imperialismo da face da Terra. E isto só será possível através da luta armada. Está provado que os imperialistas e seus aliados burgueses não entregarão o Poder pacificamente.

Contudo — e isto é muito importante — pegar em armas é a etapa culminante de uma série de lutas anteriores, também indispensáveis. Desde as simples reivindicações salariais às grandes campanhas políticas através das quais os comunistas devem se preparar e, ao mesmo tempo esclarecer, orientar e organizar o povo para a luta decisiva. Esta surgirá no momento preciso, não por acaso, mas através de uma preparação meticulosa, com as massas populares esclarecidas e dispostas ao combate, sob o comando de sua organização revolucionária, de libertação nacional, hegemônicamente impulsionada pela vanguarda do proletariado — o Partido Comunista.

"... irá de mão em mão levando pequenina chispa..."

o Isqueiro

GUANABARA — AGÔSTO 1966 — N.º 24

Leia Nesta Edição:

"UM ENCONTRO HISTÓRICO" (À PAG. 2)

"MOVIMENTO SINDICAL: NOSSA BANDEIRA É OUTRA" (À PAG. 3)

"UMA OPINIÃO SÔBRE AS TESES" (À PAG. 4)

Ouça o mundo Socialista

MOSCOU : nas ondas 31, 41 e 19 metros
19.00 às 19,300 e 21 às 21,30 horas

PEQUIM : na onda 41 metros
18.00 às 19.3o horas

HAVANA : nas ondas 19 25, 31 e 49 metros
às 19 horas

VANGUARDA

«O marxismo-leninismo parte de que o papel decisivo na história é desempenhado pela atividade e a luta de classe, das massas populares. Sòmente em ligação com a luta de classes, com a atividade das massas populares, em ligação com as necessidades sociais engendradas por esta luta, é que pode ser compreendido o verdadeiro papel dos dirigentes.

Tal concepção da história é incompatível com o culto a personalidade, com a veneração de dirigentes eminentes, atribuindo-lhes certos méritos e virtudes sôbre-humanos. O culto à personalidade é uma ideologia contrária ao marxismo, a qual tem as suas raízes na concepção feudal do mundo e no individualismo burguês.

Ao mesmo tempo, o culto à personalidade cria as condições para uma prática má, que contraria as necessidades e os interêsses do movimento socialista.

A incontida exaltação do dirigente e a exageração de seus méritos exercem, queiram-no ou não, influência nociva sôbre as massas, impedindo a sua correta educação. O Culto à personalidade gera no seio das massas concepções errôneas, como se as tarefas que se encontram diante dos trabalhadores pudessem ser cumpridas por outrem, como se as capacidades e os méritos dso dirigentes dessem a milhões de dirigidos fundamento para esperar pelo grande homem, para seguir passivamente as prescrições e indicações da «autoridade», que supostamente tudo sabe e tudo prevê, liberando, assim, os simples militantes do movimento socialista de pensar, de manifestar iniciativa, de criar, de influir ativamente no curso dos acontecimentos.»

Fundamentos do marxismo-leninismo, pág. 191. (Culto a personalidade).

VIVA A UNIÃO NACIONAL DE ESTUDANTES!

ÊSTE É UM NÚMERO ESPECIAL DE DEBATES DE "O ISQUEIRO" LEIA-O. E DIVULGUE-O.

Some Newspapers and Convention Programs and Reports Printed and Mimeographed.

NÚMERO 17
MAIO DE 1966
PREÇO Cr.$ 100

VOZ OPERÁRIA

ORGÃO CENTRAL
DO
PARTIDO COMUNISTA
BRASILEIRO

VIVA O 1.º DE MAIO! VIVA O SOCIALISMO!

CONFLITO DE FRONTEIRA

MANIFESTO DO PARTIDO COMUNISTA

Tralhadores!

A ditadura militar reacionária e entreguista continua a oprimir e esfomear a classe operária e o nosso povo. Continua a entregar nossas riquezas e o produto de nosso trabalho aos imperialistas norte-americanos. Ao comemorar a data de 1º de Maio, relembrando o passado de lutas gloriosas dos trabalhadores brasileiros, reafirmemos nossa firme decisão de intensificar a luta contra a quadrilha golpista que assaltou o poder em abril de 1964. Os inimigos do povo e traidores da pátria serão derrotados.

Olhando para o mundo, neste Dia Internacional dos Trabalhadores, vemos que são as fôrças do progresso, da democracia, da paz e do socialismo que crescem. Apesar da sua política de provocação de guerra e do furor assassino com que se atira contra os povos que defendem a independência e a liberdade, como o heróico povo do Vietname, o imperialismo é impotente para barrar a marcha da História. O mundo avança para o socialismo. Foi o hino dos trabalhadores — a "Internacional" — que o primeiro satélite da Lua, lançado pela União Soviética, transmitiu para todo o Universo. Também o povo brasileiro, ao derrotar a ditadura que o oprime, abrirá caminho para libertar-se da exploração imperialista e liquidar o latifúndio, avançando para o progresso, a democracia e o socialismo!

Trabalhadores!

Comemoremos com alegria e ânimo combativo a data internacional do proletariado.

Os comunistas vos conclamam à luta contra a ditadura, contra a fome, contra a dominação de nossa pátria pelo explorador norte-americano. Aumentai os esforços pela organização e unidade da classe operária. Pela união dos trabalhadores das cidades eo nseus irmãos os trabalhadores do campo. Pela solidariedade internacional do proletariado. Pela solidariedade aos povos do Vietname e de São Domingos. Em defesa da paz mundial.

Intensificai a luta pelas liberdades democráticas. Pela conquista de vossas reivindicações imediatas. Em defesa da estabilidade no emprêgo e dos demais direitos revogados ou ameaçados pela ditadura. Pelo direito de greve e pela liberdade sindical.

Reuni vossas fôrças e, junto a todo o povo brasileiro, levai adiante a luta pela derrota da ditadura e por um govêrno que assegure as liberdades democráticas para as massas trabalhadoras e populares.

Viva a unidade e a solidariedade da classe operária e de todo o povo!

Viva o 1º de Maio!

Viva o socialismo!

O Comitê Central do
Partido Comunista Brasileiro
Maio de 1966

A imprensa européia divulgou, há pouco, uma informação da maior gravidade: meses atrás, o sr. Lincoln Gordon, então ainda embaixador no Brasil, encaminhou um relatório ao govêrno dos Estados Unidos advertindo de que amadurecia, nos círculos econômicos e até em certos setores dos governos da Argentina, Brasil, Uruguai e Paraguai, a idéia da exploração da energia elétrica do salto das Sete Quedas — um potencial de aproximadamente 25.000.000 de quilowates. Nesse documento advertia sôbre a necessidade de medidas destinadas a impedir que isso acontecesse, dado o extraordinário fator de progresso que representaria para os quatro países, contribuindo assim, de certa forma, para subtraí-los à influência ianque.

Essa informação joga uma luz intensa sôbre as manobras que o govêrno brasileiro vem realizando nos últimos meses. Interpretando à sua maneira e de forma nova os tratados existentes, a ditadura criou um conflito de fronteiras visando aparentemente a defesa dos interêsses nacionais, mas na realidade destinado a criar maiores dificuldades à exploração do enorme manancial energético representado por Sete Quedas.

O povo brasileiro e o povo paraguaio são irmãos. Seu inimigo maior e comum é o imperialismo norte-americano, ao qual se curvam as ditaduras que infelicitam a ambos. A posição dos patriotas brasileiros não pode, portanto, ser outra senão desmascarar essa manobra vergonhosa, através da qual se procura desviar a atenção dos dois povos da luta contra a fome e à miséria, contra a ditadura e o imperialismo. Por isso mesmo, e de se estranhar que alguns reconhecidos adversários da ditadura, como o senador Aurélio Viana, se deixem envolver pela propaganda dos inimigos do povo brasileiro, chegando a afirmar que nesse caso é necessário apoiar a posição do govêrno.

EDITORIAL
EDITORIAL Solidariedade ao Vietname e a São Domingos

NOSSO DEVER INTERNACIONALISTA

Amplia-se e assume formas cada vez mais odiosas a agressão norte-americana contra todo o povo do Vietname. Mais de 300.000 soldados na guerra, usando as armas mais modernas, queimando vilas inteiras com granadas gelatinosas, destruindo pastagens e plantações com venenos e gases tóxicos, torturando publicamente prisioneiros e suas famílias, procuram desesperadamente esmagar os anseios de liberdade e emancipação de um povo. A guerra aérea não declarada contra a República Democrática do Vietname — que faz milhares de vítimas nos centros populosos, nas aldeias, nos hospitais e escolas — é um desafio cínico a tôdas as leis de convivência internacional. Os agressores ameaçam estender a guerra ao Cambodja, ao Laos e à própria China.

Até há pouco, o govêrno dos Estados Unidos afirmava que a presença de seus "assessores militares" no Vietname visava a fortalecer o govêrno de Saigon, que estaria sendo vítima de uma agressão dos guerrilheiros. Os fatos se encarregaram de desmascarar essa mentira. O povo das grandes cidades do Vietname do Sul luta nas ruas pela derrubada do fantoche Cao Ky e pela retirada das tropas norte-americanas. Até um jornalista brasileiro reacionário, levado ao teatro da guerra para dar cobertura à agressão, e obrigado a reconhecer que pràticamente já não há qualquer govêrno na-

cional no Vietname do Sul e que os elementos essenciais da máquina estatal são dirigidos pelos próprios ianques.

A outra face do problema: nem os jornalistas americanos podem esconder a realidade de que mais de 75% do Vietname do Sul estão sob o contrôle da Frente Nacional de Libertação, enquanto os feitos espetaculares dos vietcongs, bombardeando o aeródromo militar de Saigon, destruindo ali e em outros pontos do país dezenas de aviões e helicópteros, cercando e destruindo unidades inteiras do exército invasor, resistindo tenazmente a uma tremenda superioridade em homens e material bélico, refletem a férrea determinação de vencer que se apossou de todo um povo.

Mas, não é apenas na Ásia que o imperialismo norte-americano comete tais crimes. Já faz um ano que suas tropas desembarcaram em São Domingos para impedir que seu povo, já vitorioso contra as fôrças reacionárias e entreguistas, decidisse livremente de seu destino. Para defender os interêsses dos seus banqueiros, não vacilou o govêrno de Washington em tripudiar sôbre a própria Carta da O.E.A., numa agressão que foi denunciada e repudiada mesmo por grande número de parlamentares e órgãos de imprensa

(Conclui na 8ª página)

of the 1930s which condemned Left sectarianism within the Communist movement and authorized alliances with all forces opposed to fascism were quite convenient for isolating the Chinese "Stalinists" and the U.S. "Imperialists" of the 1960s. They were also calculated to squeeze the Cuban and Venezuelan Communists into less expensive popular front tactics. Castro must have been uneasy about where his harmony with the Soviets would lead him. He was sensitive about accusations that he and the Soviets confined their assistance to the rebels to mere protests at the United Nations and that revolutionaries could only expect success by rejecting the revisionist embrace of Moscow and Havana. When the Soviets began selling the popular front theme, Castro must have felt an almost unbearable psychological need to show his independence from Moscow and regain the respect of his most ardent supporters in Latin America—the guerrilla groups.

Castro must have been disenchanted with his past agreements with the Soviets, especially the one-sided Havana agreement. Just during this period when Castro felt a strong need to prove his independence of mind, another Soviet sponsored conference was due to occur—the Tricontinent Conference of January 3–15, 1966. The Soviets, apparently unaware of Castro's changing perspective, were relying on their ability to use him against the Chinese in the area of third-world radicalism. Soviet goals included creating a tricontinent movement which would be strong enough to preempt the field from other possible hostile movements yet weak enough not to threaten other more direct channels of Soviet influence with the groups involved. The ideal movement should be radical enough to provide anti-Western propaganda but not extreme enough to side with the Chinese or commit the Soviets beyond their own interests.

The alleged sponsor of the conference was the Afro-Asian Peoples Solidarity Organization (AAPSO) with headquarters in Cairo. Both Moscow and Peking were members, but by the end of 1964 their dispute had made the organization useless as a path of influence. Both the Chinese and the Soviets realized that their positions in AAPSO might be important for future Afro-Asian activities. Both had considered bringing Latin America into the organization to swing the balance in their favor, but neither was certain of the loyalties of these Communist parties. The Soviets had cause to believe the balance had shifted with the 1964 Havana Conference which had driven a wedge between Castro and the Chinese and commited the Cubans to deal through established Latin-American Communist parties. The pro-Soviet delegation was slated to be led by a rather wild third-world revolutionary, a selection whom the Chinese could not expediently refuse. At the Fourth AAPSO meeting Moscow persuaded the organization to agree to a Tricontinent Conference at Havana with "popular organizations" attending instead of traditional Communist parties. Moscow also hoped to cancel the next AAPSO meeting at Peking and make the Tricontinent Conference an official AAPSO meeting, but these measures did not pass. Undismayed by this setback, the Soviets planned to bring the proposal up again at the conference and bring AAPSO into the proposed tricontinent movement.[31]

An eighteen member preparatory committee met in Cairo September 12, 1965, to choose tentative delegates to the conference. The five Latin-American members were the Cuban PCC (Communist Party of Cuba), which Castro had just converted from the PURS shortly before the beginning of trade negotiations for the 1966 Soviet-Cuban trade agreement,[32] the Venezuelan FLN, the Chilean FRAP (Popular Action Front), the Guatemalan FAR, and the Uruguayan FIDEL (Left Liberation Front). The Cubans proposed a list of invitations composed of traditional Latin-American Communist parties or their front organizations. The Chinese challenged these pro-Soviet groups to no avail.[33] It seemed that the Soviets and Cubans were working together against the Chinese. But the final list of invitations was to be left in the hands of the members of the committee, the Latin-American members of which were controlled by Castro.

Castro, already aware of his use to the Soviets against the Chinese, began to see the conference as a chance to break his political isolation and dependence on Moscow and make a place for himself as a third-world leader of recognized consequence. His opportunities to use the conference were probably clarified after the preparatory meeting when he expressed concern over the PCV-FALN split. To insure his personal success, Castro invited any significant guerrilla groups that were unaffiliated with Communist parties in their areas. At a December preparatory committee chaired by Cubans, a traditional Communist party plea for admission was turned down in favor of a more Castro-oriented group.[34] The FALN was also invited instead of the PCV.

By the time the Conference began Moscow must have been troubled with doubts regarding Castro's behavior. They were undoubtedly delighted when Castro unexpectedly attacked the Chinese for cutting back on rice shipments to Cuba. But it was actually a matter of self-interest for Castro to deal the Maoists in his own ranks a finishing blow and to isolate the pro-Chinese factions that had sprung up in numerous Latin-American countries, thereby placing armed liberation movements on the continent clearly under the emblem of the Cuban revolution.[35] After this attack, Castro worked for the establishment of Tricontinental headquarters at Havana instead of at Cairo, the latter location being clearly preferable to the Soviets. During this Castro manipulation, the Soviets were occupied trying to insure the merger of the AAPSO into the tricontinent movement.[36] This attempt failed and the Soviets also conceded to Castro's demand to have the headquarters of the movement in Havana.

Castro and the guerrillas he had invited were setting the theme of the conference—armed struggle. Castro praised armed struggle and downgraded the Communists:

What with the ones who theorize, and the ones who criticize those who theorize while beginning to theorize themselves, much energy and time is unfortunately lost; we believe that on this continent (Latin America), in the case of all or almost all peoples, the battle will take on the most violent forms.[37]

Castro also advanced the theme that the Soviets and other developed socialist countries should fulfill their world revolutionary duty by aiding liberation movements and liberated countries. He implied that past aid to the FALN of Venezuela was motivated by political considerations rather than the desire to see it succeed. To give his comments regarding the FALN additional weight, he had made it respectable by invitation to the conference and so could safely aid it without violating the Havana agreement. Castro's most brilliant ploy, however, was in keeping the Soviets and the Chinese off the Executive Secretariat of the new organization while arranging membership for himself, North Korea, and North Vietnam.[38] The Soviets were of course expected to contribute funds to the organization.

The Soviets had been beaten at their own game. Castro had successfully used the Sino-Soviet dispute to his own advantage and was beginning to learn what Kevin Devlin calls the ungentle art of "political judo." Moscow began feeling the opprobrium of Latin-American countries, concerned at the interventionist implications of the conference. The Latin-American governments censured the conference in the U.N. and OAS.[39] Immediately the Soviets circulated a verbal note to those governments expressing dissatisfaction and disavowing Soviet delegation actions at the conference. On the same day, February 11, 1966, Castro sent a letter to the U.N. declaring Cuba's full adherence to the conference proceedings and expressing his resentment of any criticism of them. This demonstrated to the Soviets that he did not appreciate their denigrating the conference. As expected, however, the Soviets continued to play down the entire affair.

For Castro the conference provided new confidence that he was independent in mind, if not in body, from the Soviets. He became involved in international Communist politics as a world revolutionary leader and formed a new Communist alignment of the have-nots with North Korea and North Vietnam agreeing that the Communist haves should give more aid and demand less obedience. He was once again the leading undisputed advocate of armed struggle. In this reaffirmed role Castro was bound to clash with the

Soviets who were obviously more concerned with popular fronts than with costly, futile wars of liberation.

Castro involved himself in the PCV-FALN fracas again, this time over the suitability of guerrilla warfare in Venezuela. Castro was helping the FALN to reorganize and carry on the struggle without the PCV while the PCV was trying to control the dissident faction and halt guerrilla activity. The FALN requested direct aid from Castro in June and as a combined gesture and propaganda stunt twenty bearded, uniformed men landed on the Venezuelan coast July 24, 1966.[40] Castro was moving in the direction of an open renunciation of the Havana agreement. A few months later the PCV publicly insisted that there was no parallel between the Cuban revolution and the situation in Venezuela and that they were competent to handle the situation without Cuban help. They accused Castro and his Venezuelan followers of an emotionalism and infantilism which the PCV had outgrown, and referred to the Tricontinent Conference as a farce.[41] Castro, increasingly upset at having his way of revolution debunked consistently and having the Havana agreement and the Soviet popular front doctrine thrown in his face, needed a Marxist doctrine for his own thought, with which he could answer back.

When Castro assumed power his outlook was relatively non-ideological. He wanted violent revolution in Latin America, but was indifferent to whether the Communist parties carried it out. As Theodore Draper observed in his analysis of Castroism, Castro always "had a deep persistent feeling of intellectual inadequacy and inferiority, a tendency to depend on others for fundamental values or systematic thinking."[42] Until early 1965 his systematic thinker was Guevara and his thought was little more than the postulate of armed struggle as a near absolute and a how-to-do-it handbook for guerrillas. Such a limited outlook was relatively useless when Castro attempted to refute the skilled pro-Soviet dialecticians who lucidly explained how current facts required them to behave just as they always had done. Guevara was replaced by the young French Marxist convert to Castroism, Régis Debray. He helped Castro clarify his thoughts on the question of Latin-American revolutions and molded them into more sophisticated Marxist terminology in his book *Revolution in the Revolution?* This book represents a complete and authoritative statement of Castroist revolutionary doctrine as of the end of 1966.[43] Debray argued that the revolutionary theory and practice developed in other continents by the Russians, Chinese, Vietnamese, etc., were not applicable in Latin America.[44] The way ahead was that pioneered by the Cuban vanguard: "The Latin-American revolution and its vanguard, the Cuban revolution, are thus making a decisive contribution to international revolutionary experience and Marxism-Leninism."[45] But the vanguard did not have to be a Marxist-Leninist party:

J. GREGORY OSWALD

Castro says . . . this vanguard need not necessarily be the Marxist-Leninist party, and that those who want revolution have the right and the duty to establish themselves as a vanguard, independent of these parties. . . . It takes courage to state things as they are in a fearless voice, when these facts go against a tradition. There is, then, no metaphysical equation—vanguard equals Marxist-Leninist party.[46]

The guerrilla movement was to develop the political vanguard and the main emphasis was to be placed on the development of the guerrilla warfare and not in the strengthening of existing parties or the creation of new ones.[47] Most important, the guerrilla force must have its own, autonomous politico-military authority if it was to succeed:

The placement of guerrilla warfare under the strategic and tactical orientation of a party which has not radically changed its normal peacetime organization, or to make guerrilla warfare one more branch of party action will bring as its consequence a series of fatal military errors.[48] . . . the force of tradition, the habitual adherence to given forms of organization which have been consecrated and solidified by time prevents a break with the established structure and the adoption of the new form of struggle required by the war situation . . . This abstract, reformist, or contradictory political leadership transforms the revolutionary movement into a marionette without strings. . . . The armed apparatus will respond to the legalist nostalgia of the political leadership with uncontrolled terrorism in the cities and banditry in the rural sectors.[49]

Since the revolution in Latin America was to come by armed struggle through guerrilla bands in the rural areas, there would be no need for the Communist parties which would only hinder the armed struggle.[50] Debray's justification of the guerrilla movement's assumption of both political and military command is his conviction that this is the one force able to establish the worker-peasant alliance that will become the new regime. "The guerrilla army completes this alliance by action. . . . The army is in fact that alliance."[51] The guerrillas will have no trouble acquiring the proper socialistic ideological outlook because:

Under such conditions, class egoism does not last long. Petty bourgeois psychology melts like snow under the sun, undermining its very basis. . . . For the same reason, the only possible policy for a guerrilla force is a "mass line." It cannot exist without mass support and daily contact with the peoples. The vacillations of bureaucracy are too extreme even to be considered. Is this not, for a future leader or socialist official, the best of training?[52]

Debray concludes with the logical consequence of these assertions. "The people's army will be the nucleus of the party and not vice versa."[53] Finally, Debray destroys the one structure that Communists have traditionally used for involvement in armed struggles—the mass front. He terms the front "artificial and improvised." With a prestigious "independent personality" at the top as a figurehead, energy is diverted from the main task of constructing a people's army. "No deliberative political front can take charge of the effective leadership of a people's war," because any "composite national front is by nature disposed to political disagreements, endless deliberations, and temporary compromises."[54] Efforts to hold such fronts together are futile and immobilizing at the start of guerrilla action and as the guerrilla movement develops they become unnecessary.[55] In such manner Debray disposes of the standard Soviet device for squeezing armed struggle into the popular front framework. Debray deliberately attempts by rejecting Trotskyism as metaphysical and suicidal and opposing Chinese-style political factionalism not to fall into any categories of deviationism which would cause Moscow to reject his doctrine.[56] He also insists that his doctrine is not anti-Communist since the ideology of the new commanders of the Cuban rebel army is Marxist, and the Cuban Revolution that is developing is clearly socialist and proletarian.[57] He also points out that the guerrillas have not attempted to set up new parties in opposition to the established ones.[58]

Debray's book is an ideological rationalization for the Tricontinent Conference and for the neglect of the 1964 Havana Conference agreements. However, it leaves intact the one achievement in these agreements which Moscow considered most vital—the Cuban split with Peking. The writer's opinions can be seen as a conscious Cuban attempt to subvert or displace existing Communist parties and create effective guerrilla organizations which cannot be defined as competing parties or factions. It justifies Cuban aid to Latin-American guerrillas regardless of the type of government being attacked. Although Debray's book is not a complete coverage of Castro's premises, it deals with a substantial number of them. Debray alluded to two other significant Castro premises in an interview published in *Granma* in early February, 1967. One was the doctrine of placing aid to foreign revolutions above domestic prosperity, a denial of the Stalinist precept of "socialism" in one country, and the other was the refutation of Soviet leadership of the world Communist movement.[59]

In his renewed attack in March, 1967, on the PCV, Castro made use of his new tool. Castro's action was prompted by moves to expel Douglas Bravo, leader of the FALN for stepped up guerrilla violence. The PCV retaliated and a split along pro-Castro versus pro-Soviet lines among the leftist forces and Communists in Latin America was averted only by the conciliations of the Communists. The Soviets, in the *World Marxist Review* of September, 1967, indirectly supported the PCV and also denied some of Debray's contentions. The article stated that since the guerrilla group had tried to push the party into the background and destroy it, it must be expelled. The review also reiterated the Marxist-Leninist dogma that the guerrilla movement existed only as an auxiliary form of struggle and that the party would decide what form of struggle fit the reality of the moment. Obviously, the reality of the moment for the PCV was following the peaceful path and making plans to participate in the 1968 election campaign. Although the article admitted that the ultimate goals of the party could not be achieved through elections, it reaffirmed the position that "they cannot be achieved through armed struggle either, unless we achieve an uprising of the popular movement. . . ."[60] The Soviets had reiterated the very prerequisite of popular movement which Debray had denied.

One of the most complete rebuttals of the Debray guerrilla-army-as-orthodox-Communist thesis was by an old Soviet-line Argentinian Communist, Rodolfo Ghioldi. In an article in *Pravda* on October 25, 1967, Ghioldi mentions neither Castro nor Debray by name, but it is all too obvious who he is discussing. He charges:

And it is not surprising, therefore, that the so-called "left nationalist forces," acting without Communists and even against them, and being to one degree or another under the influence of Maoism, again act as levers of bourgeois nationalism. The most typical thesis of these groups is that Marxism-Leninism does not exist, or if there is something similar to it, then it is a purely Russian national manifestation, as a consequence of which Marxist-Leninists in Latin America are nothing other than agents of Moscow.[61]

Ghioldi then presents a harsh, unflattering account of left nationalist ideas:

. . . rejection of the necessity of Communist Party activity, the disparagement of the role of the working class as a revolutionary force, the negation of the theory of proletarian hegemony, the rejection of the Leninist principle of avant-garde role of the proletariat, assertion that several avant-grades exist. In this enumeration it is already evident with what contempt and ignorance this classification treats theory: once Marxist-Leninist theory does not justify their actions, down with theory.[62]

Ghioldi had already demolished Debray's assertion that guerrillas could be orthodox Communists. Now he attacked Castro-Debray on a position which Debray had purposely tried to avoid being criticized on:

The Trotskyite idea of the impossibility of building Communism in one country is resurrected. The petty bourgeois nationalists also stubbornly insist that Latin-American countries must move directly to socialist revolution, disregarding the intermediary stage of agrarian anti-imperialist, democratic revolution. In the clumsy attempt to prove the weakness of the indestructible Marxist-Leninist positions, they try more or less to reject the basic position of the unity of the world socialist system, the proletarian movement in capitalist countries, and national liberation movements in colonial countries.[63]

The Soviets had disposed of Castro's and Debray's criticisms and theories in the usual manner of relegating them to the dust-bin of Trotskyism and deviationism.

Castro, preparing for the Latin American Solidarity Organization (OLAS) Conference, seemed indifferent to these dismissing remarks. He had founded the organization at the Tricontinent Conference and organized the conference at a series of bilateral inter-party meetings ideologically and organizationally weighted against the pro-Soviet Communists. Maoist and Trotskyist organizations were not invited so as not to antagonize the Soviets any more than was necessary. Some Communist parties such as the Venezuelan PCV either were not invited or did not choose to attend. Others were divided between hard-liners and moderates, and would be neutralized on crucial issues. The OLAS Conference was held from July 31 to August 10, 1967. The conference was anti-Soviet in tone as expected. Castro made it clear that armed revolutionary struggle was the primary path of the revolution in Latin America, a path to which all other anti-imperialist activity must be subordinated. Even in those countries where this was not considered an immediate task, it must be regarded as an inevitable prospect. He also made it quite clear to the Soviets that he would not modify his views through any economic pressure they might find expedient to apply to Cuba.[64] OLAS appeared to be Castro's Latin American Comintern. But appearances were deceiving. The non-Communist groups affiliated to OLAS did not have the organization discipline or ideological cohesion of the Communist parties. They were politically insignificant locally and their militance was more apparent than real. Perhaps more significant than these limitations was the difficult reality that although the Cubans could influence their permanent representatives in Havana, they had negligible control over their home detachments. Probably the most serious weakness was Castro himself who promised many revolutions but never sat down to plan out a single one.[65] Castro, ironically, became more of a threat to traditional Latin-American Communist parties than to Latin-American governments.

At the end of the OLAS Conference, Castro had referred vaguely to an alleged conspiracy by the "pseudo-revolutionary mafia," the Cuban "microfaction," and U.S. imperialists who hoped to create a break in Cuban economic relations with the socialist camp:

This is a plot by reactionary elements within the revolutionary movement and by Yankee imperialism. It is a plot the object of which is to create an international conflict between our revolution and the states of the socialist camp, because they have already said that what they want, demand, claim and urge is that the socialist camp join the imperialist blockade against Cuba.

I ask that Mafia gang that is trying to defame Cuba with its arguments: why does it not break relations with the U.S. Government?[66]

This was an obvious attack on the Soviets and Soviet bloc countries. Castro's speech also attacked Soviet and East European efforts to improve or establish commercial and diplomatic relations with Latin-American governments. This was part of his complaint that the socialist countries did not give Cuba enough economic aid to insure his continued control. The Soviets' best counter-measure to Castro's challenges was economic pressure. In 1964 the Soviets had signed a long-term agreement for purchase of unneeded Cuban sugar at a fixed price about three times higher than the world market value. This was probably done to persuade Castro to abandon his irrational economic plans and stress agricultural production. Most trade agreements were negotiated yearly to keep some measure of control over Castro. The 1965 trade agreement gave Castro various aid from the Comecon countries in payment for his part in the Havana Conference. The 1967 agreement was a different matter. Talks began in Moscow three months ahead of time. There was a great deal of hard bargaining and political confrontation and Castro was not pleased with the agreement when it was finally signed. The trade increase was small and oil shipments were not enough to meet Cuban needs. Oil shipments were late in arriving forcing Castro to draw upon military reserves and endangering his security. This was at a period when the Soviets were seeking to increase their sales of oil to Western Europe.[67] The Soviets had paid Castro back for the Tricontinent Conference. The 1968 trade agreement was due to be negotiated, and Castro rightly believed that the Soviets would apply economic pressure on him for his behavior during 1967. Castro was determined to make the Russians pay a high political price for these pressures.

The Cuban trade delegation left for Moscow in mid-October, 1967. The talks did not go well. In retaliation Castro sent a minor official as his delegate to the Fiftieth Anniversary of the Bolshevik Revolution in Moscow. Castro was exerting counter-pressure to the Soviets hoping to disrupt their attempts to create an image of Communist solidarity. It was at this time that Castro had the counter-revolutionaries of the microfaction arrested. Those arrested were pro-Soviet Communists such as Anibal Escalante. While the Cubans and Soviets disputed over oil shipments, the prisoners were interrogated in order to form a report on their counter-revolutionary activities. The report was released in early February, 1968. The affair was used on the domestic level to discredit opposition to Castro's policies of moral incentives and mass mobilization in economic production, of personal dictatorship, and his degrading of traditional Communist ideology.[68] A statement of self-criticism by Escalante was used to explain the relative roles of the USSR and Cuba:

In the consideration of these roles, many of us have always begun, from the outside to the inside: from the USSR, the center of world revolution, toward Cuba, part of the world revolution, instead of beginning from inside and proceeding to the outside: from Cuba, part of the world revolution, to the USSR, another part of the world revolution—very large, very powerful, very respectable, but no longer an isolated socialist center today, but part of the socialist world.[69]

Castro had denied Soviet leadership of the socialist world and the socialism in one country theory, both reassertions of his independent position. To deal with his current problem, the trade negotiations, Castro presented the members of the microfaction as having hoped that "economic facts" would lead the Soviets to apply political and economic pressure to make Castro modify his mistaken policies. This affair provided Castro with a good opportunity for stirring up revolutionary morale in Cuba and Latin America and proclaiming his independent position. It did not change the outcome of the trade agreement and Moscow refused to demean herself by answering the charges. They simply tightened up the screws. The Soviet-Cuban Trade Agreement of March, 1968, increased the flow of trade and aid by a margin sufficient to preserve Moscow's role as the mainstay of Cuba, but not enough to meet the country's rapidly expanding developmental needs. The per-cent increase in trade was less than the year before. The important innovation was that Castro was required to pay interest on the trade imbalance whereas previously the Soviets had given him a hidden subsidy to fill the gap.[70] Castro had become closer economically bound to the Soviets.

It becomes increasingly apparent that a clash of national interests between Castro and the Soviet Union exists. The Soviets, obligated to fulfill the role of superpower, must promote those global interests which are expedient to the USSR. For a time they believed the Cuban revolution could be exported to the continent but the missile crisis and the failure of guerrilla struggle in a number of countries jolted them back to reality. A renewed evaluation of the Latin-American situation revealed that the Soviets had little to show in return for their economic support. They realized that the exportation of the Cuban Revolution would result in a continual and increased drain on Soviet funds—more Cubas in Latin America would expect increasing support. Perhaps most disconcerting to the Soviets was the relative unpredictability of investing in this type of operation. Obviously they could pour additional money, material, and resources into the Middle East with more certainty of their returns. Consequently, the Soviets began to play down armed struggle

J. GREGORY OSWALD

and immediate revolution. They continued encouraging Latin-American nationalism in order to counteract U.S. economic influence and gain a foothold for themselves, but they also planned to establish diplomatic and commercial relations with any government no matter what its political nature. They recently established relations with Venezuela and Colombia, two countries which were suppressing guerrilla movements in their respective areas. Castro could clamor all he liked about Moscow's betrayal of revolutionaries. The Soviets could remain indifferent as long as they had sufficient opportunity to gain more political and economic influence for themselves. The Soviets continue firm believers in the Stalinist doctrine of socialism in one country.

Castro, on the other hand, is not the most brilliant demonstration of the pure social revolutionist. It made good political sense to him to become a Communist and make his revolution a socialist one. Castro has always kept his Communist party powerless and criticized orthodox Communism because it denies individual rule of power. He became disenchanted with the Soviets because they refused to risk a war for his survival, an irresponsible reaction at best. Castro's alignment with North Korea and North Vietnam and their demands for additional aid and more Vietnams was motivated by his ability to see Cuba's situation as quite similar. And there was always the consideration that if the U.S. were not occupied elsewhere, they might invade or bomb Cuba. All Castro's talk about armed struggle and immediate revolutions can be interpreted as a power play to become the Soviet Union of Latin America. He needs Castroist revolutions in Latin America to create satellites which will give him the economic independence and security so essential for continued leadership. Popular front movements and national reformist regimes, as in Allende's Chile, are a threat to his way of revolution because they might succeed, and thus also open a means for the Soviets to gain at his expense. Next to the U.S., the Soviet Union is Castro's greatest rival in Latin America. In spite of this inherent conflict, Castro and the Soviets are inescapably bound to one another. With the effective U.S. blockade and disappointing annual sugar crops, Castro remains economically dependent on the Soviet Union with no foreseeable change. Moreover, he is militarily dependent on them for equipment and replacement parts. The Soviets, for their part, have made too substantial an investment, ideologicaly, economically, and militarily, to be written off lightly. If they attempt to eject Castro from the Socialist camp, more chaos would wrack the already disunified world Communist movement further weakening Soviet control. Castro will continue assuming the role of the leader of the Latin-American revolution and the Soviets will continue to keep him economically and militarily dependent enough so he will not have the means to completely fulfill that role.

CONCLUSION

IN CLOSING, IT MIGHT BE INTERESTING TO PLACE SOVIET RELATIONS WITH MEXICO, Uruguay, and Cuba in the general perspective of USSR–Latin-American relations since 1968. Actually, now, in 1971, more dramatic changes are occurring in countries such as Chile, Bolivia, Peru, and Ecuador than Cuba in terms of emerging Soviet relations in the southern hemisphere. In those countries, USSR influence is expanding or appears to be at least of mutual benefit to the new governments and the Soviets. The 1970 Soviet fiasco in Mexico was a setback to the USSR, but political involvement in the internal affairs of another country, however, has been a penchant of the Soviet Union since its acceptance of the need for Marxist-Leninist revolutions everywhere.

In practical ways, the USSR has made trade initiatives in Latin America since 1964 which cause one to almost wonder why. Of close to 200 million dollars credit granted to several Latin-American countries, not including Cuba, most of this sun has remained unused by the recipients. For example, it has been noted that only 4–5 million dollars out of a total 100 million dollar credit extended to Brazil in 1966 had been used by 1970. "The reason for this Latin hesitance is that the products offered by the Soviet Union have not generally been of the type required, and poor or non-existent servicing, lack of spare parts, and inferior quality have not tended to earn Soviet equipment a good reputation."[71]

Never despairing of the retarded pace of USSR practical ties with the countries of Latin America, loyal Communist adherents such as the ardent Longino Becerra expound what must be the official view of Soviet authorities. In the January, 1971, issue of the *World Marxist Review* (Prague), Becerra assures his readers that Soviet–Latin-American ties will become closer and "the support and comprehensive assistance of the USSR will serve as the necessary guarantee of successful development of the revolutionary process on our continent" (p. 116). Time will tell.

NOTES, MEXICO AND URUGUAY

1. G. V. Chicherin, *Stati i rechi* (Moscow, 1961), p. 290.

2. *Excelsior*, Dec. 31, 1924.

3. *Washington Post*, May 28, 1925. The extent of United States government and business pressures on the new Mexican administration of President Calles to oust the Soviet Minister will not be discussed in this survey, but Washington officials and U.S. editorialists were clearly opposed and fearful of the Soviet presence in America.

Pestkovsky must be considered the first genuine Soviet Latin-Americanist. After his return to Moscow, he published *A History of Mexican Revolutions* (Moscow-Leningrad, 1928), and *The Mexican Agrarian Problem* (Moscow-Leningrad, 1929), as well as several articles discussing the current labor and agrarian movements in Mexico. A devotee of historical studies, and himself a student of M. N. Pokrovsky, the founder of Soviet Marxist historiography, Pestkovsky had previously published a significant number of books, pamphlets, and articles on Polish and Russian aspects of the 1905 and 1917 revolutions in Eastern Europe. From 1926 to 1934, he served as a pamphleteer and teacher of Mexican and Caribbean affairs in MOPR (International Relief Organization of Revolutionaries). Arrested during the Stalin purges, Pestkovsky was executed in 1937. His memoirs *Wspomnienia Rewolucjonisty* (Lodz, Poland, 1961), were published posthumously.

4. J. Gregory Oswald and Anthony J. Strover, eds., *The Soviet Union and Latin America* (New York, Washington, and London: Praeger, 1970), pp. 186–87.

5. *Current Digest of the Soviet Press*, XI No. 4, p. 34, citing *Pravda*, Jan. 23, 1956, p. 6.

6. *New York Times*, April 4, 7, 9, 17, 1959.

7. *Excelsior*, April 11, 1959.

8. *Hispanic American Report*, XIII (1959), No. 8, p. 509.

9. *New York Times*, July 9, 1961.

10. *Hispanic American Report*, XVI (May, 1963), No. 3, p. 232.

11. *Foreign Broadcast Information Service*, April 9, 1963.

12. Ibid., October 11, 1963.

13. *New Times*, No. 31 (August 5, 1964), pp. 20–21.

14. *Miami Herald*, March 14, 1966.

15. *Dokumenty vneshnei politiki SSSR* (Moskva: Izdat. Politicheskoi literaturi 1966), Vol. 9, p. 393.

16. *Izvestiia*, August 26, 1926, p. 1.

17. *New York Times*, December 28, 1935, p. 1.

18. *Izvestiia*, February 13, 1929, p. 2.

19. *International Communism in Latin America*, Free Press of Glenco, 1964, pp. 158–59.

20. *New York Times*, December 28, 1935.

21. *New York Times*, July 4, 1932, p. 4.

22. Leonard Schapiro, ed., *Soviet Treaty Series: 1929–1939* (Washington: Georgetown University Press, 1955), Vol. II, p. 75.

23. Ibid., p. 128.

24. *Current History*, March, 1936, Vol. 43, p. 637. In 1930 Prestes received approximately $100,000 from Brazilians to be used in a political revolution then. He disagreed with the aims of that revolution but retained the money for a future revolution. He insists that this was the origin of money he received for the 1935 revolt. Cf. unpublished papers of J. W. F. Dulles, "Brazilian Communism," University of Arizona, 1967.

25. Jane Degras, *Soviet Documents on Foreign Policy*, Vol. III, 1933–41 (London: Oxford University Press, 1953), p. 161.

26. Dulles, op. cit.

27. *Time*, January 6, 1936, p. 20.

28. *Izvestiia*, January 2, 1936.

29. Arthur U. Pope, *Maxim Litvinoff* (New York: L. B. Fischer, 1943), p. 397; and V. V. Vol'sky, ed., *SSSR i Latinskaia Amerika, 1917–1967* (Moskva: Izdat. Mezhdunarodnye otnosheniia, 1967), pp. 91–92.

30. Vol'sky, p. 92.

31. *Time*, February 1, 1943, p. 25.

32. Robert M. Slusser and Jan F. Triska, *Calendar of Soviet Treaties* (Stanford University Press, 1959), p. 153.

33. Peter Calvocoressi, *Survey of International Affairs: 1947–1948* (London: Oxford University Press, 1950), p. 481.

34. Slusser and Triska, p. 315.

35. Robert Loring Allen, *Soviet Economic Warfare* (Washington: Public Affairs Press, 1960), p. 101.

36. Allen, p. 102.

37. *Hispanic American Report*, August, 1958, p. 342.

38. Rollie Poppino, p. 201.

39. U. S. Department of Commerce, *International Bulletin*, February 4, 1963, p. 726.

40. *New York Times*, January 2, 1956, p. 9.

41. S. S. Mikhailov, "Izuchenie problem Latinskoi Ameriki/Study of the Problems of Latin America" (*Vestnik Adademii nauk SSR*, No. 5, 1962), p. 55.

42. S. S. Mikhailov, "Izuchenie Latinosko Ameriki v Sovetskom soiuze," *Voprosy istorii* (April, 1962), No. 4, p. 98.

43. *Fundamentals of Political Economy* (Moscow: Progress Publishers, rev. ed. 1966), p. 347.

44. *U.S. News and World Report*, November 2, 1959.

45. *Hispanic America Report*, May 1959, p. 231.

46. *El Día* (January 27, 1966, p. 2), stated that the Havana Conference resolutions were a declaration of war on international law and peaceful coexistence as they encouraged violence and revolution.

47. *La Prensa*, February 16, 1966, p. 2.

48. V. V. Vol'sky, *SSSR i Latinskaia Amerika, 1917–1967* (Moskva: Izdat. Mezhdunarodnye otnosheniia, 1967), p. 6.

49. Ibid.

NOTES, CUBA

1. Wolfgang W. Berner, "The Place of Cuba in Soviet Latin American Strategy," in J. Gregory Oswald and Anthony J. Strover, eds., *The Soviet Union and Latin America*, p. 91.

2. Ernst Halperin, "The Castro Regime in Cuba," *Current History*, LI (December, 1966), p. 355.

3. *New York Times*, July 11, 1960, p. 8.

4. Herbert Dinerstein, *Soviet Policy in Latin America*, Rand Memorandum RM-4967-PR (May, 1966), p. 20.

5. *New York Times*, May 9, 1961, p. 12.

6. Dinerstein, p. 1.

7. Halperin, p. 356.

8. Dinerstein, p. 21.

9. Kevin Devlin, "The Castroist Challenge to Communism," in Oswald and Strover, eds., *The Soviet Union and Latin America*, pp. 161–62.

10. Berner, p. 92.

11. Dinerstein, pp. 15–17.

12. Bruce Jackson, "Moscow, Havana, and the Venezuelan Communist Movement" (1968—unpublished paper), p. 13.

13. *New York Times*, June 5, 1963, p. 10.

14. Berner, p. 95.

15. Peter Schenkel, "Cuban Relations with the Communist World," in Oswald and Strover, eds., *The Soviet Union and Latin America*, p. 149.

16. *New York Times*, September 29, 1963, p. 13.

17. Jackson, p. 17.

18. Dinerstein, p. 28.

19. Ibid., p. 29.

20. A. Sivolobov, "Krestianskoe Dyizhenie v Latinskoi Amerike," *Kommunist* (August, 1964), p. 107, as quoted in Jackson, p. 16.

21. Palmiro Togliatti, "On International Working Class Unity," *Political Affairs*, XVIII (October, 1964), pp. 38–40.

22. Bruce Jackson, "Whose Men in Havana?" *Problems of Communism*, XV (May–June, 1966), pp. 1–3.

23. Daniel Tretiak, *Cuba and the Soviet Union: The Growing Accommodation*, Rand Memorandum RM-4935-PR (July, 1966), p. 10.

24. Ibid., pp. 10–12.

25. Jackson, "Moscow, Havana, and the Venezuelan Communist Movement," p. 23.

26. Ibid., p. 26.

27. Adolfo Gilly, "A Conference Without Glory and Without Program," *Monthly Review*, XVII (April, 1966), pp. 27–29.

28. V. Listov, "Big Stick Diplomacy Against A Small Nation," *New Times*, XX (May 17, 1965), p. 11.

29. J. M. Fortuny, "Has the Revolution Become More Difficult in Latin America?" *World Marxist Review*, VII (August, 1965), p. 44.

30. B. T. Rudenko, "The Ideas of the Seventh Comintern Congress and the Anti-imperialist Movements in Latin America," Joint Publications Research Service (JPRS) 36, 691 (July 26, 1966), pp. 88–92.

31. Jackson, "Moscow, Havana, and the Venezuelan Communist Movement," pp. 58–60.

32. Berner, p. 96.

33. Council of the OAS, *Report on the First Afro-Asian-Latin American Peoples Solidarity Conference and its Projections*, 2 vols. (Washington: Pan American Union, 1966), vol. I, pp. 10–11.

34. Ibid., p. 18.

35. Schenkel, p. 9.

36. Ch'en Lo-min, "The Struggle of the Asian, African, and Latin American Peoples Solidarity Conference," *Shih-chieh Chih-shih*, Peking (February 10, 1966), pp. 15–18. Translated in JPRS 10,010.

37. OAS Report, vol. II, pp. 47–50.

38. Ch'en Lo-min, p. 9.

39. OAS Report, vol. II, pp. 285–88.

40. Jackson, "Moscow, Havana, and the Venezuelan Communist Movement," pp. 77–87.

41. Carlos Valencia, "The Effectiveness of the Venezuelan CP is not under Discussion," *Que*, Caracas (September 23, 1966), pp. 6–7. Translated in JPRS, 5058, 1966.

42. Theodore Draper, *Castroism, Theory and Practice* (New York: Praeger, 1965), p. 50.

43. Regis Debray, *Revolution in the Revolution?* (New York: Grove Press, 1967), p. 7.

44. Regis Debray, *Revolution Within the Revolution?* JPRS 40, 310 (March 20, 1967), p. 28. (This is the edition used in this paper.)

45. Ibid., p. 72.

46. Ibid., p. 65.

47. Ibid., p. 81.

48. Ibid., p. 41.

49. Ibid., pp. 46–47.

50. Ibid., p. 69.

51. Ibid., p. 75.

52. Ibid., p. 76.

53. Ibid., p. 81.

54. Ibid., pp. 54–57.

55. Ibid., p. 55.

56. Ibid., pp. 17–21.

57. Ibid., p. 73.

58. Ibid., p. 71.

59. Jackson, "Moscow, Havana, and the Venezuelan Communist Movement," p. 111.

60. Juan Rodriguez, "The New in the Political Line of the Communist Party of Venezuela," *World Marxist Review*, X (September, 1967), pp. 78–82.

61. Rodolfo Ghioldi, *Pravda*, Moscow, October 2, 1967, p. 4, as quoted in Flor-

ence Memegalos, "Regis Debray: The Phophet of Castro Communism," in Oswald and Strover, eds., *The Soviet Union and Latin America*, p. 183.

62. Ibid.

63. Ibid.

64. Devlin, p. 169.

65. Ibid., p. 171.

66. Havana Radio August 11, 1967, as quoted in Devlin, "Castro Strikes at the Communist 'MicroFaction' in a Challenge to Moscow," *Radio Free Europe Research Paper*, 1968, p. 2.

67. Devlin, "The Soviet-Cuban Confrontation: Economic Reality and Political Judo," *Radio Free Europe Research Paper*, April 1, 1968, pp. 4–8.

68. Ibid., pp. 8–10.

69. *Granma*, Havana, January 31, 1968, as quoted in Berner, p. 5.

70. Devlin, "The Soviet-Cuban Confrontation: Economic Reality and Political Judo," pp. 15–16.

71. The author is highly indebted to his former graduate student, John P. Jurecky, for his past insights and exposition on this subject. For more analysis of economic ties of USSR and Latin America, see Oswald and Strover, eds., *The Soviet Union and Latin America*, pp. 185–88.

BIBLIOGRAPHY

I. PRIMARY SOURCES

Documents

Council of the Organization of American States. *Report on the First Afro-Asian-Latin American Peoples Solidarity Conference and its Projections.* 2 vols. Washington: Pan American Union, 1966.

Books

Debray, Regis. *Revolution within the Revolution?* Joint Publications Research Service (JPRS) 40, 310, March 20, 1967.

Debray, Regis. *Revolution in the Revolution?* New York: Grove Press, 1967.

Articles

Fortuny, J. M. "Has the Revolution become more difficult in Latin America," *World Marxist Review*, VIII (August, 1965), 38–45.

Gilly, Adolfo. "A Conference Without Glory and Without Program," *Monthly Review*, XVII (April, 1966), 21–34.

Listov, V. "Big Stick Diplomacy Against a Small Nation," *New Times*, XX (May 17, 1965), 8–11.

Ch'en Lo-min. "The Struggle of the Asian, African, and Latin American Peoples Solidarity Conference," *Shih-chieh Chih-shih*, Peking. Translated in JPRS 10,010.

López, Carlos. "The Communist Party of Venezuela and the Present Situation," *World Marxist Review*, VII (October, 1964), 18–25.

"Resolutions of the Seventh Plenum of the Central Committee of the PCV," *Confidencial*, Caracas, June 30, 1965. Translated in JPRS 10,564, 1965.

Rodríguez, Juan. "The New in the Political Line of the Communist Party of Venezuela," *World Marxist Review*, X (September, 1967), 78–82.

Rudenko, B. T. "The Ideas of the Seventh Comintern Congress and the Anti-imperialist Movements in Latin America," JPRS 36, 691, July 26, 1966, 82–92.

Togliatti, Palmiro. "On International Working Class Unity," *Political Affairs*, XVIII (October, 1964), 38–49.

Valencia, Carlos. "The Effectiveness of the Venezuelan CP is not Under Discussion," *Que*, Caracas, September 23, 1966. Translated in JPRS 5058, 1966.

Volsky, V. "New Stage of the People's Struggle," *Pravda*, March 10, 1968, p. 4. Translated in *Current Digest of the Soviet Press*, XX (April 10, 1968), 19–20.

Newspapers

New York Times. 1960–64.

II. Secondary Sources

Books and Monographs

Dinerstein, Herbert. *Soviet Policy in Latin America.* Rand Memorandum RM-4967-PR, May, 1966.

———. *Castro's Latin American Comintern.* Rand Paper P-3678, September, 1967.

Draper, Theodore. *Castroism, Theory and Practice.* New York: Praeger, 1965.

Goldenberg, Boris. *The Cuban Revolution and Latin America.* London: George Allen and Unwin, 1965.

Lockwood, Les. *Castro's Cuba, Cuba's Fidel.* New York: MacMillan, 1967.

Oswald, J. Gregory, Compiler-translator. *Soviet Image of Contemporary Latin America: A Documentary History, 1960–1968.* Published for the Conference on Latin American History by the University of Texas Press, Austin and London, 1971.

——— and Anthony J. Strover, eds. *The Soviet Union and Latin America.* Praeger, 1970.

Tretiak, Daniel. *Cuba and the Soviet Union: The Growing Accommodation.* Rand Memorandum RM-4935-PR, July, 1966.

Articles

Burks, David. "Cuba Seven Years After," *Current History*, L (January, 1966), 38–44.

Cattell, David. "Soviet Policies in Latin America," *Current History*, XLVII (November, 1964), 286–91.

Devlin, Kevin. "Castro Strikes at Communist 'Microfaction' in a Challenge to Moscow," *Radio Free Europe Research Paper*, 1968.

———. "The Soviet-Cuban Confrontation: Economic Reality and Political Judo," *Radio Free Europe Research Paper*, April 1, 1968.

Halperin, Ernst. "The Castro Regime in Cuba," *Current History*, LI (December, 1966), 354–59.

Jackson, Bruce. "Whose Men in Havana?" *Problems of Communism*, XV (May–June, 1966), 1–10.

Oswald, J. Gregory. "Contemporary Soviet Research on Latin America," *Latin American Research Review*, I (Spring, 1966), 77–96.

CHAPTER IV

THE LEFT WING AND THE COMMUNISTS IN MEXICO

Donald L. Herman

HERE IS A CURRENTLY POPULAR THEORY THAT THOSE COUNTRIES OF LATIN America which have strong and dynamic liberal movements, or native social revolutionary movements, under the guidance of democratic left wing political parties, can offer the strongest resistance to the influence of Communism. Since this theory, in part, seems to have influenced current United States policy toward Latin America, particularly in the early 1960s, it behooves the student of Latin-American politics to test the theory in specific cases to determine whether or not the basic premise is valid or whether events dictate that a modification is in order.

The administration of Lázaro Cárdenas of Mexico (1934–40) affords an excellent opportunity to put the theory to the test.[1] During that period, several basic industries were nationalized and more land was distributed to the peasants than during all the previous administrations combined. President Cárdenas placed a great deal of emphasis on the development of the collectivized ejido, in which the land was owned by the village and cultivated by the peasants in common. Labor was represented in the official government party, and the workers received considerable benefits compared to previous years. The government made great strides in alleviating the problem of illiteracy and generally in improving the condition of the mass of the people. The social promises of the Revolution of 1910 were pushed forward by the government and the official party.[2]

The Cárdenas administration accordingly appeared to represent a democratic left wing political party leading a social revolutionary movement. The lessons to be drawn from the development of the Mexican Communist movement during that period are particularly germane in the consideration of the theory.

THE POPULAR FRONT IN MEXICO

THE TACTICS OF THE POPULAR FRONT ERA, WHICH LASTED FROM THE SEVENTH Congress of the Comintern in Moscow in the summer of 1935 until the signing of the Nazi-Soviet Pact in August, 1939, were based on one main theme: Fascism was to be opposed at all costs and on all levels, whether this signified denouncing the Fascism practiced by Nazi Germany or supporting the forces opposed to Franco in the Spanish Civil War.

Five main tactics were decided upon during the Seventh Congress, most of which were attempted, with varying degrees of success, by the Mexican Communists. Firstly, the Communists were called upon to make an effort to form a United Front in their respective countries; they were expected to cooperate with "bourgeois" leaders and Socialists on all levels. Communists were even encouraged to participate in election campaigns. The call for a proletarian revolution, one of the slogans of the previous period of the Comintern, was dropped; nationalism was to be the new slogan of the Popular Front era. Secondly, the United Front was to merge into the People's Front (Popular Front). Thirdly, it was hoped that the Communists in the various countries would be able to realize a government of the United Front or People's Front. Fourthly, Communists were to strive to bring about trade union unity; Communist trade unions had to be abolished. Fifthly, Communists were to join with other elements to form a single party of the proletariat.

The Mexican Communist leaders went through two phases in trying to explain to their followers the best methods to be used toward realizing a Popular Front in Mexico. At first, they hoped to create a broad movement which would include the official government party as one of several groups. However, after the government party was reorganized and the Party of the Mexican Revolution (Partido de la Revolución Mexicana, or PRM) came into being in the spring of 1938, the Communists changed their tactics. They began to think in terms of infiltrating the new party, and, according to their interpretation of conditions in Mexico, to make the PRM into a Popular Front which would include Communist and non-Communist groups.

The new government party was organized into four sectors—peasants, labor, military, popular. The Communist party tried to enter the PRM, but it was rejected unanimously by the various organizations which comprised the four sectors. Nevertheless, the rejection of the Communist Party of Mexico did not prevent individual Communists from working within the PRM. Furthermore, as far as the Mexican Communists were concerned, the new official government party was synonymous with the Popular Front:

The Party of the Mexican Revolution has been set up as the special form of the People's Front in Mexico. . . . The Party of the Mexican Revolution represents a bloc of all the organizations of the people, with one million workers and employees, 1½ million peasants, and a great number of groups of women, youth, intellectuals, and the whole army. The Communists belong to the Party of (the Mexican) Revolution through the workers' and peasants' organizations in which they are working . . .[3]

Throughout the remainder of the Popular Front era, the Communists called upon their followers to support the official government party. They continued to stress the theme that the form of the Popular Front in Mexico was the PRM. It followed, then, that the PRM had to be strengthened to carry on the struggle against Fascism and to realize the goals of the Mexican Revolution.

By their own admission the Communists believed that a Popular Front, that is, the form in which they perceived it, did not exist in Mexico until the official party was transformed into the PRM. This was the Communist version of the "special form of the Popular Front in Mexico." Although the Communist party as such never joined one of the sectors of the official government party, individual Communists and Marxists who supported Soviet foreign policy were very active in the PRM. As we shall observe at a later point, the labor sector was dominated by the Confederation of Mexican Workers (Confederación de Trabajadores Mexicanos, or CTM) which, in turn, was heavily infiltrated with Communists and with those who closely adhered to the policies of the Comintern.

The question arises, were the Communists successful in realizing a Popular Front in Mexico? If one thinks of a Popular Front in terms of the movements which existed in France and Chile, several political parties and groups working in common to support particular candidates and to realize certain programs, then a Popular Front did not exist in Mexico. One Latin-American specialist believes there were several reasons why a "real" Popular Front did not become a reality—the rejection by the army of any coalition including the Communists; the presence of Leon Trotsky, which split the Leftists:

Most important of all the concept of a Popular Front simply did not fit the needs of Mexican political conditions. It had developed as a political device in countries where an institutionalized multiparty system already existed. Rather than a device of this sort, which would turn interest groups into competitive hard-core class parties, during this period Mexico required some sort of political mechanism that could channel the activities of the developing specialized interests into a constructive and integrated political system. As a consequence, President Cárdenas gave the projected Popular Front the "finishing stroke" when, in December, 1937, he called for dissolution of the PNR [Partido Nacional Revolucionario] and formation of a new revolutionary party.[4]

DONALD HERMAN

The writer agrees with this interpretation; a Popular Front, in the strict sense of the term, did not exist in Mexico. Nevertheless, the environment of the Popular Front era, a phenomenon which occurred in many countries throughout the middle 1930s, did exist. It was this environment, the importance of which transcends the question of whether or not a true Popular Front came into being, which concerns us at this point. Many anti-Fascist groups were prone to accept the cooperation of the Communists. This facilitated the efforts of the Communists to move into positions of strength in the labor movement, particularly in the CTM, and to participate in the labor organization which was the main factor in the labor section of the newly-formed PRM. Thus, the Communists received the benefits of a Popular Front, although a Popular Front movement did not exist in Mexico as originally envisaged by the leaders of the Comintern. The Communist party was legal, its members were influential in the organs of the official government party (and in the government itself); the Communists were identified with other popular forces opposed to Fascism. The Communists, on their part, gave almost unqualified support to the Cárdenas government.

THE COMMUNISTS AND THE CÁRDENAS ADMINISTRATION

THE MEXICAN COMMUNISTS SUPPORTED THE CÁRDENAS GOVERNMENT, FOR THE most part, during the life of the administration. However, as Hernán Laborde, secretary-general of the Communist Party of Mexico, stated in January of 1936, the Communists were being realistic in supporting such a government:

Comrades: It is said that this is an engagement or an alliance of the proletariat with a class foreign to it and it is true: It is an engagement, but it is one of those engagements which Lenin considered not only admissible, but necessary. . . . But, Comrades, this does not mean that we are Cardenistas: We are Communists . . . We support Cárdenas as conscientious allies, because we have certain common immediate objectives. . . .[5]

The Communists generally backed the Cárdenas administration's strongly anti-Fascist foreign policy. Cárdenas personally attended the CTM's "Congress Against Fascism and War," opposed the forces of Franco in Spain, and welcomed the Spanish refugees to Mexico. In the League of Nations, Mexico voted for the application of sanctions against Fascist Italy for its colonial exploits. Since all of these policies were in accord with the foreign policy of the Soviet Union during that period, the Mexican Communists did not find it difficult to applaud most of the proclamations and actions of the government.[6]

Generally, the domestic policies of President Cárdenas were also well received by the Communists. In particular, they praised the land distribution policy of the government:

Cárdenas follows a definite national revolutionary policy. He is engaging in agrarian reform and in anti-imperialist measures of the widest consequences. Cárdenas is granting land to peasants who were outside of the scope of the agrarian laws. He has established collectivization of land besides establishing collective ownership.[7]

When the government nationalized the railroads and the petroleum industry in the spring of 1938, however, the Communists reacted somewhat strangely at first. They called a strike in support of the expropriation of the petroleum industry, but, according to one close observer of the scene, this was at best a token strike. It is his impression that the Communists opposed the expropriation.[8] If this interpretation is correct, it would be very difficult, in the writer's opinion, to determine the reason of the Communists. One could argue that they were correct in an ideological sense. At least since the period of War Communism in the Soviet Union, the Communists have not urged direct workers' control of particular industries. That is Syndicalism or Guild Socialism, rather than Marxism-Leninism. Therefore, the Communist Party of Mexico's opposition to workers' control of petroleum and railroads was not inconsistent with its basic ideology. But perhaps they felt that the more the non-Communist government realized such programs, the less would be the attraction of Communism for the mass of the people. For they might well have asked themselves, what can we offer the masses in view of such accomplishments of the Cárdenas administration? In time, however, the Communists joined other non-Communist groups within the country in support of the nationalization policies of the government.

The Communists supported the Mexican government against internal revolts. When President Cárdenas dismissed General Saturnino Cedillo as Minister of Agriculture, the latter raised a private army in order to oppose the government. The revolt was easily crushed by loyal government forces. The Communists fully supported the government, identifying the rebels with a variety of "evil" forces.[9]

Besides supporting the Cárdenas government, the Communists also backed candidates of the PRM in the various elections. This policy began in the summer of 1937, before the government party was reorganized, when Laborde withdrew as the Communist candidate from the Federal District in an election for the Chamber of Deputies. He decided to support the candidates of the government. At the Seventh Congress of the Communist party, Laborde proclaimed his famous slogan: "United Behind a Single Candidate" (Unidos Tras un Solo Candidato). It signified that the Communists would support the candidate of the PRM as a successor to President Cárdenas.

DONALD HERMAN

THE GROWTH OF THE COMMUNIST MOVEMENT
DURING THE CÁRDENAS ADMINISTRATION

THERE ARE TWO METHODS OF MEASURING THE GROWTH OF A COMMUNIST MOVE-
ment under a non-Communist government. One is to analyze Communist
strength in specific organizations—the Communist party, labor and agrarian
organizations, institutions of the government, and so forth. The other method,
to be discussed later, involves a consideration of whether the non-Communist government's ideological position has contributed to or hindered the
growth of Communism.

During the administration of Lázaro Cárdenas, the Communists were very
strong in the CTM, which became the dominant labor organization in the
country. The CTM and the role of the Communists will be discussed in detail
when we analyze the labor movement at a later point. Since the main strength
of the Mexican President was with labor, the more influential the Communists
could become in the labor movement, particularly within the CTM, the
greater would be their influence during the Cárdenas administration.

Although the reliability of figures from Communist sources leaves a great
deal to be desired, the use of both Communist and non-Communist sources
provides us with a general view of Communist party growth during that
period. A general trend can be observed. In the summer of 1937, Laborde
spoke of the rapid growth in Communist party membership since the latter
part of 1935. Total membership was placed at 17,000 by the party newspaper.[10] By the summer of 1938, the Communist party was claiming a larger
number: "Before the VII Congress of the CI, the CPM numbered 2,000
members. By July, 1938, it had more than 27,000 members."[11] Less than one
year later, the Communists reported 33,000.[12] Although the above figures
may not be accurate, it seems safe to conclude that the Communist Party of
Mexico grew in numbers under the administration of Lázaro Cárdenas.

The Communists were able to move into positions of influence on both a
national and state level. The following quotation shows the broad area of
Communist political activity during the Cárdenas administration:

The growing influence of the Mexican Communist Party can best be illustrated by
part of the organizational report made before the Congress (i.e., Seventh Congress
of the party). According to this report the membership of the Party includes the
presidents of 73 municipalities, 23 syndicates, 178 aldermen, and 17 other city officials. In the National Chamber of Deputies, the Party has two members. Fourteen
deputies of various state legislatures are also included in the ranks of the Party.
The influence of the Party in important trade unions is strong and growing. The
present development leaves no doubt that the Mexican Communist Party has already become a vital factor in the life of the nation.[13]

Miguel Aroche Parra, who rose in the Communist hierarchy to become a member of the Central Committee of the Communist party, has written that the greatest number of militants in the history of the Communist Party of Mexico adhered to its banners during the period 1934–40. According to Aroche Parra, Communist elements participated in the following organizations: trade unions of Miners, Petroleum Workers, Electricians, Tramways, Railroads, Textiles; trade unions of Workers at the Service of the State, particularly the trade unions of Teachers, of Communications, of the Central Department, in the leadership of the majority of the Federations of Workers of the CTM in the states, in the Federations of Workers at the Service of the State, in the CTM. In addition, members of the Commuist party "participated in the leadership of the ejidos, cooperatives, societies of ejidal credit, Leagues of Agrarian Communities and Peasants Syndicates, in the most important student organizations, organizations of youth and women."[14]

Even though the Communists were espousing a popular cause by opposing Fascism and, as a result, cooperating with various non-Communist groups within the country, their efforts could have been hindered if the government in power had taken an anti-Communist attitude. On the other hand, Communist influence within the country at large would have been greater and the Communist dogma more attractive if the ideological propensity of the government had been in accord with Marxist doctrine.

THE IDEOLOGICAL ORIENTATION OF THE CÁRDENAS GOVERNMENT

THE REVOLUTION MADE MANY PROMISES IN THE CONSTITUTION OF 1917 AND the Six-Year Plan. President Cárdenas chose to emphasize those concerning agrarian reform, labor, economic nationalism, and education. We have already dealt with the Communist reactions to the agrarian reform (land distribution program) and economic nationalism (expropriation of the railroads and petroleum industries); a separate section will deal with the labor movement. This discussion will be concerned with the government's attitude toward education.

When Lázaro Cárdenas was nominated by a convention of the government party for the presidency, the party pledged itself to work for "the abolition of the lay school and the establishment of the socialist school as the basis of education." Two weeks after the new President assumed office, the Constitution was amended to provide: "The State shall impart socialist education and, in addition to excluding all religious instruction, shall combat fanaticism and prejudice, so that the school . . . may imbue the youth with a rational and exact conception of the universe and social life."[15] This amendment stayed in force during the six years Lázaro Cárdenas was President of Mexico.

Various political leaders had used the word "Socialism" throughout the Mexican Revolution. To some it signified an aggressive economic nationalism; others thought in terms of a vaguely conceived social justice; however, the group which identified "Socialism" with the Marxist idea of a classless society strongly influenced the Secretariat of Education during the Cárdenas administration.

Many Communists were officials within the Secretariat of Education. In 1939 José Mancisidor, a member of the Communist party, became Chief of the Department of Secondary Schools (Departmento de Secundarias). Marco Arturo Montero, the former Secretary General of the Anti-Imperialist League and member of the Communist party, became Chief of the Radio Section. Roberto Reyes Pérez, also a member of the Communist party, directed the "España-México" School.[16] In addition, there were many other lesser Communist officials who were employed by the Secretariat.

In 1938 the Secretary of Education, Gonzalo Vásquez Vela, declared that dialectical materialism was the philosophic groundwork of Mexican education.[17] This decision was soon reflected in the hundreds of thousands of low-cost pamphlet texts which were published through the Secretariat of Education and distributed throughout the country. The writings of Marx, Lenin, and Stalin reached the hands of the rural population. Virtually every phase of Mexican social life was written from a Marxist viewpoint.

Let us analyze a significant one of these publications in some detail: *Detalles de la Educación Socialista Implantables en México* (Feasible Details of Socialist Education in Mexico). Luis G. Monzón, at one time a Communist Senator, and a member of the Communist party, was a functionary of the Secretariat of Education when he wrote the book.

It states that Capitalism has produced the class struggle: the people, the exploited class, must fight to free themselves from the miserable existence in which Capitalism has placed them.[18] Furthermore, it is the duty of the Polytechnic Schools to join the proletariat in the struggle. The new imperialist war, dooming Capitalism, can have only one conclusion: a classless society.

We are facing the danger of a new world conflict (October of 1935). The great thieves, the lords of monopoly capitalism have realized that if the planned conflagration breaks out and they send the great masses of workers to the fields of battle, as it would have to happen, the latter would turn their arms against their tyrants, in order to convert the imperialist war into a world socialist revolution, which would end once and for all the corrupt regime of capitalist exploitation, that is, that it could end the shameful period of the Salary, in order to open the doors to the New Era, in which humanity may constitute a society without classes, composed only of the men who work and produce.[19]

Imperialistic Capitalist wars and Fascism are linked in Monzon's book with Mexico's enemy: the Anglo-Americans.[20]

The progress of the Soviet Union stands in contrast to the evils of Capitalism and Fascism, guiding Mexico with shining examples of Soviet education[21] and the way to a classless society: "In the world there should not exist exploiters and exploited, but only men of work, absolute owners of their own destinies, who labor for the benefit of the proletarian communities, such as is happening in the exemplary territories of the USSR."[22]

According to the interpretation of this publication, Socialism cannot be separated from Communism. When one speaks of Socialism, he is speaking of a single process, or system, which inexorably moves toward a culmination in Communism. Thus, pushed to its logical conclusion, "Socialist education" does not differ significantly from "Communist education":

It is said that Socialism is one system and Communism another, but that Socialism is a period of transition which the workers need to go through in order to enter, perfectly prepared, the field of Communism. We differ very slightly with such an opinion, since we believe that Socialism is a sole system although divided into two periods: Socialism and Communist Socialism . . .[23]

The process of "Socialist education" also involves the primary symbol of the hammer and sickle, the primary slogan calling for the workers to unite, and the hymn of combat—*The Internationale*. But the main battle cry is that which was proclaimed in the *Communist Manifesto*:

The proletariat cannot withdraw from the last imperialist conflict, which will mark the cessation of "the exploitation of man by man," by means of which their tyrants and hangmen will lose all, including their lives, and in which "the proletariat cannot lose more than their chains, having, on the other hand, a world to win."[24]

Reference is also made to the Comintern, considered to be the basis of the national and international United Front. It should include workers, peasants, school teachers, office workers, and so forth, grouped into the Workers' and Peasants' United Front of the Third International.[25]

And finally, the importance of the CTM, in relation to the Comintern, is brought into clear focus:

The CTM cannot be with the First International, less with the Second and much less with Fascism which longs to constitute the Fourth. Then ideologically, it is with the Third International, and it will be with it frankly and formally, when it consolidates its structure, incorporating also in its center the strong, the dense, the formidable mass of the national peasantry and joins its action with that of the rest of the organized sections of the same tendency and by organizing in all the regions of the planet.[26]

It is quite obvious that the Communists could only benefit by the ideological orientation of the Cárdenas administration in the field of education. It would be impossible to measure how many people in the rural areas were attracted to Communism because of the government's educational program. And how many intellectuals looked to Communism because they believed this was the "natural inclination" of the masses?

The last quotation is particularly germane to the next section to be considered. Communists and Marxists of all hues were very active in the labor movement, particularly the CTM, during the Cárdenas administration. The labor movement is most vital in the analysis of Communist influence during the Popular Front era.

THE LABOR MOVEMENT

ONE OF THE MOST IMPORTANT TACTICAL DECISIONS DURING THE SEVENTH CONgress of the Comintern was to change from having Communist trade unions oppose "reformist" labor organizations to trade union unity. In his speech to the Comintern Congress, Laborde called for trade union unity as the basis of the Popular Front in Mexico.[27]

The change in Communist tactics in Mexico was first noticed in the labor movement. In 1935 Communist and non-Communist labor officials formed a National Committee of Proletarian Defense (Comité Nacional de Defensa Proletaria). The Committee produced a "Pact of Solidarity" which was signed on June 15, 1935, by various Marxist and Communist labor officials including Fernando Amilpa of the Marxist-oriented CGOCM and Valentín Campa of the Communist-controlled CSUM. During the meeting, preparations were begun for the calling of a National Workers' and Peasants' Congress, which would establish one central labor organization.[28]

From the National Congress, held at the end of February, 1936, by the National Committee of Proletarian Defense, emerged the Mexican Confederation of Workers (CTM). Lombardo Toledano was elected Secretary General, and two Communists were on the Executive Committee.

It would not be beneficial, in the writer's opinion, to become involved in polemics for the purpose of determining whether or not Lombardo Toledano was a Communist. He denied the charge on several occasions; he never belonged to the Communist party. By his own admission, Lombardo Toledano believed in Marxism-Leninism as a solution for the social problems of Mexico.

But he added that one must think in terms of Mexican conditions and not be limited by the dogmatism of the Communist Party of Mexico. In addition, he believed that what the Soviet leaders did had been good for Russia. But their solutions to the problems in their country might not have been the solutions for Mexico—Mexico should seek its own way.[29] One could argue that Lombardo Toledano was a "national Communist," and perhaps this is true in a sense. However, for the purposes of this study any discussion of Lombardo Toledano will be based upon one factor—What, if any, was his influence in shaping the Communist movement in Mexico? In order to answer this question, his activities and speeches will be referred to intermittently. His orientation takes on more importance with his rise to power in the labor movement.

An analysis of the reasons behind the formation of the CTM can shed more light on the tactics of the Communists in the Mexican labor movement during the Cárdenas administration. Most writers agree that President Cárdenas encouraged the formation of the new labor organization in order to obtain unified labor support for his government during the power struggles with Calles. However, it must also be kept in mind that the CTM came into being approximately six months after the termination of the Seventh Congress of the Comintern and the proclamation of the "line" of the Popular Front.

One of the organizers of the CTM, Fidel Velázquez, told the writer that neither the Seventh Congress of the Comintern nor President Cárdenas influenced the formation of the labor organization. He stated that various labor leaders and groups representing Communists, Anarchists, Syndicalists, and so forth, merely came together to form a new trade union, each with its own ideas.[30]

Lombardo Toledano generally agreed with Fidel Velázquez that the Seventh Congress of the Comintern was not an influence. According to Lombardo he wished to help form the CTM to bring all the elements of the working class, regardless of their ideological beliefs, into one labor organization. He also stated that he wanted to give all types of workers a political party and a political education so that they could not only help themselves, but could become a vanguard to solve the problems of the rest of the country.[31]

These interpretations of two very influential labor leaders can be challenged on several grounds. The view of Fidel Velázquez, that neither President Cárdenas nor the Comintern was an influence in the formation of the CTM, requires little comment. Besides the strong need for labor support which the Mexican President sought during his term in office, no major labor organization has ever been formed in Mexico without government encouragement and support. Furthermore, the formation of the CTM followed too closely on the heels of the Seventh Congress of the Comintern and the "line" of the Popular Front. How can one doubt that the proclamation of the Popular Front was not an influence in the establishment of the CTM, particularly so when the Mexican Communists took an active part in its creation?

It was also during that period that Lombardo Toledano made a trip to the Soviet Union, ostensibly to study. Upon his return to Mexico, the Communists welcomed him with open arms thinking that he had been won over to the cause of Communism, but Lombardo Toledano stated emphatically that the Mexican Communists had been incorrect in this assumption.[32] Be that as it may, Lombardo Toledano wrote from Moscow in September, 1935, that he had been in contact with Losovsky.[33] He also wrote of his intention to speak to Stalin and the leaders of the Comintern. The letter concluded that he was so impressed with the Soviet Union that he would "redouble work in favor of the proletarian revolution."[34] Shortly after his return, he became very active in the formation of the CTM.

In addition, Lombardo Toledano's explanation that he wished to create a party for the workers is a little lame, since the PNR, the official government party, already existed, and when the CTM was formed, it affiliated with the PNR. It is more plausible that Lombardo Toledano wanted to bring the workers into an organization which he could mold according to his own ideological beliefs.

It is the writer's contention that the CTM was the product of the coincidence of political reality as interpreted by President Cárdenas and the "line" of the Popular Front as handed down by the Comintern. Communists, Marxists, and non-Communists came together for diverse reasons to create a new labor organization, which was to receive the encouragement and support of both the Mexican government and the Comintern leaders.

At the outset, the CTM was very close to the orientation of the Comintern.[35] It supported the policies of President Cárdenas and declared itself in favor of the Popular Front. In addition, the leaders of the new labor organization declared ". . . the Committee has tried to base its activities in all cases on the principle of recognizing the contradiction which exists between the interests of the proletarian class and those of the exploiting class, between which, therefore, there is no possible collaboration."[36]

There is strong evidence that Lombardo Toledano and the Communists worked closely within the CTM after the Communists reentered the organization.[37] *Acción Social* reproduced a photostat of a letter written by Lombardo Toledano on May 16, 1939, to the Federation of Workers of the State of Oaxaca asking their leaders to cooperate with and have confidence in a representative of the Communist party, Graciano G. Benítez, in his organizing efforts in Oaxaca. Lombardo Toledano signed the letter as Secretary General of the CTM.[38]

The CTM expanded during the Popular Front era. The Workers University (Universidad Obrera), established with financial support from the government, became the cultural center of the CTM, offering courses in Marxism and publishing a variety of material. The periodical, *El Popular*, was established as the official organ of the CTM, also with the governmental financial aid. Lombardo Toledano was the nominal director, but he was out of the country when it was founded by several anti-Communist leaders within the CTM—Rodolfo Piña Soria, Benjamín Tobón, Señor Manrique Páramo, and Rodrigo García Treviño. At first, *El Popular* reflected the political orientation of its founders and was anti-Communist, although somewhat modified by the influence of the Popular Front environment of the Mexican labor movement. A short time later, when the anti-Communist group and Lombardo Toledano were in opposing camps, *El Popular* came under the strict control of Lombardo Toledano and was usually in accord with the Comintern "lines."

When the CTM became part of the official party and one of the main pillars of President Cárdenas' strength, the Communists were very optimistic. They were now back in the good graces of the CTM and they were working closely with its secretary general, Lombardo Toledano. Furthermore, the Communists viewed the new official party, the PRM, as the form of the Popular Front peculiar to Mexico, and the CTM as the bedrock of the Popular Front policy.[39] In addition, as the CTM became more influential in government circles and the country at large, the Communists, already a powerful force within the CTM, increased their influence within the labor movement.

According to the tactics of the Popular Front, complete backing was given to the government against the threats of revolt. As a result, the CTM gave its full support to the government's crushing of the revolt led by General Saturnino Cedillo. An interesting article in *El Popular* explained the defeat of the fallen general in Marxist terms:

It may perhaps be said that the punishment meted out to Cedillo—exposure to the finger of ridicule—is even worse [than execution]. Cárdenas was able to use the weapons of dialectic because history is with him. Heroes triumph when they know how to interpret history, when they recognize the historic moment; but when they forget this, they fall with a resounding crash, never to rise again. In Mexico, we have just had an example of this fact.[40]

The leaders of the labor organization strongly supported a Popular Front for Mexico. They hoped that the peasant groups, other labor organizations, the CTM, the Communist party, and the official government party might be brought into one broad organization. A formal invitation was actually sent by the CTM to the Communist party to form a Popular Front[41] approximately one year before the PRM was created as the "Mexican form of the Popular Front."

Lombardo Toledano was a strong advocate of the Popular Front, as indicated by his report to the Fourth National Council of the CTM in 1939. His views were similar to those of Hernán Laborde, expressed to the Seventh Congress of the Comintern:

What is the program of International Communism at present? The program of the Popular Front is the program of the petitions of those who agree with all the sectors not proletarian, like the middle class and the sector of the petty bourgeoisie. The Popular Front is not, therefore, a tactic of retrogression nor counter-revolution, because the working class, at the moment, and inclusive of breaking with its circumstantial allies, can go to the true revolution and transform the bourgeois regime.[42]

As mentioned previously, the CTM, as labor groups almost everywhere, supported the forces opposed to General Franco in the Spanish Civil War. It was not just propaganda: When the Cárdenas government took a strong stand in favor of Republican Spain, the CTM held pro-Loyalist demonstrations all over the country. The workers within the labor organization also pledged to work without pay to send munitions to the Loyalists.

The CTM strongly supported President Cárdenas' welcome of Spanish refugees into Mexico, many of whom joined the trade unions of the CTM and found positions with Lombardo Toledano's Workers University. Aiding the Spanish refugees was a popular cause, and the Communists within the CTM were able to bask in the light of this favorable propaganda.

CONCLUSIONS

THE COMMUNIST MOVEMENT OF MEXICO REACHED ITS PEAK IN STRENGTH DURING the administration of Lázaro Cárdenas and began to wane with the signing of the Nazi-Soviet Pact in August of 1939. The process was accelerated when Leon Trotsky was assassinated one year later. The Communists were able to recoup some of their losses with the initiation of the "people's war," when the Soviet Union entered World War II in June of 1941, but, through the end of 1945, they never regained the strength they enjoyed earlier.

When Lázaro Cárdenas was President of Mexico, the Communist party had more members than at any other time before or during World War II. Communists were very strong in the CTM, itself a powerful force in the official government party. Communist officials were found on all levels of government, in labor and agricultural organizations, in student organizations, and so forth. Furthermore, as we have seen, the Communists were very influential in the Secretariat of Education; their doctrine was preached throughout the country under the guise of "Socialist Education." Added to these factors was the influence of Communism with a substantial number of articulate middle class intellectuals, who, in reality, comprise the public opinion of Mexico.

It would be difficult to ascertain how the Communist movement would have developed during the administration of President Cárdenas without the Popular Front environment. One might argue that, due to the Popular Front era, the Communists would have gained strength regardless of who was President of Mexico. On the other hand, did the Popular Front environment require placing several important Communists in the Secretariat of Education? Might it not be assumed that the Communists eventually would have supported the policies of the President, i.e., the land distribution policy, nationalization of some basic industries, and thereby strengthen their own position, regardless of the Popular Front era? In the writer's view, the Communists identified themselves with the policies of the government and benefited as a result. In addition, the ideological orientation of the government, as exemplified through the Secretariat of Education, proved to be advantageous to the Communist movement. The Communist movement of Mexico would have been strengthened during the Cárdenas administration, although possibly to a lesser degree, in the absence of the Popular Front environment.

In the light of the current interpretation of the theory under consideration, the Communist tide should have been stemmed during that period. And yet the growth of Communism, through the end of World War II, was at its peak during the Cárdenas administration. As previously pointed out, the Popular Front environment was an influence in the spreading of Communism. However, there were other influences which were more dominant, such as the ideological orientation of the government. Thus, the growth of Communism during the Cárdenas administration indicates that the theory is in need of qualification. For if the ideological orientation of the government, while not Communist in the strict sense of the word, nevertheless makes possible an environment which favors the growth of Communism, then such a left of center democratic government does not offer the best resistance to Communism. Furthermore, the non-Communist revolutionary movement may be led by a democratic left wing party, but the party may be weakened by Communist elements within the official circles which affect the party's ability to struggle against the spread of Communism. In the case of Mexico, we saw that the Communists were very strong in the CTM, and the labor organization was one of the vital parts of the official government party.

DONALD HERMAN

The theory is also in need of qualification in another sense. One must analyze the government's attitude toward the Communist movement within the country in order to determine if such a government offers effective resistance to the growth of Communism. If the left of center democratic government is sympathetic to Communism, as exemplified by the Cárdenas administration, the growth of Communism will not be effectively resisted by such a government. On the contrary, the Communist movement will probably increase in strength. However, if the left of center democratic government wants to be the best answer to Communism, if it actually fights the Communist movement within the country, then such a government can offer the best means of resisting Communism. Examples of the latter were the recent governments of Rómulo Betancourt and Raúl Leoni of Venezuela. The government of Lázaro Cárdenas was sympathetic to Communism, and, as a result, it was easier for the Communist movement to increase in strength during President Cárdenas' term of office. The governments of Rómulo Betancourt and Raúl Leoni were anti-Communist; they actively struggled against the Communists of Venezuela, and, as a result, Communism had been effectively resisted within the country. Thus, the attitude of the left of center democratic government toward Communism is an extremely important consideration in the application of the theory.

The conclusions drawn in the case of Mexico, under a particular government, may not be applicable to other countries of Latin America. Admittedly one cannot generalize about the relationship between the Communists and the left wing of Latin America based on the findings in one case study. Further testing in specific cases will be needed.

Nevertheless, the findings under the Cárdenas government of Mexico indicate that the theory must be utilized with a note of caution. One cannot make a blanket statement that native social revolutionary movements, under democratic left wing political parties, are the answer to Communism in Latin America. They may be the answer in certain countries, given particular conditions, but this interpretation does not necessarily apply to all countries under any conditions. Mexico, under the Cárdenas administration, again teaches us the lesson that no theory pertaining to Latin America is sacrosanct and beyond re-examination.

NOTES

1. For an analysis of the early Communist movement in Mexico see Donald L. Herman, *The Comintern in Mexico* (Washington, D.C.: Public Affairs Press, 1972).
2. The Mexican Revolution, as distinguished from numerous upheavals in Latin America, was a true social revolution. It began as a simple movement for political

reform. But it developed into a movement for land reform, economic development, the integration of the Indian into national life, and the weakening or elimination of class barriers.

3. *World News and Views*, Vol. 18, No. 42, September 3, 1938, p. 979.

4. Robert E. Scott, *Mexican Government in Transition* (Urbana: University of Illinois, 1959), p. 130. The PNR or National Revolutionary Party (Partido Nacional Revolucionario) was the original name of the official government party which was formed by President Calles in 1928.

5. Cited by Ricardo Treviño, *El Espionaje Comunista y La Evolución Doctrinaria del Movimiento Obrero en México* (México, 1952), p. 182.

6. *World News and Views*, Vol. 18, No. 41, August 27, 1938, p. 963.

7. *World News and Views*, Vol. 17, No. 51, November 27, 1937, pp. 1257–58.

8. Interview with Rodrigo García Treviño. García Treviño also told the writer that the CTM, under the leadership of Vicente Lombardo Toledano, wanted to stop the strike of the petroleum workers, which was proving effective. However, the workers refused to stop the strike and it continued. The same point was made by Rodolfo Piña Soria in his article "Viaje Por Suscripción Popular," *Acción Social*, Marzo 15 de 1943. On the other hand, Fidel Velázquez, the present secretary general of the CTM, stated that the organization supported the strike of the petroleum workers and the expropriation from the beginning. Interview with Fidel Velázquez.

9. *World News and Views*, Vol. 18, No. 36, July 23, 1938, p. 860.

10. *El Machete*, Junio 26 de 1937, suplemento.

11. *World News and Views*, Vol. 18, No. 42, September 3, 1938, p. 979.

12. *World News and Views*, Vol. 19, No. 10, March 11, 1939, p. 204.

13. *World News and Views*, Vol. 19, No. 10, March 11, 1939, p. 205.

14. Miguel Aroche Parra, *Unidad Anti-Imperialista! Unidad Proletaria!* (México, D. F., 1962), pp. 28–29.

15. Nathaniel and Sylvia Weyl, *The Reconquest of Mexico: The Years of Lázaro Cárdenas* (London: Oxford University Press, 1939), p. 315.

16. Bernardo Claraval, *Cuando Fuí Comunista* (México, D. F., Ediciones Polis, 1944), pp. 175–77.

17. Weyl, p. 316.

18. Luis G. Monzón, *Detalles de la Educación Socialista Implantables en México* (México, D. F., Secretaría de Educación Pública [SEP], Comisión Editora Popular, Talleres Gráficos de la Nación, 1936), p. 19. The stamp of SEP which appears in the publication signifies the Secretariat of Education. The "Comisión Editora Popular" is a branch of the Secretariat in charge of books. The "Talleres Gráficos de la Nación" is the government printing office.

19. Monzón, p. 381.

20. Monzón, p. 458.

21. Monzón, p. 52.

22. Monzón, p. 170.

23. Monzón, p. 428.

24. Monzón, p. 382.

25. Monzón, pp. 244–46.

26. Monzón, p. 459.

27. *The Communist*, Vol. XV, No. 1, January, 1936, p. 80.

28. *El Trabajador Latino Americano*, Nos. 60–61, Octubre-Noviembre, 1935, p. 18.

29. Interview with Vicente Lombardo Toledano. He died in December, 1968.

30. Interview with Fidel Velázquez.

31. Interview with Lombardo Toledano.

32. Ibid.

33. The Red International of Trade Unions was dissolved in 1934. Losovsky, however, remained very influential in high Comintern circles.

34. The letter was reprinted by *Acción Social*, Número 14, Marzo 15 de 1941, p. 16.

35. The organization supported the position of the Comintern, but this does not necessarily mean that it was an instrument of the international Communist organization. Although infiltrated with Communists, the CTM was not officially connected with the Comintern.

36. *C.T.M. 1936–1941*, (1936) (México, D. F. Talleres Tipográficos Modelo, S.A.), p. 37.

37. In April of 1937, a split occurred within the ranks of the CTM. The Communists and the trade unions under their influence walked out of the organization. The breach was healed with the assistance of Earl Browder, secretary general of the Communist Party of the United States and a Comintern official.

38. *Acción Social*, Número 14, Marzo 15 de 1941, p. 14.

39. *The Communist*, Vol. XVII, No. 11, November, 1938, p. 1013.

40. *El Popular*, Junio 10 de 1938, p. 2.

41. *El Machete*, Enero 23 de 1937, p. 1.

42. Alfonso López Aparicio, *El Movimiento Obrero en México* (México: Editorial Jus, 1952), p. 223.

CHAPTER V

THE BRAZILIAN LEFT: EFFORTS
AT RECOVERY, 1964–70

John W. F. Dulles

JUST BEFORE THE BRAZILIAN MILITARY ACTION OF MARCH 31, 1964, OVER-
threw the regime of President João ("Jango") Goulart, concern was
expressed in anti–far left military and civilian circles about "the Communist threat" in Brazil. Men close to Goulart (wealthy friend of organized
labor) had been encouraging forces sympathetic to Communism in order to
find backing for "basic reforms." It appeared to many (including the head
of the Brazilian Communist Party) that these forces would soon be in complete control of the country.

The forces which were felt to make up this "threat" did not put up any
resistance during the brief and bloodless military movement, a fact which
subsequently bothered Communists engaged in writing self-criticisms. All
looked to the Army to decide the issue, and when it did decide the issue,
with encouragement from many alarmed citizens, the odds against would-be
defenders of Goulart were too great. It was not even clear at the moment
that Goulart's overthrow would bring an end to the kind of electoral democracy in which the supporters of Soviet Communism, Fidel Castro, Mao Tse-
tung, Trotskyism, and various brands of national Marxism had been able to
live.

Those who were worried about a "Communist threat" would have had
much more to worry about had Communists and their allies penetrated the
ranks of Army officers as effectively as they had penetrated the top echelons
of labor and student organizations.

As it turned out, most of the Army officers were not disposed to support a
President who encouraged military indiscipline by favoring mutinying sailors
—and who chose his Navy Minister in accordance with the wishes of Communist labor leaders. And so Goulart, despite glowing reports rendered by his
chief military aide, could not rely on any huge military apparatus (*dispositivo*). In the state of Minas Gerais at the end of March, 1964, a few anti-

Goulart Army leaders, speaking against Communism, took the initiative and marched with a small force against the President. Most of their fellow-officers preferred to join them rather than shoot them on behalf of a President who appeared to think more of Communist labor leaders than he did of military discipline.

PART 1. FORCES MAKING UP "THE COMMUNIST THREAT" BEFORE THE 1964 MILITARY ACTION

THE FAR LEFT FORCES WHICH WERE ADVERSELY AFFECTED BY GOULART'S OVER-throw had not been well united; but they had, early in 1964, found a good deal to agree about as far as a program was concerned. Important points of the program had long been advocated by the Brazilian Communist Party. These included the expropriations of large estates so that those who worked the land could own parcels of it. The program also called for the nationalization of all important foreign enterprises, and state ownership of utilities. Petrobrás, the "glorious" state petroleum extraction monopoly (whose management was riddled with corruption and partial to Moscow-line Communists), should become the owner of those oil refineries which remained in private hands. The program defined the United States as imperialistic, and the Brazilian Constitution as obsolete and feudal. The Brazilian Congress, branded as reactionary, was to be replaced by "authentic" representatives of laborers, peasants, soldiers, and sailors. The program called for legalization of the Brazilian Communist Party, enfranchisement of Brazil's illiterates (who made up about 47 per cent of the population), and national plebiscites to resolve important issues.

Symbolic of other basic changes, "agrarian reform" became the loudest of the battle cries. Marxist historian Leôncio Basbaum describes a Congresso Camponês (Peasant Congress) at which the slogan was: we want land either by law or else by violence. Peasants, some without shoes, came from great distances. They listened to the outstanding national leaders who were associated with "land reform." The trouble, Basbaum asserts, was that every one of these leaders wanted to be the one and only leader.[1]

The far leftists saw themselves as the advocates of reform. As Congress was cool to their favorite schemes, they espoused a "crisis climate" (induced by constant strikes and stirring rallies) as a means of exerting pressure.

They disagreed as to whether violence would have to be used to achieve their program. Among those who favored peaceful evolution were the Brazilian Communist Party (PCB—Partido Comunista Brasileiro) and Miguel Arrais, governor of the restless northeastern state of Pernambuco.

BRAZILIAN COMMUNIST PARTY. The Moscow-affiliated PCB continued to be headed by Luís Carlos Prestes, who had become known as the "Cavalier of Hope" after leading a band of revolutionary fighters in the mid-1920s, and who had headed the bloody and unsuccessful Communist rebellion of 1935. Past 65, he was no longer the frail little "martyr" who endured nine years of jail (1936–45); nor was he any longer the fugitive who spent ten years (1948–58) hiding from the law. He spoke frequently on national issues, and continued to radiate an air of earnestness.

Prestes, while preserving his undemocratic leadership of the Party and while adhering to the Moscow line, had witnessed serious Party dissensions in the 1950s and early 1960s.[2] Particularly after Khrushchev had criticized "the cult of the personality," Prestes' role and leadership qualities had come under attack by former associates.

But his prestige was high again during the Goulart regime. From time to time the President conferred with him. The Party's support of candidates and political rallies continued to be important. The PCB's ULTAB (União dos Lavradores e Trabalhadores Agrícolas do Brasil) assisted the Goulart administration to form unions of agricultural workers and these unions helped create a confederation of agricultural workers whose directorship was dominated by Communists. Above all, the PCB was strong in urban labor organization.

The Party had been declared illegal in 1947, after two years of legal life. But ever since 1958, when the courts had dismissed charges against Prestes and other Communists, the Party and its members operated fully in the open. Party membership in 1963 was estimated to be around 30,000. Many of these worked in industrial São Paulo and the nearby port city of Santos.

The Party found itself unable only to run political candidates on its own ticket. This limitation it sought to overcome by revising its statutes to conform with Brazilian customs. In Brasília in July, 1962, Prestes presented, on behalf of the Party's legality, a petition signed by 53,367 voters. While awaiting a decision of the Superior Electoral Tribunal, Prestes announced that in the congressional elections of October, 1962, seventeen PCB members had been elected to the federal Congress on other party tickets.[3]

President Goulart appeared to be more than sympathetic to the PCB, which had such a strong foothold in labor organizations. The PCB had helped make his political rallies successful, and had filled these rallies with placards calling for a legal status for the Party. In March, 1964, Goulart asked Congress to facilitate the legalization of the Party.[4]

Prestes was ever ready to attack Goulart when he seemed to back anyone who might listen to the International Monetary Fund or stray from the program of the PCB. But, speaking on the radio in January, 1964, before going abroad to be received by Khrushchev, Prestes declared that he did not believe that a violent revolution would be necessary for the implantation in Brazil of the type of regime he favored. Socialism, he said, was victorious and was being achieved peacefully.[5]

Since its inception in 1922, the PCB had held only five national Party Congresses (including the first—organizing—Congress of 1922). The Congresses, theoretically making the top policy decisions, ordinarily adopt a program and new statutes, and choose the members of the Central Committee.[6]

Late in March, 1964, the Party's weekly newspaper *Novos Rumos* published the "theses" which were to be discussed and presumably approved with few or no modifications at a Sixth Party Congress scheduled for later in 1964. The proposed theses considered the invasion of landholdings by armed bands legitimate and healthy, for the PCB then believed that no rural property should exceed 500 hectares (1236 acres).[7] The theses emphasized the need of a "Nationalist and Democratic United Front," which in politics would be made up of the Communist and Socialist parties, a majority of the Labor party, and "nationalist" (minority) elements of other political parties. The United Front was to battle against "concessions" made by "the present Government to imperialism and to reactionary forces." It would welcome non-commissioned men of the Armed Porces as well as the small bourgeois leftist movements "which have developed in recent years." However, the theses warned against "ultra-leftist platforms," frequently presented by radical small bourgeois groups "in the name of Marxism."[8]

MIGUEL ARRAIS. Recife, the capital of troubled Pernambuco, was sometimes described as the "reddest" of Brazilian cities even though PCB membership in Pernambuco was less than that in Guanabara and far less than that in São Paulo. In Recife Prestes was well received by the masses when he went to campaign on behalf of politicians who were favored by the PCB because of monetary or other considerations.

One of these politicians was Miguel Arrais, elected mayor of Recife in 1959 and governor of Pernambuco in 1962. His dedication and apparent sincerity made up for his lack of oratorical skill. Although he was not a member of the PCB, he worked closely with it and was one of those persons who was often called a Communist by people who worried about "the Communist threat." These people would explain that Arrais "surrounded himself with Communists, and spoke and acted like a Communist."

Arrais condemned the Alliance for Progress, the United States wheat shipments to Brazil, and the short-lived effort of Finance Minister San Tiago Dantas to reduce inflation by means of financial austerity. President Vargas's suicide (1954) and President Quadros's resignation (1961) he blamed on "financing by imperialists." "Large landownings," he said, "are allied with North American imperialism and must be liquidated." He got the federal government to decree a relatively high minimum wage for Pernambuco, and he tried to make employers observe it. Downtrodden peasants found in him a friend.

Hopeful of achieving the presidency in 1965, Arrais preached the same peaceful line which was being recommended by Prestes and the Soviet Union. He spent much time addressing audiences outside of his state. His chief rival among the prominent far leftists was Congressman Leonel Brizola, an advocate of violence. Arrais often felt that Brizola's brother-in-law, President Goulart, was scheming to depose him from the Pernambuco governorship.

LEONEL BRIZOLA. Oratorical ability and drive made Brizola the outstanding leader of the radical left. But he was constitutionally ineligible to run for the presidency in 1965 because his wife was a sister of Goulart.

As governor of the southernmost state of Rio Grande do Sul, he achieved fame by expropriating (with practically no payment) a United States–owned telephone company, by praising Cuba and attacking the United States, and by urging that landed estates be broken up for the benefit of peasants. His views, violently presented, were popular in centers of organized labor; and he went on, in 1962, to be elected federal congressman from the geographically small state of Guanabara, which includes the city of Rio de Janeiro. He received by far the largest vote ever recorded in such an election. With this handsome showing, and his frequent and lengthy Castro-like radio diatribes, he was able to make life difficult for Goulart, especially when the President tried to be conciliatory with the anti–far left forces. Brizola repeatedly insisted that Congress was reactionary, and urged peasants to use arms to seize lands for themselves. He encouraged sergeants to fight for rights which the Constitution denied them.

While he unsuccessfully sought to gain from Goulart national control of the Brazilian Labor Party, he engaged in forming and directing leftist *frentes* (fronts). Among these were the Frente de Libertação Nacional (1961–62) and the Frente de Mobilização Popular (1962–64).

At the end of November, 1963, Brizola, with the help of Rádio Mayrink Veiga and a nationwide network of forty stations, issued a call to the people to organize themselves into "Groups of Eleven Companions" (Grupos de Onze Companheiros). In his widely-circulated 11-page brochure, "nationalist leader" Brizola explained that an upheaval was in the offing and that the people must organize to avoid being oppressed. The Groups of Eleven were to help bring about agrarian reform and "free Brazil of international spoliation."[9]

Within a few months Rio's Rádio Mayrink Veiga received several thousand forms, filled in by Groups of Eleven, many of them made up of misfits who were in no condition to do anything.[10] They were asked to listen regularly to Brizola's broadcasts. The movement, described by Brizola as attracting 200,-000 members, put fear into Brizola's rightist opponents and leftist rivals.

Shortly before the 1964 military uprising, "secret instructions" to the Groups of Eleven were issued in the name of Brizola, the "Supreme Commander of National Liberation." The Groups of Eleven were told to saturate themselves with mystical feeling, and to arm themselves. A general strike was to be the signal for them to start their work. Special groups, "humble, strong, and full of hatred of the powerful" were assigned special tasks. They were to back those authorities who cooperated with the "liberating movement" and they were to seize all other influential people.

These instructions told Brizola's followers that surprise was the principal factor for initial success. And they reminded the Groups of Eleven that "today we have everything in our favor, including the goodwill of the Government and the complacency of powerful civilian and military sectors, frightened and fearful of losing their present and ignominious privileges."

The "secret instructions" spoke poorly of Prestes, blaming him for turning the PCB into quarrelling factions. The China-line PC do B (Partido Comunista do Brazil) was praised and called "our chief ally." Daily, Brizola's followers were told, "it grows with the help of the ideas of Mao Tse-tung and Stalin, which are, in the last analysis, those of Marx and Engels. In this wing, today much more powerful than that of Moscow, we shall seek the source of material and military potential for the struggle of national liberation. Happily it is completely cohesive, at our side, for its militants have the same fierce determination that we have."[11]

PARTIDO COMUNISTA DO BRAZIL (PC DO B). The PC do B, of which Brizola spoke so glowingly, had only about one thousand members. Its formation in February, 1962, following plans made late in 1961, coincided with quarrels between leaders of the Soviet Union and Red China. Had it not been for the Sino-Soviet split it is unlikely that a few PCB dissidents could have formed when they did a second Brazilian Communist party which has lasted until today. But the PC do B's founders had been unhappy about the PCB well before the Sino-Soviet split occurred.

The dissidents—João Amazonas, Maurício Grabois, and Pedro Pomar—had been among the top figures in the PCB from 1945 to 1957. They had benefitted from the PCB's structure: one in which a few men, dominating the Secretariat and Presidium (later called the National Executive Commission) ran the Party. Occupying important PCB posts along with Carlos Marighela, they had carried out directives favored by Moscow and issued by Prestes and Diógenes de Arruda Câmara. While doing this in 1957 they had helped shove aside those who had wanted to turn Khrushchev's de-Stalinization speech into a call for democracy in the Party. However, following the loss in membership caused by this episode, Prestes in 1957 demoted Arruda Câmara and most of Arruda's chief associates, and in their place he set up the so-called Group from Bahia: Carlos Marighela, Jacob Gorender, Mário Alves de Souza Vieira and Giocondo Alves Dias. At the Fifth Party Congress of the PCB, held in 1960, Prestes and the Bahia Group completed their work against the fallen leaders: twelve of the twenty-five voting members of the Party's Central Committee were replaced.[12] In the next year, as part of the campaign to obtain legal recognition, the Central Committee changed the Party name from Partido Comunista do Brasil (the form called for by the Communist International in Moscow in 1920) to Partido Comunista Brasileiro. It issued new statutes which omitted references to Marxism.

João Amazonas, Maurício Grabois, Pedro Pomar, Lincoln Cordeiro Oest, and other ex-leaders of the PCB had been criticizing their successors for "revisionism" and for favoring bourgeois concepts. In 1961 these ex-leaders pointed out that only a National Congress, not the Central Committee, was empowered to change the Party's name and statutes. They took the former party name and claimed to be carrying on with the authentic party. They also were able to take the venerable PCB monthy newspaper, A Classe Operária, because it had been registered in the name of Grabois. With the help of some funds from Communist China they made it a fortnightly. They started sending groups of ten to train, generally for six months, in China. The trainees spent their time in barracks learning about making bombs and guerrilla warfare, and sometimes returned with small parcels of money for the PC do B.

Chinese Communist agents who visited Brazil spoke highly of Amazonas, Lincoln Cordeiro Oest, and Grabois and suggested that they be trained in China to be "special agitators." A couple of Brazilian sergeants, one the leader of an unsuccessful sergeants' rebellion in Brasília in 1963, were also highly regarded by the Chinese Communists.

The diary of a Chinese Communist agent, captured in Brazil in April, 1964, tells of his meetings with leaders of peasant leagues (ligas camponesas), and of invitations which he received to lunch with Goulart and the Presidential Press Secretary, former Communist Raul Riff.

FRANCISCO JULIÃO. The diary also makes references to Francisco Julião, who had made a name for himself in the Northeast as an organizer of numerous peasant leagues: "Those responsible for the peasant movement in Pernambuco are politically backward. Francisco Julião is afraid of his staff. The work of Julião is very important, but he pays no attention to organization. He likes fame and bragging. . . . Julião speaks and shrieks, but . . . Julião does not want an armed movement; that is my impression. But I do not think we should criticize Julião openly. His influence is relatively large. . . ."[13]

Julião, lean and bright-eyed, was a spirited orator. Belonging to a family of large landowners, he had become a lawyer-politician whose legal practice included the defense of peasants against large landowners. Beginning in 1955 he urged the formation of peasant leagues.[14] Effective, bitter speeches had already gained him a seat in the Pernambuco state legislature when he was discovered in 1960 by socialist writers and much of the United States press, and was pictured as the great and mystical leader of Brazilian peasantry.

Seeking financial assistance for the peasant leagues, he visited Red China in 1960 and made a number of trips in 1960 and 1961 to Cuba (where he put his four children in school). He was full of praise for Mao Tse-tung and Fidel Castro. He repeatedly declared himself a Marxist and once stated that if the Brazilian people could express their views, they would invite Castro to run the affairs of Brazil.

Julião's election, in October, 1962, to be federal congressman from Pernambuco coincided with the gubernatorial election of Miguel Arrais, who over-shadowed him as the radical left's leader in the Northeast. It also coincided with a great surge of activity on the part of Julião's rivals, who put on better organized campaigns to create leagues, "circles," and other bodies of suddenly discovered peasants. One of these rivals, the PCB, gained control of the Federation of Peasant Leagues in Paraíba, a state adjoining Pernambuco.[15] In other northeastern states (such as Rio Grande do Norte, Alagoas, and Sergipe) the rising tide of "progressivism" in the Catholic Church, inspired by the Pope John XXIII's *Mater et Magistra,* resulted in the organization of many peasant unions by Catholic "progressives."[16] At the same time Catholic conservatives organized peasant "circles."

Julião's influence fell further in 1963, when the federal government, the PCB and Ação Popular (radical leftist offspring of Catholic University Youth), all assisted by federal funds, bounced around Brazil in jeeps, madly organizing official *sindicatos* (unions) of agricultural workers.

By that time Julião's Tiradentes Radical Movement, financed by Fidel Castro, had turned out to be a great fiasco, and some Brazilians who had worked with it were among those who were wondering whether a violent peasant upheaval was what Congressman Julião really wanted. They might well also have wondered whether the Brazilian peasants had much interest in participating in a violent upheaval.

THE CASTRO-SPONSORED GUERRILLA TRAINING CAMPS. As a result of conversations in Cuba in 1960 and 1961, Julião and Clodomir dos Santos Morais (another Pernambuco politician) headed a Castro-supported program for preparing Brazilian peasants to make a violent revolution as members of the Tiradentes Radical Movement. One of the first steps was the training of twelve Brazilians in Cuba during August, 1961.

Young Tarzan de Castro, an aide in the Goiás state government, was for a while in charge of making fighters out of peasants in that state in the Brazilian interior. There and in other parts of Brazil much Cuban money was spent foolishly in 1961 and 1962. The sad state of affairs was revealed in the report of a Fidelist agent, whose baggage was found after the crash (near Lima, Peru, on November 27, 1962) of the plane in which he had left Brazil.

"The recruitment of the forces has been carried on by telling the future *guerrilheiros* that when they arrived at the encampment they would find a Cuban instructor who would give military classes and they would have a political instructor for the political development of the combatants; that there existed a national military directorship oriented by a Cuban, and a national political directorship; that as for money there need be no worry, for Cuba would give enough to make the revolution in Brazil."

According to this report, and other evidence, money was generously supplied for a while. The report states that, for training purposes, *fazendas* (ranches) were purchased, sometimes for three times their value. Local peasants were contracted "and sometimes they were paid wages five times as high as those prevailing in the region." At correspondingly high prices old rifles were purchased from local political chiefs or large landowners. All the neighbors became aware of, and generally hostile to, these encampments. They reported what they knew to the police. Actually little training or work was done by the peasants, some of whom felt lost and bewildered, and a few of whom were pleased to find themselves in training centers which resembled centers of gambling and revelry.

The signer of the report concluded that the work should be overhauled. He asserted that, at the time he wrote, no more than fifty peasants could be found at all such centers, located in the states of Goiás, Maranhão, Mato Grosso, Rio de Janeiro, and Bahia. Ten men were reported to be at three properties near Dianópolis, Goiás, "all willing to support an insurrection, but not knowing what they should do, although they have been there almost a year."[17]

The training centers and the areas surrounding them were well covered with Communist propaganda, such as that prepared in Prague under the direction of long-time PCB member Pedro Mota Lima and printed in

Havana. In spite of complaints by some anti-Communists, the Brazilian authorities showed little concern about machine guns at the installations near Dianópolis, relatively close to Brasília. Eventually, in 1963, a private plane flew the guns to Julião's peasant league headquarters in Recife.[18]

TROTSKYITES (PORT). In addition to the Soviet, Chinese, and Cuban Communist influences, there was in Brazil a band of Trotskyites, whose membership did not exceed one hundred. Since its inception, in the late 1920s the Brazilian Trotskyite movement, always small and often containing some well-known intellectuals, had from time to time found adepts who came from the PCB.

Persuasive speaker José Maria Crispim associated himself with this movement for a while, after being expelled from the PCB in 1952 for a show of independence. But others dedicated more time and energy in Brazil to Trotskyism. In the early 1960s they established PORT—Partido Operário Revolucionário Trotsquista, "Secção Brasileira da IV Internacional"—and maintained close ties with the Latin-American Trotskyite headquarters in Montevideo. Among PORT's Brazilian leaders were some São Paulo residents, such as Professor Tomás Maack, Tulo Vigevânia, and Sidnei Fix Marques dos Santos. Tulo Vigevânia maintained contacts in peasant circles in the Northeast, where PORT had a following. Sidnei Fix directed the Brazilian Trotskyite publication, *Frente Operária*. Three thousand copies of *Frente Operária*'s May, 1963, issue were printed, and they were distributed without charge in barracks and factories, often by students who were influenced by a number of Trotskyite professors.

PORT's program was simple. It called on the sergeants and soldiers to revolt against their superiors, and to give military assistance to the industrial workers and peasants; the industrial workers were to form committees which were to run the plants; peasants were to form armed militias and take possession of lands and rural properties; Congress and the Government were to be made up of industrial workers, peasants, sergeants, and soldiers; students were to take over the directive organs of the universities.[19]

ORGANIZED LABOR. The PC do B and PORT had little strength in comparison with the PCB. This becomes apparent from a look at organized labor during the Goulart regime.

In the 1963 election for the presidency of the powerful São Paulo metalworkers' union, the successful candidate, a member of the PCB, far outdistanced the PC do B rival. This union was Brazil's largest, with an active membership of 25,000; and it was wealthy—receiving its share of the *impôsto sindical* (union tax) from the approximately 200,000 metalworkers of the city. The staff of the union was made up of Party activists, and the money was used by the PCB to strengthen its labor activities throughout the state.

According to the labor laws, the top labor organizations were the confederations. Brazil had six of them at the end of 1963. Of the six, four were considered to be Communist-dominated. That domination was pronounced in the confederation of credit (or financial) workers; also in the confederation of air, maritime, and river transport workers, whose Osvaldo Pacheco, PCB leader and king of the stevedores, appeared to have the greatest influence in the Goulart regime just before its fall. Communists also dominated the confederation of agricultural workers, hastily put together late in 1963 after the aging PCB and the youthful Ação Popular had helped the Goulart administration in the feverish creation of over a thousand *sindicatos* (unions) of agricultural workers.

The largest labor confederation is the CNTI (National Confederation of Industrial Workers) and a glance at its affairs may help in understanding the role of Communism during Goulart's presidency.

The CNTI had been founded by anti-Communists in 1946 with the help of the Communist-hating Dutra regime (1946–51). During the Kubitschek regime (1956–61), when Goulart was Vice President, the anti-Communist "old guard," entrenched at the top of the official hierarchy of labor organization, was challenged by dynamic nationalistic "renovators"—many of them able Communist leaders. These "renovators," unable to dislodge the anti-Communists, established in the late 1950s a number of informal, unofficial "united labor fronts" which were known as "horizontal" labor organizations because they were made up of leaders from different occupational categories. The best known "horizontal" groups—all Communist dominated—were the PUA (Pact of Unity and Action), influential among maritime, port, and railroad workers, and run by Osvaldo Pacheco; the CPOS (Permanent Commission of Syndical Organizations), a Guanabara council headed by Roberto Morena and Hércules Correia dos Reis; and the FSD (Forum Sindical de Debates) of Santos.

Vice President Goulart, seeking to preserve unity in labor, urged the anti-Communists in the official hierarchy to work together with the growing "renovator" force. For the "renovators" coexistence was a means of getting much more power than the anti-Communists ("democrats") could concede; and in 1960 the anti-Communists, provoked by the aggressive tactics of the "renovators," broke with coexistence and with Goulart. It was hardly surprising that late in 1961, soon after Goulart became President, the "renovators" took over the CNTI.

This important change assured the formation of an over-all directive body for organized labor, a long-time dream of Luís Carlos Prestes and such veteran Communist labor leaders as Spanish-born Roberto Morena. The new leaders of the industrial workers (Clodsmidt Riani, Dante Pelacani, and Benedito Cerqueira) joined with the Communists and pro-Communists who headed maritime workers and workers in ports, railroads, banks, and air transport to establish an over-all unofficial ruler of Brazilian labor: the CGT (Comando Geral dos Trabalhadores—General Labor Command). It was the CGT which in 1962 called for "general" strikes and demonstrations in support of Goulart and against "imperialism"; and it was the CGT which in 1963 began to find itself in a position to tell Goulart what to do. Besides running the pension institutes and the Labor Ministry, it had influence in other ministries. Unions could get the loans they wanted only if their requests were approved by the CGT.[20] The so-called "leftist popular fronts" looked powerful on paper; but it was the CGT which had the funds and organization for mobilizing masses for leftist rallies.

During 1963 the CGT opposed Goulart on some important issues. Goulart encouraged his labor affairs adviser, Gilberto Crockatt de Sá, to build up a counter force in organized labor: the UST (União Sindical dos Trabalhadores). In December, 1963, Crockatt de Sá, moving against what he called the Communist "imbeciles" and "idiots" of the CGT, had Dante Pelacani removed from his government post of Director General of Social Welfare Funds. The wrath of Brazil's dynamic Communist and "renovating" labor leaders, in and out of the CNTI, was immediately directed against Goulart, who at the time was under plenty of fire from almost every other quarter.

Goulart's big decision was made in January, 1964, when the CNTI prepared for its biennial election of officers. Crockatt de Sá had the votes of enough industrial federations in his pocket to defeat the CGT in the CNTI. But a UST victory would have caused an acrimonious split in organized labor, and at the last minute Goulart backed the CGT. The election did more than preserve the Communists' power. It resulted in Cerqueira's replacing Crockatt de Sá as Goulart's labor affairs adviser. And it brought to top CNTI and CGT circles Luís Tenório de Lima, who, like Morena and Pacheco, served on the Central Committee of the PCB. In the CNTC (National Confederation of Workers in Commerce), theretofore considered one of the two non-Communist confederations, the pro-Communists became stronger; they gained an election tie with the anti-Communists, and, as the tie could not be broken in repeated ballotings, the CGT-dominated Labor Ministry "intervened," taking over the CNTC.

The CGT came out of it all in the driver's seat. Decisions little related to labor matters, such as the naming of the new Navy Minister in March, 1964, were made when the CGT gathered in its exclusive rooms in the CNTI offices in Rio. The men who had been meeting there were: Osvaldo Pacheco, of the stevedores and the PUA; Clodsmidt Riani and Pelacani of the CNTI; Roberto Morena and Hércules Correia dos Reis of the informal Guanabara CPOS (Permanent Commission of Syndical Organizations); Humberto Menezes Pinheiro of the workers in financial establishments; Commander Paulo de Melo Bastos of the air transport workers; Rafael Martineli of the railroad workers; Severino Schnaipper of the maritime workers; and Benedito Cerqueira of the CNTI and the Guanabara metalworkers. Men like Morena, Pacheco, and Martineli had taken training courses in the Soviet Union; but by early 1964 a good many CGT leaders, not wanting to be accused of backwardness, showed the influence of the more violent ideas supplied by Red China.[21] Pelacani, a Red China enthusiast and an electrifying speaker, was the Brazilian who made a trip to Chile to work for the foundation of CUTAL, the Communist labor center for Latin America which was receiving the praises of Roberto Morena.

Communist victories in labor union elections were not a reflection of the ideological views of a majority of the workers. While the victories were due in part to government assistance, they were due also to hard and effective work by Communist leaders. Labor union presidents in the state of São Paulo, polled by an anti-Communist United States–supported institute, voted Pacheco Brazil's best labor leader, and gave two of the next three places to Pelacani and Morena.[22]

STUDENTS.[23] Most of Brazil's students did not participate in student politics. Those who did placed the leadership of the official student organizations in the hands of Catholic far leftists, Communists, Marxists, and Castro devotees. For years the PCB had given careful attention to students. At the same time other forces, within the church and outside of it, led politically-conscious Catholic and non-Catholic youths to feel the need of a radical change of Brazil's social structure. This need was felt strongly by members of Juventude Estudantil Católica (JEC) and Juventude Universitária Católica (JUC), two of the youth sections of Ação Católica (Catholic Action).

Although at lower levels the PCB was frequently strongly at odds with JEC and JUC, agreements were reached at upper levels. Thus, for some important secondary school union elections JEC and the PCB formed a united front. And elections to the directing board of the National Union of Students (UNE), official voice of Brazil's 100,000 university students, confirmed agreements which the PCB reached first with JUC and, after 1962, with Ação Popular (formed when bishops told JUC leaders that they had been misusing JUC). A majority of the UNE directorship posts was customarily divided evenly between the Moscow-line Communists and Ação Popular, with an Aãço Popular representative in the UNE presidency; a few posts were allotted to members of Política Operária (POLOP), a hardhitting independent Marxist revolutionary organization established in 1960 by a group which included a former Trotskyite.

The UNE, its leaders extolling Castro and denouncing the Alliance for Progress, was courted by Brizola and other radical leftists. As an official organ it received, through the Education Ministry, federal budget funds; Petrobrás also helped it financially. It retained strong ties with the Communist International Union of Students, based in Prague, and with Peking.

That radical leftist groups, although split by rivalries, were able to work together against worried opponents was apparent from the makeup of the victorious UNE directorship slates; it was apparent to members of the anti-Marxist Frente da Juventude Democrática when at meetings they found the UNE directors being protected by Osvaldo Pacheco's stevedores.

PART 2. EFFECTS OF THE 1964 MILITARY ACTION ON "THE COMMUNIST THREAT" FORCES

WITH THE OVERTHROW OF GOULART IN 1964, MANY OF THE BEST-KNOWN LEADERS of "the Communist threat" went into hiding, rushed to find asylum in embassies, or managed to get out of Brazil. Others were arrested.

GOVERNMENT INVESTIGATIONS. São Paulo's DOPS (Departamento de Ordem Política e Social, a section of the state Secretaryship of Public Security) assigned men to watch the house where Prestes had been living with his wife and young children. They did not capture Prestes, but on April 9, 1964, searching the house, they found numerous papers, and nineteen spiral notebooks in Prestes' handwriting. The notebooks provided detailed descriptions of all that had been said and decided at meetings and conferences which Prestes had attended during the previous three years.[24]

DOPS inspectors in São Paulo spent about six months studying these documents and noting how many times each prominent Communist was mentioned in the Prestes notebooks. Then they produced a 2,087-page study. Based on this study, approximately sixty individuals were tried in mid-1966 in a military court in São Paulo. At about the same time President Castelo Branco cancelled, for ten years, the political rights of 59 Communists, whose rights had not been cancelled earlier in the regime. The new list included Carlos Marighela, Jacob Gorender, João Amazonas, Maurício Grabois, José Maria Crispim, and the inactive Diógenes de Arruda Câmara.

Famed old lawyer Heráclito Fontoura Sobral Pinto, who had been busy defending imprisoned Miguel Arrais and Red Chinese agents, joined ten other lawyers in defending those accused in the "case of the notebooks." From his place of hinding (probably known to less than five people), Prestes addressed a long letter to Sobral Pinto and it was read in the military court. Prestes pointed out that the PCB "had no subversive intent, or desire for insurrectional combat. We were convinced that the best and most rapid advance of the revolutionary process in our country was by legal methods and not by illegal ones or subversion." The actual conspirators, according to Prestes, had been those generals who had worked for the 1964 rebellion which had toppled a legal regime. Prestes spoke of his patriotism, his hopes of improving the lot of the Brazilian masses, and asked what his crime had been.[25] He quoted Pope Paul VI. In court, defense lawyers quoted Pope John XXIII and pointed out that it was not a crime to be a Communist.

But the military trial ended in July, 1966, with almost all of the defendants receiving jail sentences. Prestes was sentenced to serve 14 years. Such PCB stalwarts as Carlos Marighela, Dinarco Reis, Giocondo Alves Dias, Roberto Morena, and Mário Alves de Sousa Vieira received 7-year sentences; theoretician Jacob Gorender received 5 years. Leaders of the China-oriented PC do B, which had favored a violent insurrection, were more fortunate. João Amazonas was sentenced to two years, and Maurício Grabois was absolved because of insufficient evidence against him. Intellectual Astrogildo Pereira, who had headed the PCB in the 1920s, was not sentenced because he had died shortly after being released from a twelve-week detention in a Rio prison hospital.

Like Astrogildo Pereira, some of those condemned in 1966 had been held for a while by the authorities in 1964. Carlos Marighela, the big, active mulatto, put up physical resistance when he was arrested in a Rio theater in 1964 and was wounded by a bullet.[26] Practically every one of these men had been released on appeals based on habeas corpus.

The outcome of the trial of 1966 did not alter the fact that leading Communists continued to remain outside of the jails, most of them in Brazil but a few of them abroad. Paris was the new home of balding, paunchy Roberto Morena (who, as a carpenter, had joined the Brazilian anarchist movement before the PCB was born in 1922). Stevedore leader Osvaldo Pacheco, already sentenced on another judgment, remained in Uruguay.

Only one accused man, São Paulo PCB leader Luís Tenório de Lima, was present at the 1966 sentencing. This labor leader was already serving a 30-year term as the result of another conviction. Soon after, his long sentence was reduced, on appeal, to three years, and then it was further reduced for good behavior, allowing him to go free. Tenório de Lima's experience, and that of the other convicted Communists, the large majority of whom remained "in hiding" in Brazil, revealed no strong official desire to have Communist leaders in jail. (There was nothing resembling the police searches for Communists which had followed the 1935 rebellion.)

The only well-known Communist in jail in 1967 was aging Gregório Bezerra, a long-time militant in the Northeast.[27] After being seized and publicly tortured in 1964, he was still in a Recife jail awaiting the outcome of an appeal for the reduction of a 19-year sentence handed out early in 1967 by the Military Region of the Northeast. Ex-Army Sergeant Bezerra, who had bitter military foes because he had been found guilty of killing an Army officer during the 1935 uprising, was not among those listed in the accusation based on the Prestes notebooks.

The overthrow of Goulart was followed by numerous military investigations and the ill-treatment of some far leftists and Communists.[28]

Military investigations looked into the affairs of Brizola's Groups of Eleven, Communism in education, and the ultra-nationalist Instituto Superior de Estudos Brasileiros. Ferdinando de Carvalho, the gentlemanly "hard line" colonel who headed the military investigation of Communism in Brazil, kept his group in Rio at work beyond the time limit desired by the Castelo Branco government. During his investigation the colonel became convinced that Francisco Negrão de Lima, seeking to be elected governor of Guanabara in 1965, had purchased Communist electoral support to strengthen his campaign. He therefore prepared to make a sensational TV revelation shortly before the election of October 3, 1965. But the Castelo Branco government, much to the annoyance of Governor Carlos Lacerda (whose candidate opposed Negrão de Lima), stepped in to prevent the colonel's investigation from thus involving itself in current politics.

Complaining of a lack of government co-operation, Colonel Ferdinando de Carvalho wound up his work in 1966.[29] The two years, he felt, had not been sufficient for a thorough investigation. Just before being transferred to Curitiba, Paraná, in October, 1966, he delivered to the Military Justice system 157 volumes, containing accusations against 140 people, including ex-Presidents Kubitschek and Goulart. Press reports about the colonel's study were confusing and misleading. In Rio in November, 1966, the Supreme Military Tribunal dismissed the charges against Negrão de Lima, who had been victorious in the 1965 election and was serving as governor of Guanabara. One of its judges stated that Colonel Ferdinando de Carvalho had been "subject to passions which produced and nourished injustices."[30]

At his Curitiba post (for training Army inductees) Colonel Ferdinando de Carvalho persevered zealously with the investigation of Communism. Late in 1967 he issued a report on the organization and activities of Communists in the state of Paraná.[31] The Party there had been much alive, with the violent line (which included students) taking courses in the preparation of Molotov cocktails. This line had been gaining the upper hand over the "moderate Communists" who were apt to have business or professional interests as well as Party interests.[32]

BRAZILIAN COMMUNIST PARTY. Most of the PCB leaders, including Prestes, remained in hiding in Brazil. In mimeographed documents, or in modest monthly issues of *Voz Operária* and other publications, printed and distributed clandestinely, they heatedly debated future policy and the causes of the 1964 setback. Prestes was subject to some attacks and was criticized for having allowed his notebooks to be seized. Many leaders proposed a wave of violence which Prestes continued to be hesitant to sponsor. After the numerous setbacks during its 42-year existence, PCB self-criticisms had blamed excessive leftism or excessive rightism, depending on what the policy had been before the setback. Quotations from the works of Marx and Lenin had been found to support one viewpoint or the other. Now the time had come to assail recent "opportunistic rightism."

A "Thesis for Discussion" was issued by David Capistrano da Costa and other discontented Pernambuco Party leaders in May, 1964. This document lashed at the Party's national leadership, blaming it for the setback resulting from the "coup of April, 1964." That leadership, it said, had been guilty of opportunism, "illusions of class," a lack of revolutionary vigilance, and the advocation of a peaceful course. "Under those conditions we did not politically prepare the proletariat and working masses to face violent clashes." "We absurdly relied on the apparatus of the large landowners and the bourgeois State—the so-called military *dispositivo* of Jango." The document stated that, had the national situation been properly explained, it would have been "relatively simple" to mobilize the workers and peasants to fight on behalf of the Goulart government and "vacillating" Miguel Arrais. National Party leaders were blamed for failing to appreciate the positive aspects of Goulart's policies. This "thesis" concluded that "North American imperialism brought powerful forces together, taking advantage of the PCB's errors and the left's weakness, a weakness caused by disagreements as to the tactics to be adopted for the Brazilian revolutionary movement."[33]

A mimeographed reply denied a lack of "revolutionary vigilance" based on "illusions of class." It condemned the Pernambuco "thesis" as erroneous and in violation of Marxist-Leninist theory.

"The 'vacillations of Arrais' were not vacillations; his attitude resulted from a carefully made and correct evaluation, whose correlation with the social forces the author of the thesis can best appraise." "Of all the states, Pernambuco is the least indicated for preparing an armed struggle. The peasants have to learn about handling arms and the tactics of guerrilla warfare. This preparation takes time. . . . To submit the masses to a 'bloodbath' on account of an illogical 'leftism' would have greatly retarded the revolutionary process. . . . The deviations of the left do not speed up, but retard, the revolution."

This mimeographed reply went on to say that readers of Rio's *Novos Rumos* and São Paulo's *A Hora* would have known the untruth of the charge that "we did not clearly appreciate the positive aspects of Goulart's policies." It pointed out that, although the PCB national leadership had trusted the increasing nationalist current in the armed forces, it had distrusted Goulart's so-called "military *dispositivo*" and had fought in every possible way to improve its composition.[34]

The Party's Central Committee (CC), elected at Party Congresses, was supposed to meet, together with non-voting alternates, at least twice yearly.[35] The first meeting to follow the 1964 revolution was the one which began in São Paulo on May 5, 1965, and ended two weeks later. Thirty-two members and alternates attended. The sessions promised to be stormy because Party dissensions had torn not only the CC but also the potent, and smaller, National Executive Commission.

In preparation for this meeting some Party leaders had issued a "Scheme for Discussion," proposing that the PCB become part of an anti-Government united front. Meanwhile Executive Commission members Mário Alves de Sousa Vieira and Manoel Jover Teles, differing with Moscow, had come out in favor of violence and been supported by brilliant linguist Jacob Gorender and Rio journalist Neri Reis de Almeida.

At the CC meeting in São Paulo in May, 1965, the opposition to Prestes was led by Gorender. Early in the discussions, Prestes set the tone for the sessions by providing a criticism of two articles which Gorender had written praising ex-Colonel Jefferson Cardim, the unsuccessful leader of a recent tiny uprising in the south of Brazil. Gorender had since revised his opinion of Cardim. Prestes let the CC know that Cardim was a "reckless adventurer."

The majority, including Prestes, backed a long resolution which admitted many of the "past mistakes" already recorded in the thesis from Pernambuco. This resolution favored working with the broadest possible "anti-dictatorial" front, participating in elections, and "using the most varied forms of struggle and all legal possibilities, not necessarily restricted to the 'legality' accorded by the dictators." It stressed the need of preparing the masses, and it reflected the views of those who felt that quick "leftist" violence was unwise.[36]

When a vote was taken, most of those present went along with Prestes' position. Gorender opposed it and five abstained from voting.

Among those dropped from the Executive Commission were Mário Alves de Sousa Vieira and Manoel Jover Teles, but they continued to be members of the CC chosen at the Fifth Party Congress in 1960. A new Executive Commission was formed: Prestes, Carlos Marighela, Giocondo Alves Dias, Dinarco Reis, Orlando Bonfim Júnior, Geraldo Rodrigues dos Santos, and Jaime Amorim de Miranda. The new Secretariat was made up of Prestes, Giocondo Alves Dias, Dinarco Reis, and Jaime Amorim de Miranda.

This new leadership emphasized the importance of participating in the October, 1965, gubernatorial elections, not mentioning, of course, the monetary importance to the Party of participating in elections. After the elections, when the leadership felt pleased with Negrão de Lima's victory in Guanabara, it prepared a new "scheme of discussion" which expressed satisfaction at "the reopening of the democratic road" and proposed to back the Castelo Branco Government against the "hard-liners." But no sooner had copies of this "scheme of discussion" been distributed than the PCB rushed to recall them because President Castelo Branco issued Institutional Act Number Two which dissolved all political parties, gave dictatorial powers to the government and again provided for the cancellation of the political rights of individuals. The PCB's "scheme of discussion" was replaced by a note affirming that "all the democratic possibilities have now been closed to the people."[37] However, Prestes continued to advocate the PCB's participation with the bourgeoisie in a broad anti-dictatorial front.

When the Central Committee of the Party met in January, 1966, it was, as before, in São Paulo and with thirty-two participants. It had been called to approve a set of theses which had been prepared by the leadership for the discussions which were to precede the Sixth Party Congress. Mário Alves de Sousa Vieira and Manoel Jover Teles stated that the proposed theses did not reveal an understanding of the Brazilian political situation. They submitted their own proposed set of theses. Another proposed set was offered by Orestes Timbaúba Rodrigues, but his theses were not critical of the ideas of the Party's national leadership.

At Prestes' suggestion a commission was named to study the various proposals and submit a recommendation at the next CC meeting. Members of the commission were Prestes, Antônio Chamorro, Orlando Bonfim Júnior, Orestes Timbaúba Rodrigues, and Dinarco Reis. The meeting ended with Prestes' announcement that the Party's principal representative at the Tricontinental Congress in Havana was to be Ivan Ramos Ribeiro, and that Giocondo Alves Dias would be a leading representative of the PCB at the Twenty-third Congress of the Communist Party of the Soviet Union.

The 1964 military action and its aftermath stirred the PCB leadership into giving great attention to what it called Trabalho Especial (Special Work). The first job of this "permanent front" of the Party, headed by Salómão Malina, was to build up "self-defense" groups which would physically resist violent efforts by the authorities to hamstring the Party or break up mass meetings. "Clubs, stones, scythes, knives, gasoline, etc., are sure tools within the reach of the workers in general. The use of firearms should be restricted to those who have previously used them." "Self-defense . . . does not imply any change in our political orientation," the PCB leaders added.[38]

The unpopularity of these PCB leaders and of their political orientation was becoming the subject of more and more articles. *Arma da Crítica*, organ of the cell of Communist students attending the National Law School in Rio stated that the Party leaders, guilty of "opportunism and treason," were systematically repressing discussion and acting against "the true revolution-aries." The Communist law students noted that in April, 1966, the PCB's Executive Commission had "intervened illegally" in the directorship of the Rio maritime workers' cell, and that, even then unable "to quiet the true revolutionaries," had engaged in "a shameful campaign of slander unsuited to a true Marxist-Leninist party."[39]

Another Rio cell (B8), rebuking the party leaders for their position regarding the maritime workers, made public its letter advising the CC and the Executive Commission to revise its position and to join with all those "who struggle on behalf of the construction of a real Marxist-Leninist party."[40]

When the CC met in June, 1966, it approved a set of theses recommended by the commission appointed in January, and it decided that the Sixth Party Congress should be held nine months later. The PCB municipal and state organizations prepared to meet to comment on the theses and to choose over one hundred delegates to the Sixth Congress.

The theses recognized that all forms of struggle, legal and illegal, could be used. The PCB was to prepare itself and the masses for a possible civil war. In order to reach understandings with all "anti-dictatorial" political currents, a "minimum program" was advocated for Brazil: democratic liberties, freedom of opinion, "independent" economic-financial development, the combat of inflation, and a foreign policy which affirmed national sovereignty.

The theses attributed numerous current "deviations" in Party sectors to the "complex situation," the defeat in 1964, and the weakness of political work done by the CC.

The sins which preceded the "April 1 military coup" were listed. The CC had behaved "immodestly" and had sought to bring about "the revolution not as a phenomenon of the masses but as a result of top-level action." Within the Party ranks there had been illusions about the bourgeoisie and the "military *dispositivo*" of the government. The masses had not been properly prepared. The "pacific path" had been erroneously interpreted so as to imply that the revolution would come about easily and without conflicts. Goulart had not been fully appreciated, and demands made of him had been extreme. Holders of medium-sized properties had been alienated, weakening the "united front." Instead of alerting the masses against a coup by the right, the Party had pushed too aggressively for more and more "advanced" measures on the part of the government. Threats against Congress had allowed the reactionaries to pose as the defenders of legality.

The big dangers of 1966 were declared to be sectarianism, leftism, and small bourgeois radicalism. Due to increased police reprisals, "leftist tendencies are apt to increase, above all in the small bourgeoisie, particularly among intellectuals and students, and they will hamper the activity of the masses of the Party unless the Communists engage in a firm and effective fight against leftism . . ., against the inclination to make use of immediate action by small groups instead of developing popular mass action and the organization of laborers and all the democratic and patriotic forces."[41]

PREPARING FOR THE SIXTH NATIONAL CONGRESS OF THE PCB. The great debate was formally opened with the publication of the theses in *Voz Operária*, the official organ of the Party. Like the internal debates of 1928 and 1957, this one promised to hurt the PCB, whose estimated membership had already fallen to 20,000 (compared with 30,000 before Goulart's overthrow).

In *Voz Operária* and the other clandestine publications prominent Communists, using names which were not their own, defended or attacked the theses. Prestes, signing his articles "Antônio Almeida," wrote that the great masses should work together with all the antidictatorial forces to isolate the Brazilian regime and bring about its fall. "It would be the most stupid sectarianism to suppose that the dictatorship could be beaten only by a systematic and methodically organized action of the masses. It is perfectly possible, and even more probable historically, that the overthrow of the dictatorship be provoked by a spontaneous explosion or by the contradictions within the dominant classes themselves and even among the *putschistas*."[42]

Mário Alves de Sousa Vieira wrote that "if one examines the form in which the theses of the CC view the essential question of the perspectives of the revolution, one can easily see the opportunistic character which is hidden behind the beautiful words about the revolution."[43] Theoretician Jacob Gorender asserted that "Comrade Prestes has lost sight of the essence of reality and thus passes from truth to error."[44]

Another critic of the theses, writing in *O Isqueiro*, stated, "In considering an armed conflict as only a possibility, which might or might not become a reality, the authors of the theses continue to admit the possibility of a peaceful path for the Brazilian revolution. . . . For the revolution in Brazil, I am convinced that the idea of a peaceful path is not realistic."[45]

O Isqueiro ("The Lighter") was the official organ of the PCB's committee for the Central Zone of Guanabara. This committee used this organ to describe the theses as "a dose of cold water" and to denounce the "opportunistic" majority of the CC.[46] That majority, it said, was preparing for the Sixth Congress by reorganizing cells in a manner to maintain control over the state committee.[47]

Combater, the organ of the Pernambuco State Committee of the PCB, came out for a "Popular Front against the Dictatorship," and it analyzed the theses without attacking the Party's national leadership.[48] However, throughout Brazil in 1967 the most noise in PCB circles was made by partisans of violence who were unsparing in their denunciation of the Party's national leadership. In the south the PCB of Rio Grande do Sul released a stiff resolution in opposition to the CC's "anti-Marxist" theses. Above all, it concluded, the fire should be aimed at the "rightist opportunism and revisionism" in the top directorship of the Party.[49] PCB leaders in Paraná called on the Party to modify its "small-bourgeois" composition ("responsible for the funereal line of conciliation which led to the defeat of April, 1964") and to become a genuine worker and peasant party which would take over Brazil by means of armed struggle.[50]

For Prestes the most serious explosion was in São Paulo, which had more PCB members than any other state. There popular, brave Carlos Marighela, aged 55, came out for violent revolution. In December, 1966, after the PCB supported the anti-dictatorial Broad Front (*Frente Ampla*) being proposed by Carlos Lacerda and Juscelino Kubitschek,[51] Marighela left the PCB's National Executive Commission. In his letter of resignation, Marighela accused the PCB leadership of flouting Marxism and believing in the leadership of the bourgeoisie. He declared: "I wish to state publicly my will to fight, as a revolutionary, along-side the masses; and in doing so, I want also to express my disgust with the political, bureaucratic and conventional play-acting that is going on among the leadership. . . . For Brazil there is only one possible solution: armed struggle. We have to prepare for an armed rising by the people, with all that that implies."[52]

In March, 1967, the CC declared that Marighela was no longer an Executive Commission member because he had not been attending meetings and had abandoned his post. The CC also declared an end to the debate, in the Party press, about the theses. It ordered the São Paulo Committee to recall all copies of its recent publications.[53]

In April, 1967, when Marighela and Prestes confronted each other at the Conference of the São Paulo State Committee, the official PCB theses were overwhelmingly voted down in spite of Prestes' defense of them.[54] Marighela, who declared that it was time to stop submitting the proletariat to bourgeois tactics and leadership,[55] was elected secretary of the State Committee.

Then, under Marighela's leadership, the São Paulo State Communist apparatus issued a series of documents and resolutions stressing what it called "the ideological divergences between the majority of the Party and the group dominating the Central Committee.[56]

Marighela further irked the PCB leadership by attending the LASO (Latin-American Solidarity Organization) conference in Havana (July 31 to August 10, 1967). The PCB had sent no representative because it had learned that LASO intended to set up a Brazilian committee in which the PCB would be an equal with "well-known renegades and fractionalists."[57]

In Havana Marighela was quoted as asserting that the PCB's "opportunistic" leadership was not interested in knowing about revolution and did not "desire armed struggle or the preparation for it."[58] The PCB's Executive Commission retaliated on August 15, suspending Marighela from all of his Party posts. On the 18th Marighela, still in Havana, wrote to "Dear Comrade Fidel" to express his complete agreement with Castro's closing speech and with the LASO resolutions, and to advise that he had sent a letter from Havana breaking with the CC of the PCB. "As I see it," Marighela wrote Castro, "guerrilla warfare is the only means of uniting all the revolutionaries in Brazil, and bringing the people there to power."[59]

The CC, at its September, 1957, meeting, expelled hard liners Marighela and Manoel Jover Teles from the Party. Gorender, found guilty of "divisionist activity," was "suspended" from voting on the CC. Three other CC members were censured.

The CC, in a bad mood, declared that unruly state organizations, such as those in São Paulo, Rio Grande do Sul, and the state of Rio de Janeiro, had been sabotaging the distribution of *Voz Operária*. Trying to strike against rival publications, the CC ratified a recent Executive Commission prohibition against the distribution of material issued by the PCB state committees of São Paulo and Rio Grande do Sul. And it agreed that *O Isqueiro*, "at the service of fractionalism," no longer had any connection with the PCB.[60] The CC also supported a decision, already made by what it called the Guanabara State Committee, to fire eleven Guanabara PCB leaders from their Party posts.

These and other expulsions cleared the way for the leadership to call the delayed Congress.

THE SIXTH NATIONAL CONGRESS OF THE PCB was held in São Paulo in the first part of December, 1967. It was held in great secrecy. Forty-three per cent of those attending had prison sentences issued against them, and seventy-six per cent were "being sought" by the police.[61]

After Ho Chi Minh had been named "honorary president" of the Congress, those present ratified a CC decision to expel from the Party seven who had been elected to the CC in 1960: Carlos Marighela, Manoel Jover Teles, Mário Alves de Sousa Vieira, Jacob Gorender, Joaquim Câmara Ferreira, Apolônio Pinto de Carvalho, and Miguel Batista. Two others (including journalist Neri Reis de Almeida) were expelled for having furnished the police with information about the Party when they were in jail.

Fraternal messages were exchanged with the Communist Party of the Soviet Union.

Prestes, whose pro-Moscow will had once more prevailed and who would become seventy on January 3, 1968, was the object of praise. It was generally felt that the Party's day-to-day affairs would be run by Giocondo Alves Dias, who was named First Secretary of the Party. Giocondo (about whose activities the police had received information from Neri Reis de Almeida) had gotten his start in Communist work as a 22-year-old Army corporal participating in the short-lived uprising in Natal in 1935; he had learned to read and write when he was in jail following that uprising.

With no immediate hope of achieving legality, the Party reverted to statutes which described it as guided by Marxism-Leninism. The PCB's turn from the extreme right of the Goulart years was also reflected in its latest declaration of purpose: "the conquest of political power in order to establish Socialism and Communism in our country."[62]

While the expelled leaders of the past gathered elsewhere to argue about theories of terrorism and sabotage, the PCB, at its Sixth National Congress, gave serious attention to the possible use of violence. The Political Declaration, adopted by the Congress, stressed that conditions for struggle varied in different areas of Brazil and that in each area the most appropriate means, whether violent or non-violent, should be used. "The essential thing is that the form of struggle should be in accordance with the demands of the concrete situation."

The PCB was to participate in the limited elections allowed by the "dictatorship" and co-operate with opposition politicians when that seemed useful. "But the dictatorship might force on the people the path of armed insurrection or civil war. The situation therefore requires that the Communists prepare the Party and the masses, and also enter into understandings with the different currents of the anti-dictatorial front, to prepare for this eventuality.[63]

It might be well to add that the PCB, in seeking to prepare the masses, was faced with a problem which had troubled and perplexed its organizers for decades: that of exciting the interest of the very people who, it felt, had the most reason to espouse its cause. A contemporary poll hardly indicated that a state of poverty induced such an interest, and it made it clear that a lack of education was a serious barrier. The poll, conducted among Brazilian women by *Realidade* magazine, included the question: "Do you fear Communism?"[64] Affirmative replies are shown below:

all those questioned	72%
the poor	75%
those with university education	41%
those with secondary education	67%
those with primary education	76%
illiterates	81%

MIGUEL ARRAIS was released in April, 1965, after having been held on Fernando de Noronha Island and in other prisons. The release of Pernambuco's far leftist ex-governor infuriated some "hard line" colonels. Colonel Osneli Martineli, who headed an investigation of Brizola's Groups of Eleven, had his men seize and hold Arrais in Rio, while the ex-prisoner underwent long questioning by military investigators. But the federal government, not appreciating Martineli's intentions, locked up the colonel in Rio's Copacabana Fort. And Arrais issued a defiant manifesto, belittling the investigators and refusing to give further testimony. Instead, he found asylum in the Algerian embassy.

In July, 1965, he issued a pronouncement from Algeria, where he settled. He declared that Brazil, fifteen months after the "coup of April, 1964," was in the same situation that Cuba had been under the Batista dictatorship: it was a country militarily and economically occupied by an oligarchy tied to the interests of the large North American monopolies. The Brazilian military dictatorship, he added, would have to be overthrown, and he called on the Brazilian people to participate in the struggle so that it would be successful.[65]

Russian Communists who approached him found that he had switched from his past legalistic and peaceful line, a line the Soviet Union continued to advocate. Acting like a man the Soviet agents would be unable to control, Arrais got in touch with Brizola, who was in exile in Uruguay.

LEONEL BRIZOLA worked hard to assume the leadership of exiles and others willing to use force to overthrow the "dictatorships" of Marshal Castelo Branco and of Marshal Costa e Silva (who succeeded Castelo Branco in 1967). Brizola hoped that the Frente de Libertação Nacional, whose headquarters he set up in Montevideo not long after Goulart's overthrow, would bring far left forces together. Representatives came to Brizola from PORT, POLOP, PC do B, Ação Popular, and other groups interested in an armed uprising.

While rancher Goulart, also in Uruguay, seemed inclined to relax and watch his cattle fatten, military figures who had once supported Goulart's regime conspired with Brizola. In February, 1965, the Brazilian Government persuaded the Uruguayan Government to "intern" Brizola at Atlantida, an hour's drive from Montevideo; in spite of this restriction, Brizola made frequent trips to Montevideo (explaining that he was auditing a course at the University Law School).

A Brazilian government prosecutor, after investigating a small armed invasion which penetrated Brazil from Uruguay late in March, 1965, was generous in distributing the blame. Seldom has such wide-scale backing been attributed to so few invaders. The prosecutor announced that the invasion had been planned by members of Groups of Eleven under Brizola's leadership and had been financed by Cuba, Communist China, and countries of Eastern Europe. After questioning captured raiders, including ex-Colonel Jefferson Cardim de Alencar Osório, he placed the responsibility on thirty-eight prominent Brazilian exiles in Uruguay. Besides Brizola the list included a former cabinet minister, a former president of the UNE (National Students' Union) and far leftist Darci Ribeiro, the anthropologist who had been Goulart's chief administrator of the presidential office and was now being accused by the Brazilian Supreme Military Tribunal of having taken government funds into exile.

Even after the invading group of the overly impetuous Jefferson Cardim had crossed from Uruguay into Rio Grande do Sul and found some adherents in that state, it consisted of only fifteen men. They had little difficulty in stealing police weapons in the small town of Três Passos, in the north of the state; there they cut telephone wires and used the local radio station to broadcast ex-Colonel Cardim's proclamation in the name of the "Army of National Liberty." As they proceeded in a truck north and into the state of Paraná they were untroubled until, near the Iguaçá River in southwest Paraná an Air Force plane spotted them. Soon they were shooting at Army soldiers who moved against their improvised camp. After one soldier had been killed, a part of the "Army of National Liberty" was captured and a part of it disappeared.

Two tiny "guerrilla camps," uncovered in Brazil in 1967 by the authorities, produced better evidence of the interest shown by Brizola and Cuba in 1966 in aiding Brazilian "Marxist-Leninists" and others eager to use violence. The authorities, after questioning members of the 14-man "guerrilla front" in the

Caparaó mountains in the east of Minas, reported that some of the revolutionaries had been trained in Uruguay and some in Cuba. Later in 1967 federal cavalry and police arrested twenty so-called guerrilla fighters in Goiás. Again arrested conspirators reported that Brizola, with whom they had conversed in Uruguay, had supplied leadership and funds.

Partido Comunista do Brazil (PC do B). Following the 1964 military move, the Red Chinese gave up the task of selecting a building to serve as their future embassy in Brazil; and they showed less interest in financing the PC do B. But the PC do B, its membership down to around 750, continued its practice of sending men to China for training in guerrilla fighting. Although two of these were caught by the authorities upon their return to Brazil, later they both ended up finding asylum in the Embassy of Uruguay. One was Tarzan de Castro, who had once belonged to the PCB and later, until he broke with Francisco Julião, had headed the training of guerrilla fighters in the state of Goiás. In order to reach the embassy, Tarzan de Castro had to make an escape from one of Rio's forts.

Late in May, 1965, right after Prestes-led PCB leaders expelled two partisans of violence from their Party's Executive Commission, the PC do B also held a meeting of its CC. This meeting took place in Santo Amaro, São Paulo, and was attended by nine members including Amazonas, Grabois, Lincoln Cordeiro Oest and two who had just returned from Communist China. The CC expelled one absent member ("for demonstrated inefficiency"), and resolved to increase its total CC membership from twelve to twenty.

In June, 1966, while the PCB's CC was approving theses to be debated in connection with the Sixth Party Congress, the PC do B held what it called "the Sixth National Conference of the Communist Party of Brazil." (Thus it emphasized again that it was the continuation of the true party.) The "Sixth National Conference" was made up of the PC do B's CC and representatives of its regional committees. It approved new statutes and produced a political resolution: "Union of Brazilians to Free the Nation from the Crisis, the Dictatorship, and the Neocolonialist Threat."

This union was to be made up of those who favored violence and who recognized that peaceful coexistence with the United States was a mistaken policy. It could include PCB militants who opposed the "opportunistic line" proposed by the "revisionists" who headed the PCB.

After the fall of Khrushchev, his "mistaken revisionist" ideas had, the PC do B said, been continued by his successors in the Soviet Union. In Brazil, Prestes, embracing "the opportunistic theses of the Communist Party of the Soviet Union," had likewise "abandoned Marxism-Leninism." The PC do B quoted Lenin's warning against opportunism, and his affirmation that "the unity which the workers' cause needs is the unity of the Marxists and not of Marxists with adversaries and renegades of Marxism."

Fidel Castro was scolded for his "open and unjustifiable attack on the Communist Party of China and on Marxist-Leninists throughout the world." Trotskyites, seeking to "create leftist fronts, of a sectarian form," were accused of provoking confusion and spreading "slanders against the Communist leaders."[66]

FRANCISCO JULIÃO, like Goulart, Prestes, Brizola, Arrais (and ex-President Quadros), found his name on the April 10, 1964, list of one hundred: the first list of those deprived of their political rights for ten years.

After two months of hiding, Julião was caught in Goiás. The treatment of far leftist prisoners, seized after Goulart's fall, was not always pleasant. Julião complained of three violent blows on the head, as well as some time spent in a cell which was uncomfortably small even for a man of his short stature.[67] To investigators, connected with the Fourth Army (in the Northeast), he spoke of his admiration of Castro, Mao Tse-tung, and Khrushchev. He compared Brizola's "vigor" with Goulart's "lack of energy"; he said that he had never belonged to the PCB.

Early in 1966 Venezuelan leftist revolutionaries (of FALN) reported that Julião was in Castro's bad graces because he had not properly accounted for money received from Cuba in 1962. By this time Julião (who had been released from prison) was in exile in Mexico. His absence from Brazil was probably a good thing for him because early the next year (1967) a military tribunal in Recife condemned him, along with such Communists as Bezerra and Capistrano, to 19 years in jail. (The absent Arrais was condemned to 23 years.)

TROTSKYITES (PORT). In April, 1965, Government investigators claimed that 35 military men, most of them sergeants, had been so moved by PORT propaganda in the São Paulo area that they had made plans before April, 1964, to revolt against their superiors.

In September, 1964, five months after Goulart's overthrow, PORT leaders from São Paulo and the Northeast met in São Paulo, studied the situation, and sent Cláudio Vasconcelos Cavalcanti to participate in conversations with Brizola and other violent-minded conspirators in Montevideo. (Vasconcelos Cavalcanti, a member of PORT's top *Bureau Político*, had participated in the Trotskyite "World Congress" in Montevideo just before Goulart's fall.)

Under the leadership of Pedro Makovsck Clemachuk, PORT's political secretary in the Northeast, the state committees of Pernambuco and Paraíba were reorganized. In spite of anti-Communist military alertness in the Northeast, PORT had some success in attracting members of the Airforce Sergeant's Club in Recife.

PORT's small mimeographed publication, calling on the proletariat of all countries to unite, reflected the views issued by The Fourth International's Montevideo headquarters under the name of Juan Posadas. Early in 1966 Posadas attacked Castro for doing nothing to promote the revolution and, instead, "stupidly" entering into dialogues with members of the bourgeoisie. Posadas said that a sector of the Brazilian bourgeoisie, including Goulart, sought a peaceful, electoral solution to the Brazilian crisis. Posadas insisted that the bourgeoisie lacked the influence to persuade the masses to take such a mistaken path. He added that the Brizola nationalist sector might possibly be strong enough to induce an electoral victory, and he warned that an electoral solution was just what the bourgeoisie wanted in order to paralyze a more virtuous sector which favored a violent uprising on behalf of the ideals "of Trotskyism and revolutionary Marxism."

The Brazilian Trotskyites recognized that their group was small. But they saw hope in "Groups of Five" among the workers of Santos. Such "Groups of Five, of the Popular Liberation Front," should be organized elsewhere. A "class united front" should prepare to form a revolutionary, anti-imperialist, and anti-capitalistic party, together with the labor unions and PORT. True nationalists, rejecting elections, should help in this work.[68]

ORGANIZAÇÃO REVOLUCIONÁRIA MARXISTA—POLÍTICA OPERÁRIA (POLOP), which was sometimes considered to be Trotskyite because of the Trotskyite background of director Luís Alberto Moniz Bandeira, suffered an internal split after 1964. Earlier, this pro-Castro, anti-Stalinist group, which called for "Marxist renovation" on a revolutionary basis, had grown to become a second-rate power, exceeded only by Ação Popular and the PCB in the UNE (National Students' Union). It had come out in favor of the Chinese Communists in their conflict with the USSR Communists.

POLOP's experience reflects the strain which affected communist organizations after March, 1964. Some of POLOP's important directors were seized and questioned. Their answers helped the authorities draw up cases against Brizola, Paulo Schilling (Brizola's aide), and POLOP's Moniz Bandeira, all three of whom had left Brazil. In 1967 a mimeographed paper ("School of Informers"), reflecting Moniz Bandeira's views, appeared. It declared that POLOP was dead, betrayed by directors who did not understand that good Communists tell nothing to their foes, even should they be tortured as Harry Berger had been in the late 1930s. The paper quoted Carlos Marighela and cited his steadfast refusal to answer questions put to him by the authorities in 1964.[69]

Moniz Bandeira's declaration of the demise of POLOP was ignored by many of his former associates. In July, 1967, POLOP placed three of its members on the UNE's ten-man board of officials. Two months later POLOP leaders held the Fourth National Congress of their organization. At this Congress they issued a call for a strictly proletarian uprising to bring about a dictatorship of the proletariat. POLOP felt that in the course of the struggle, which might well be started as a guerrilla movement in the interior, a truly Marxist-Leninist party would emerge in Brazil.[70] "Workers of the world, unite!" concluded POLOP.

POLOP, however, was far from united. Dissidents at its Fourth National Congress accused the directorship of erroneously wanting to rely largely on urban insurrection instead of on guerrilla warfare in the countryside.[71] They prepared to go their own separate way.

ORGANIZED LABOR. As a result of Goulart's overthrow, the CGT, which had never achieved official status in the labor laws, was eliminated. So were the other informal "horizontal" labor organizations, such as the Communist-dominated PUA (Pact of Unity and Action), CPOS (Permanent Commission of Syndical Organization), and FSD (Forum Sindical de Debates) of Santos.

The new military government intervened in the affairs of all "red" unions, such as those affiliated with Rafael Martineli's National Federation of Railroad Workers and with the confederations of industrial workers, financial workers, agricultural workers, and workers in air, maritime, and river transport. Sometimes the government appointed slates of union officers to run these unions; sometimes it asked the non-Communist factions to organize committees. In all cases the government asked for reports on earlier "subversion."

In the case of CNTI (Confederação Nacional dos Trabalhadores na Indústria), the largest labor confederation, the Labor Ministry acted quickly, wanting the installation of a slate which it felt might influence elections to be held in the industrial workers' unions and federations. The climate in mid-1964 was right; also, "red" labor leaders had fled and been deprived of their political rights. By July, 1964, a CNTI "election" had given victory to a slate which satisfied the Labor Ministry.

The Ministry also moved quickly in the case of the confederation of agricultural workers (CONTAG). It declared that all but seven of the thirty agricultural workers' federations had been "paper" federations, hastily put together for Goulart's political purposes.[72] With their elimination CONTAG's administration ceased being Communist.

In the case of some of the intervened unions, "unity" slates were worked out. Thus in the huge São Paulo metallurgical workers' union four contending groups got together, eliminating the fifth (the PCB). After much negotiation, this union's governing body found itself having representatives of the Socialists (long-time allies of the PCB), two rival "anti-Communist" groups, and the PC do B.

Benedito Cerqueira, after coming to rest in Prague with a job in the World Federation of Trade Unions, continued, through followers in Brazil, to influence the Guanabara Metalworkers' Union. This union turned down a "unity slate" and a Christian Democratic slate in favor of a Communist slate. The government then declared that elected Communists could not take office. It did the same in the case of Communists elected by Guanabara shipyard workers and by Guanabara and São Paulo textile workers.

The Guanabara bank workers in 1966 chose between a "green slate," in which Colonel Ferdinando de Carvalho was actively interested, and a "blue slate," made up of Communists and other far leftists. After the "blue slate" won, the government intervened again, declaring that there had been no quorum and therefore no legal election. In an effort to end the intervention in this union, which represented 20,000 workers, negotiators discussed a "unity slate." The Communists, with about 1,200 Party members in the Guanabara banks, were in a strong position because non-Communist leftists were very willing to enter into coalitions with them. The leadership of the militant left had a record of having done something for the bank workers.

Non-Communist labor leaders were able to establish themselves in those situations where, before 1964, Communist domination had been artificially produced by Labor Ministry assistance. However, before long it became evident that association with the Castelo Branco regime was not an asset to labor leaders. That regime, seeking to reduce the rate of inflation, established a system under which the workers were in no position to strike for higher wages, and under which they were being allotted wage increases, based on government coefficients, which did not keep them abreast of cost of living increases.

In Paris late in 1966, Communist Roberto Morena took note of the unhappiness of Brazilian labor; in a letter to Brazil he therefore expressed satisfaction with the Brazilian situation.[73]

UNIVERSITY STUDENTS. In 1964 Castelo Branco's first Education Minister, Suplici de Lacerda, regulated arrangements for student organizations. To prevent these organizations from being controlled by minorities, the Lei Suplici (Suplici Law) required that all students vote in student elections. It provided for a Student Central Directorship at each university; these Directorships would choose State Directorships, which in turn would choose the National Directorship of Students.

The UNE, objecting to the new arrangements, decided to remain outside of the Lei Suplici. In January, 1966, the UNE was dissolved by a judicial body. But nevertheless its enthusiastic supporters kept it going and it played a role in the student anti-government demonstrations of 1966. In July, 1966, it held its clandestine Twenty-eighth National Congress in a Dominican convent in Belo Horizonte.

During the November, 1966, congressional elections the UNE, defying the PCB, participated in a campaign to have voters invalidate ballots by writing "Down with the Dictatorship" on them. This campaign was supported by sixteen PCB cells in Guanabara universities, reportedly representing 85 percent of the Party strength among Guanabara university students.[74] The PCB leadership expelled all these cells from the Party. The UNE retaliated by expelling from the UNE those who supported the theses advocated by the Party directorship.[75]

Student leaders, agitating for improvements in education and calling for a "worthwhile dialogue," were reported to regret having lost in April, 1964, the ability to get things done by going directly to the government.[76] On the other hand, one improvement was noted by the leaders of the new, post-Goulart student movement. They saw this new movement, including the sensational contributions made by the now illegal UNE, as a genuine movement —much more genuine and popular than what had been provided before 1964 by a legal UNE with close ties to politicians.[77] The new anti-government movement, strong in many of the university student Directorships, revealed a nationalist sentiment which was widespread. It was directed against the United States, whose ideas and business interests were said to have been favored by the Castelo Branco regime to the detriment of Brazil.

The UNE was much in the news in the latter part of 1967, after it was learned that its clandestine Twenty-ninth Annual Congress, attended by about 400, had been held at a retreat of the Benedictine Order in the state of São Paulo.[78] At this time the influence of Ação Popular in the UNE was considerable.

Ação Popular (AP) had been organized on May 1, 1962, at a meeting, held at the University of Minas Gerais, by Catholic University Youth (JUC) leaders whose political use of JUC displeased bishops. These young people had been influenced by a Brazilian Jesuit Father, Henrique de Lima Vaz, and by the visit made to Brazil by Father Thomas Cardonnel, a French Dominican; also by the writings of French philosophers Emmanuel Mounier and Pierre Teilhard de Chardin.[79] After AP was established it found some warm friends in Goulart's cabinet. Education Minister Paulo de Tarso and Labor Minister Almino Afonso were particularly helpful.

Early documents, such as those issued at AP's First National Congress (1963), called on AP to lead a socialist revolution. Socialism and Christianity were declared to be compatible, whereas capitalism was to be condemned by good Christians.[80]

Before Goulart's overthrow, AP, under its dedicated young "National Coordinator," Herbert José de Sousa, made a name for itself by providing UNE leaders; also by organizing peasant federations which, after displaying a keen rivalry with PCB peasant federations, finally collaborated with the PCB in an arrangement which put the Moscow-line Communists in control of the agricultural workers' confederation.

Following Goulart's overthrow, a good number of students and some Catholic priests, who had been connected with AP, were seized and interrogated.[81] Father Francisco Lage Pessoa, associated with AP in Minas Gerais, was jailed, sentenced to serve 28 years in prison, and allowed to find exile in Mexico.

AP leaders met and turned AP into a violent revolutionary secret organization, which carefully checked on the merits of would-be members. At the base of its structure were cells of five or less militants. Some of them helped to arrange the sensational escape by means of which young José Anselmo dos Santos, leader of the March, 1964, sailors' mutiny, reached asylum in the Mexican Embassy.[82] Brazilian Government intelligence services worried more about AP than they did about the PCB. Some of them estimated AP to have 1,200 or 1,500 militants.

AP's sophisticated literature appealed to intellectuals and university students. Some students, driving flashy cars, called themselves "extreme Marxists." The literature of 1966 called for the complete overthrow of Brazil's social and political structure in order to install a pure socialism—one which would not, as under Stalin, limit the dignity of man. Brazilian workers, peasants, and intellectuals were to be prepared, not only ideologically, but also militarily—by learning guerrilla warfare and by other means—to bring about the ultimate violent overthrow of "United States–supported" capitalism and imperialism. "It is necessary," AP wrote, "to place our militancy at the vanguard of the revolutionary work."[83] Basic training courses, usually lasting about three weeks, were given to small groups.

Intensely nationalistic, and bold in its theory-filled declarations, AP found encouragement in 1967 in the increasing number of statements by Brazilian Catholic priests who flayed the existing order of things and who attributed hunger in Brazil to United States "imperialism."

Although AP held Mao Tse-tung in high esteem, it was inclined to look down on the PC do B, considering it to be led by "old men" (Amazonas and

Grabois). It was was especially contemptuous of the PCB. While the Prestes faction was busy in November, 1966, instructing followers to vote for certain anti-government candidates, AP played an important role in the campaign to get voters to nullify ballots as a protest against a "farce." Prestes could hardly agree with AP's self-appointed "vanguard" role, and he repeatedly expressed concern about the "leftism" of AP.

When the outlawed UNE met at the Benedictine retreat in São Paulo in July, 1967, it gave comfort to AP and none to the Prestes wing of the PCB. The victorious slate of ten new officers was made up of four AP members, three POLOP members and three followers of what was then the Marighela wing of the PCB. The UNE refused even to analyze the proposed program which the PCB had drawn up for students, and promptly disassociated itself from the International Union of Students in Prague.

AP's literature in 1967 sought to prepare the militants for a Second National AP Congress. One pre-Congress resolution declared that "theoretical and ideological deficiencies now constitute the fundamental problem of our organization." To rectify this situation, the militants were told to learn about the true views, not the distorted versions, of Marx, Lenin, and Mao Tse-tung. Militants were to read Marxist texts, debate them in cell meetings, and forward reports of these debates to AP units immediately higher in the hierarchy. In this way each layer of units was to debate and report; the zonal committees would report to the regional committees, and these would finally report to AP's top National Committee.[84]

All of this study and debate of Marxism was supposed to help the Second National Congress give AP an "ideological definition." However, it contributed to internal fighting. Herbert José de Sousa and other AP leaders, absorbing ideas propounded in France by Professor Louis Althusser, opted for a Marxism said to be closer to that of Mao Tse-tung than to anything recently produced by the Soviet Union. When they finally proclaimed AP a Marxist organization, objections came from within the ranks. Priests, such as Henrique de Lima Vaz, long influential in AP, opposed Marxism.

PART 3. THE 1964–67 SPLINTERING AND ITS EXTENSION IN 1968

IN SPITE OF BICKERING AND RIVALRIES, FORCES WHICH EARLY IN 1964 WERE SAID to make up "the Communist threat" managed to demonstrate a certain amount of cohesion in working for program points about which they agreed.

Thus in January, 1964, the Frente de Mobilização Popular (Front of Popular Mobilization) met at Brizola's Rio residence. It included representatives of the CGT, the UNE, the Liga Feminina Nacionalista, UBES (União Brasileira dos Estudantes Secundários) and Ação Popular. This Frente heard from Arrais and Brizola, and then presented demands to Goulart.[85] One of these called for the expropriation of the largest petroleum refinery which was in private hands. The Frente reminded Goulart that his executive power allowed him to carry out many things; among these, the Frente said, was the much discussed expropriation of lands adjacent to federal railroads, highways, and irrigation works.

On March 13, 1964, leaders of the Frente de Mobilização Popular gathered to address a great crowd which had been brought together by the CGT. On that occasion they heard Goulart announce, in the final speech, that he had decreed the expropriation of all private petroleum refineries, and of lands, in excess of 500 hectares, which adjoined federal railways, highways, and irrigation works. At Goulart's side, actively assisting him on the speakers' platform, was PCB leader Osvaldo Pacheco, "the master of ceremonies."[86] It was a display of unity which helped to unify those who opposed the Frente, Pacheco, and their ideas.

By late 1966, over two years after the overthrow of Goulart, political leaders who had long been foes, but who had been shoved aside by the Castelo Branco regime, were deciding to unite for political action. Carlos Lacerda and ex-President Juscelino Kubitschek, whose differences had been great, smilingly shook hands and prepared to work together. This "Frente Ampla" (Broad Front) was extended in September, 1967, when Lacerda and Goulart, whose past differences had been extreme, issued a joint statement in Montevideo.

However, as we have tried to show in detail, those who proposed to make Brazil a Marxist country were more split than every by late 1967. The 1964–67 period produced nothing like the old AP-PCB alliance, so effective in the period before Goulart's fall. The more AP came to admire Marx and Lenin the less it would have to do with the PCB. Up through 1967 the principal troubles of Brazilian Marxists came not from arrests by the police but from clashes between the Marxist groups themselves and internal dissensions within the groups.

Adepts of the Moscow line, adepts of the Peking line, and Trotskyites continued to devote much time to attacking each other and Castro. All these Communists were apt to be criticized by an unorganized province of Brazilian Marxism, made up of men such Agildo Barata who had broken with the PCB in the late 1950s and had remained on the sidelines. Groups suffered from internal struggles, such as those in POLOP and AP. One of the things which contributed most to the fragmentation of Brazilian Marxism was the bitter battle within the PCB, a battle brought on not only by differences concerning policy but also by a struggle for power.

The 1964–67 period was characterized by two trends: (a) a move away from the cautious Moscow line; and (b) fragmentation on the part of opponents of the Moscow line.

The first trend was confirmed by estimates of PCB membership given in 1968. The figures mentioned were below 13,000, the lowest since the end of World War II.[87] The PCB hoped to reverse this trend by appealing to those who abhorred violence; however, in September, 1968, when Prestes presided over the first CC meeting following the Sixth Party Congress, a resolution was adopted supporting the Soviet invasion of Czechoslovakia.

The year 1968 also confirmed the already evident inability of non-PCB Marxists to work together. Those expelled from the PCB late in 1967 established not one, but two new formal Brazilian Communist Parties. One of these was the PCBR (Partido Comunista Brasileiro Revolucionário) headed by Mário Alves de Sousa Vieira, Jacob Gorender, and able Apolônio Pinto de Carvalho, a veteran of the Spanish Civil War and the French Resistance. The other was the POC (Partido Operário Comunista—Labor Communist Party) in which former PCB leader Joaquim Câmara Ferreira and PCB dissidents of Rio Grande do Sul and elsewhere joined up with a part of POLOP.[88]

Carlos Marighela kept in close touch with Joaquim Câmara Ferreira. As for the parties, he felt critical of the "traditional left-wing organizations in Brazil, whose functions revolved round meetings to discuss documents and conduct other more or less bureaucratic business dictated to them by the leaders and never put into practice."[89] While so many were theorizing, he decided that the time had come for revolutionary action. For this reason he organized an informal group which came to be called the ALN (Ação Libertadora Nacional).

AP (Ação Popular) became torn by internal strife in 1968. Although it continued with some strength in Minas Gerais, its overall collapse was such that one expert on its affairs pronounced it "dead" in its Regional Command No. 4, which covered the states of Guanabara, Rio de Janeiro, and Espírito Santo. A group of ex-members from this region joined the PCBR.

Internal strife was rampant in the illegal university student organizations. Luís Travassos, the ultra-radical AP adherent who had been elected UNE president in 1967, lost influence in the UNE's executive and in the state organizations. The São Paulo organization (UEE) held a stormy election during which half of the delegates walked out and the remainder gave the most votes to José Dirceu, an opponent of Travassos. For a while, São Paulo had two UEEs, until the UNE's national executive officially confirmed Dirceu's election.[90]

In Rio Vladimir Palmeira, head of the União Metropolitana dos Estudantes, attained national fame and a strong following for his able leadership during formidable student demonstrations of protest (in which one student was killed by the authorities).

During the preparations for the Thirtieth UNE National Congress, scheduled for the latter part of 1968, Palmeira supported Dirceu for the UNE presidency; Travassos supported Jean-Marc van der Weig, of Rio. Palmeira and Dirceu, critical of Travassos' calls for "struggle in the streets,"[91] spoke of the need of reforming universities, restructuring the UNE, and developing an anti-imperialistic middle class which would support labor.[92] Travassos' proposals about place (Belo Horizonte) and agenda for the Thirtieth Congress were defeated.[93] Splits in state student organizations affiliated with the UNE were serious. Both factions tried to mobilize the widest support and participation for the UNE's Thirtieth National Congress, where executive elections would decide which of the two trends would prevail as UNE's new direction.

When the Congress was held in the countryside in São Paulo in October, 1968, the state authorities arrested 720 raindrenched delegates (out of an estimated total of 1,000) before an election of new officers could be held. Among those arrested was José Dirceu whose election had seemed likely at the start of the Congress.

The UNE failed in its subsequent efforts to hold clandestine elections on a nationwide, representative basis. The split continued to be evident. In late 1969, Jean-Marc van der Weig (who later ended up in Chile) was generally being called UNE president.[94] But when Dirceu landed in Mexico in September, 1969, on his way to Cuba from a Brazilian jail, he, too, called himself the president of the UNE.

The China-line PC do B, although it suffered from a squabble between Amazonas and Grabois, gained some adherents in 1968, due in part to Manoel Jover Teles. Teles, after his expulsion from the PCB in 1967, helped organize the PCBR and became head of its Guanabara State Committee. But almost immediately after he assumed his post, he accused fellow PCBR leaders of taking an "intermediate position" between the "revisionist line" and the Marxist-Leninist line.[95] During the ensuing wrangle he took most of the PCBR's Guanabara Committee into the PC do B, and then he himself made a trip to Peking.

Thereupon the "Central Committee" and the "National Executive Committee" of the PCBR following the familiar path, adding to the abundant literature in which self-proclaimed Marxists attack other self-proclaimed Marxists. Once again the old question was raised about whether or not to work for a "two-stage" revolution with the first stage including the "national bourgeoisie" among the revolutinaries. The PC do B's directors were accused of favoring this idea and therefore of being "incapable of freeing themselves from the opportunistic strategic concept of the party of Prestes."[96] The PC do B's "inability to become a revolutionary party" was given as a reason why, "among the various leftist organizations, it is one of the smallest and least connected with the masses."[97]

Thus spoke one very small new Brazilian Communist party about a small six-year-old Brazilian Communist party in the middle of 1968. The declaration from which these words are taken is not likely to end up in a documentary history. But it is highly significant, nonetheless, for it reflects, as well as anything, what had been taking place.

In his article, "There'll Be Many Communisms in 1984," Milovan Djilas predicts "the decline of the influence of Soviet Communism in world Communism." Writing in this article about "the existing Western Communist parties," he states that "all sort of groups will splinter off from them."[98] Before Djilas made these forecasts, Brazil was fulfilling them well.

PART 4. TERRORIST GROUPS, 1968–70

WHILE THE SPLINTERING OF THE COMMUNIST MOVEMENT IN BRAZIL KEPT MANY occupied, arguing and drawing up documents, it did not seem to harm the effectiveness of the small minority which decided to engage in action. Perhaps the only "violent revolutionary" activities possible under the circumstances then existing in Brazil could best be carried out by a number of independent bands. At least this fractionalization allowed various leaders, familiar with local situations, to act with flexibility, and it eliminated the problems which arise when an overall structure seeks to force adherence to particular lines.

As stated above, Carlos Marighela formed his group, the ALN (Ação Libertadora Nacional), in 1968. It began carrying out what it called "urban guerrilla activities" in São Paulo. Of the thirty-one "terrorist explosions" (which killed three people and wounded 266) in Brazil between July, 1966, and mid-October, 1968, seventeen ocurred in São Paulo in the first nine and one-half months of 1968.[99] In the same nine and one-half months the terrorists stole 1,448 kilograms of dynamite (of which the police recovered 485 kilograms).[100]

A flurry of robberies, mostly of banks, began in São Paulo on February 8, 1968.[101] Among the spectacular ones was a train robbery yielding 110,000 New Cruzeiros ($30,000) and the robbery of 185,000 New Cruzeiros ($50,000) from a branch of the Banco do Estado de São Paulo.[102] Within one year of terrorist operations the equivalent of $600,000 was stolen from fifty São Paulo banks, and $360,000 from banks in Rio.[103] (More remunerative for the terrorists would be burglarly of cash left in a house safe by the late governor of São Paulo, Ademar de Barras, which occurred a little later.)

In São Paulo in October, 1968, terrorists machine gunned United States Army Captain Charles R. Chandler in the driveway of his home and in front of his wife and nine year old son.[104] The captain, who was studying at São Paulo University after having served in Vietnam, had never hesitated to defend United States policy in Vietnam. Marighela, in a "Call to the Brazilian People," issued after the killing, incorrectly described Chandler as a "spy for the CIA in Brazil" and said that his "execution" demonstrated "the revolutionary groups' concern to defend national sovereignty and interests."[105]

In December, 1968, when Marighela listed the aims of "the revolution," he said, "We shall publicly try to execute CIA agents found in the country and police agents responsible for torturing, beating, and shooting prisoners. We shall expel North Americans from the country and confiscate their property. . . . We shall confiscate private Brazilian companies which collaborate with the Americans or oppose the revolution."[106] In a broadcast from a captured radio station early in 1969, he asserted that "North American landowners must be attacked and killed, as well as the estate owners' agents and stooges. The same punishment should be given to foremen, administrators, and bailiffs who persecute peasants and destroy their goods."[107]

"Our forces," the ALN wrote in January, 1969, "have not ceased to increase, our zone of influence has grown, and the same can be said about popular backing. . . . We have gained a year on the reaction, catching it by surprise with our expropriations [bank robberies], our seizure of arms and explosives, without ever leaving any traces. . . . Starting from nothing, we have become a national organization."[108] Marighela, optimistic, spoke of having "baffled the dictatorship" by terrorism. He foresaw the completion of "the first stage of the guerrilla war," that is, "the urban guerrilla and psychological warfare." The year 1969, he declared, would witness the development of the urgently needed "second phase": rural guerrilla action.[109]

When bombs exploded, when weapons disappeared, or when banks were robbed, it was usual for the press, and not infrequently with reason, to explain these events as the work of Marighela's group. But other groups were doing the same things. One of them was the VPR (Vanguarda Popular Revolucionária), founded in 1968 by some POLOP members, who were eager for action, and MNR (Movimento Nacional Revolucionário), made up of military men who had lost their political rights.[110] The VPR, like the ALN, started out in São Paulo. It grew to such an extent that one of its former members wrote elatedly in 1969: "It has won a notoriety which assures it virtually inexhaustible possibilities of recruitment among the younger generation of revolutionaries in Brazil."[111]

Late in 1968 the "Leninist wing" of the VPR argued that the VPR had become so important that the time had come to emphasize political theory. This wing feared that the "militarist wing" might lead the VPR to "a pure empiricism in which 'urban actions' became ends in themselves." The "Leninist wing" argued that a plan to "expropriate" arms from an infantry regiment was "purely tactical, since VPR already disposed of a large number of automatic weapons for the level of the struggle it had reached."[112]

This "expropriation" attempt failed when authorities caught VPR cell members painting a truck in Army colors. Arrests followed by confessions and more arrests seriously threatened the VPR for a while. However, the VPR survived, and it survived with the "military wing" on top because leaders of the "Leninist wing" were purged.[113]

In July, 1969, the VPR joined with other forces to form VAR-Palmares. (VAR stands for Vanguarda Armada Revolucionária; Palmares was a seventeenth century "republic" of runaway slaves.) Uniting with VPR in establishing VAR-Palmares was COLINA (Comando de Libertação Nacional—which also included some former POLOP members). The new group attracted dissidents from Ação Popular, the PC do B, and the PCB. Captain Carlos Lamarca, who had been secretly associated with VPR while he worked in the Army to defend banks, brought Army rifles to VAR-Palmares when he formally joined it.[114]

VAR-Palmares members, according to one of them, carried out bank robberies efficiently: "In one case they surrounded a whole block and robbed four banks at the same time."[115]

The supplier of this information, "a young Brazilian intellectual revolutionary," stressed the role of young women who participated in these activities. He went on to say that VAR-Palmares was fighting "directly for socialism in Brazil, while Marighela thought that socialism must be the second phase of the movement, following the unification of all popular forces and the establishment of a popular government without a clear socialist organization." "We think in terms of working internationalism, but this internationalism must respect national differences, and differences of strategy. It's true that Brazilian revolutionaries are very critical of the orientation given by the Soviet Union to the international movement. They generally are closer to Cuban or Chinese orientation, but this doesn't mean directly accepting the international strategies defended by the Cubans or the Chinese. And they want to make their own criticisms and have the opportunity to judge independently what is happening in international affairs."[116]

Marighela told the urban guerrilla fighters to attract popular support by stressing their efforts to help the ordinary people against high taxes, the increasing cost of living, low wages, and high profits. He gave this advice in his

Manual do Guerrilheiro Urbano, a booklet released in June, 1969.[117] The *Manual* spoke of shooting as the "be-all and end-all" of the urban guerrilla, and discussed such topics as the most suitable weapon (the sub-machine gun .45 INA) and the need for quick, offensive movements by "firing groups," made up of not more than four or five people. Ambushes, Marighela wrote, could best be carried out by snipers working alone, and he suggested that they trap their victims by issuing false appeals for help. The Seven Deadly Sins of the Urban Guerrilla were listed: inexperience, boastfulness, over-valuing the urban struggle (at the expense of fighting in the countryside), "disproportion between our action and our available logistic infra-structure," precipitateness, temerity, and improvisation.[118]

It seemed to Marighela, who had a high regard for student revolutionaries, that the urban guerrilla movement could only benefit from Decree Law 477 of February 26, 1969, because students expelled from universities under this decree found themselves automatically prevented from rematriculating at any Brazilian university for three years.[119] In his *Manual* he wrote: "The students with their well-known sharpness discard pacifist and opportunistic taboos with ease, and rapidly acquire good political, technical, and military training. And since they do not have much to do once they have been expelled from the schools where they have been studying, they can devote themselves entirely to revolution."[120]

Marighela's *Manual* discussed kidnapping: "Kidnapping American personalities who live in Brazil, or who have come to visit here, is a most important form of protest against the penetration of U.S. imperialism into our country."[121]

The kidnapping of United States Ambassador Charles Burke Elbrick on September 4, 1969, was carried out by Marighela's ALN and a Rio group of former PCB members: MR8 (Movimento Revolucionário de 8 de Outubro—honoring Ché Guevara, killed on October 8, 1967). The kidnapping plan is said to have been elaborated by Joaquim Câmara Ferreira, who, after helping to found the POC (Partido Operário Comunista) in 1968, became a close associate of Marighela.[122] In carrying out the plan, three terrorists held up the Embassy limousine when Ambassador Elbrick was being driven to the chancellery after lunching at the Embassy residence. Transferred to a Volks-wagen station wagon, the Ambassador was struck with a pistol butt for refusing to close his eyes, and was bound in large piece of canvas. He was taken to a house, which the terrorists controlled, and confined to a room.[123]

At midnight the Brazilian government released for widespread publication and broadcast, as demanded by the kidnappers, a declaration drawn up by the MR8 and the ALN. It offered to release the Ambassador if, within twenty-four hours, "the dictatorship" would agree to fly fifteen political prisoners to a nation where they could enjoy asylum; otherwise, the declaration said, "we shall execute the ambassador."[124] The government accepted the terms, and fifteen political prisoners were quickly released from jails and flown to Mexico City (from where they made their way to Cuba). Elbrick was released.

Among the fifteen freed prisoners were terrorists who had been involved in the assassination of Captain Chandler and in an assassination attempt against Brazilian President Costa e Silva.[125] Others released were one PCB member (Gregório Bezerra) and some student leaders, such as Luís Travassos, Vladimir Palmeira, and José Dirceu, who had been arrested at the UNE National Congress of 1968. News items furnished by representatives of Bezerra and a few of the student leaders, who hoped for early liberty under regular legal procedures, suggested that they were not keen on the flight to Mexico, which would ban them from returning to Brazil, but were cooperating in order that the whole deal not collapse.

According to one report, the list of prisoners to be freed was drawn up by Joaquim Câmara Ferreira and reflected his belief that all leftists should work together in the "revolutionary war." Marighela, described as favoring a "Cuban line," was said to have been angry about the list and to have called Câmara Ferreira "insubordinate, no longer respecting the ideas of the leader."[126] But Marighela's "revolutionary greeting to the fifteen patriots exchanged for the U.S. ambassador" makes it clear that he, too, wanted all leftists to work together.

Marighela's "revolutionary greeting," issued in the name of the ALN, reflected its author's pleasure at the "humiliation" suffered by the "Brazilian dictatorship" and the United States government. It expressed support for OLAS, and declared that "the Brazilian people . . . are advancing resolutely, side by side with the peoples of Latin America, with their gaze firmly fixed on the Cuban revolution, symbol of the triumph of the armed revolutionary movement."[127] It called for unity: "not simply unity among revolutionaries, but the unity of the whole Brazilian people, in order to establish a revolutionary people's government."

Following the kidnapping of Ambassador Elbrick, the authorities intensified the hunt for Marighela and suspected terrorists. The capture of twenty-three individuals on the weekend starting Friday, October 31, 1969, brought to the jails twelve seminarians of the Dominican Order and—more importantly—a Dominican priest and a former Dominican priest, both of whom had been associated with the ALN and close to Marighela.[128] These two men were forced to lure Marighela into a trap.[129]

In São Paulo on November 4, when Marighela and members of his guard walked toward a parked car where the priest and former priest sat waiting, they saw some loving couples in cars, and laborers working with bricks. They were all men and women of the São Paulo DOPS (Departamento de Ordem Política e Social). While about forty of them threatened to shoot, Marighela's surrender was demanded. But Marighela refused to yield. In the shooting which followed, Marighela and a passer-by were killed. A young woman of the DOPS died of wounds soon after.

Later a DOPS official told Cardinal Agnelo Rossi and another visitor that the Dominicans had not betrayed Marighela but that some members of the order "had become enmeshed in a plot which had been well-mounted by the inspectors and commissioners of the political police."[130] The enmeshment was denied by Catholic spokesmen.

Some of the government authorities said that the shooting of Ché Guevara had been the death-blow of continental rural guerrilla warfare and that, similarly, the shooting of Marighela would be the death-blow of Brazilian urban guerrilla activities. However, just about when they were uttering these thoughts, and while the DOPS young woman was being buried at services attended by leading police officers, terrorists carried out another sensational bank robbery.

There was no immediate slowing down of the terrorist movement following the shooting of the man who in 1966 and 1967 had so vigorously rejected the PCB's peaceful path and then gone on in 1968 and 1969 to practice what he had preached. Indeed, the kidnapping of foreign diplomats in Brazil reached a high point in 1970, provoking Germany's Foreign Minister to ask: "Should the Ambassador go around inside a tank?"[131] The victims were the Japanese Consul General in São Paulo (seized on March 12), the German Ambassador (seized on July 11), and the Swiss Ambassador (seized on December 7). Following the example set by the kidnappers of Ambassador Elbrick, the abductions were carried out by closing in on the victims while they were in their automobiles. A guard of the German Ambassador and a guard of the Swiss Ambassador were killed while trying to resist the kidnappers.

The Japanese Consul General was released on March 16 after five Brazilian political prisoners, selected by the terrorists, were flown to Mexico City. One of the freed political prisoners had been involved in the abduction of Ambassador Elbrick. Two of the five were women. One was the widow of a terrorist killed by the police in February; she was accompanied to Mexico by her three small children. The other woman was Maurina Borges da Silveira, the Mother Superior of an orphanage in Ribeirão Prêto in São Paulo State, who had been arrested for hiding terrorists in the orphanage. Upon reaching Mexico City she told the press that she had been tortured in the Ribeirão Prêto jail.

The abduction of German Ambassador Ehrenfried von Holleben by men associated with Carlos Lamarca[132] in June, 1970, was followed by the release, at the kidnappers' demand, of forty political prisoners. This release was said to have been "the stiffest price ever paid in ransom for a diplomat" in Latin America.[133] Among the forty were at least three men who had been jailed for their roles in abducting Ambassador Elbrick. Spokesman for the forty was Apolônio Pinto de Carvalho, the 58-year-old co-founder of the PCBR who had distinguished himself in the Spanish Civil War and French Resistance.

To be the host country, the kidnappers chose Algeria over Mexico and Chile. After a Varig Airlines plane brought the released prisoners to their destination, Apolônio de Carvalho said: "We don't have anything against the Ambassador or West Germany. It so happens that in Brazil the kidnapping of prominent foreigners is the only way to free our revolutionaries."[134] Some of the released prisoners complained of having been tortured. Dulce de Sousa said that she had helped kill Charles Chandler as an act of "revolutionary justice for the crimes committed by Chandler in Vietnam and Bolivia."[135]

On June 13, after an ordeal of 123 hours in the hands of terrorists in a small house near Rio's Maracanã soccer stadium, the German Ambassador to Brazil was set free. Contributing to the delay had been mixups about the names of two men on the list of forty and a complaint by the kidnappers about "too much policing" in Rio.

The authorities stepped up the fight against the terrorists. Among those arrested in October, 1970, was Joaquim Câmara Ferreira, considered to be Marighela's successor. Soon after his arrest he died, reportedly of a heart attack. In November, 1970, approximately 4,000 suspects were rounded up and held briefly to prevent an outbreak of abductions, rumored to be planned by the ALN for the first anniversary of Marighela's death.[136]

The kidnapping of Swiss Ambassador Biovanni Enrico Bucher in Rio on December 7, 1970, was carried out by seven terrorists, including one woman, during an attack in which his car was surrounded by four other cars in the midst of rush hour traffic. The Ambassador, his bodyguard mortally wounded, shouted while being forced into the kidnappers' Volkswagen: "I never thought this would happen to me in this country."[137] In the Ambassador's limousine the kidnappers left pamphlets issued by the ALN, the Operação Joaquim Câmara Ferreira, and the Comando Juarez Guimarães. (Guimarães was one of the growing number of terrorists who had recently met death in Brazil.)

On behalf of the kidnappers the VPR demanded that seventy political prisoners be flown to asylum in Chile. This time the negotiations took over five weeks mainly because the Brazilian government established the principle that some prisoners had committed crimes, such as murder, which were "too serious" to permit their release;[138] furthermore, the government refused to release prisoners who preferred to remain in Brazil rather than be banished from the country. While 1,500 policemen undertook a house-to-house search in Rio in an attempt to locate the Ambassador, the kidnappers submitted several lists.

The original list of seventy included eight who chose to remain in Brazil and sixteen who for other reasons were unacceptable to the Brazilian government. Only after the terrorists had submitted their fourth list on January 11, 1971, was agreement reached on seventy names. Among them were twelve women and two foreigners. President Emílio Garrastazú Médici banned the sixty-eight Brazilians from Brazilian territory and declared the two foreigners expelled.

At the airport in Santiago, Chile, on January 14, 1971, the released prisoners showed clenched fists and sang the *"Internationale"* for the benefit of the press. The warm welcome they received was in contrast to the treatment given by the Chilean authorities to the Brazilian security agents who had escorted the liberated prisoners. Only one Brazilian agent was permitted to leave the plane. Seeking to deliver a document to the Brazilian Military Attaché in Chile, he was detained for three hours in a room at the airport while a crowd chanted that the Brazilian agents were "torturers."[139] According to one report, a Chilean police agent tore up the document which the Brazilian agent hoped to deliver.[140]

Late in December, 1970, before the Swiss Ambassador was allowed to depart from the small, poorly ventilated room where he spent forty days, Luís Carlos Prestes' views on terrorism were given wide publicity. Acts of terrorism by urban guerrillas, Prestes wrote, were having no "lasting consequences." They showed no sign of being able to topple the government. According to Prestes they stimulated "the idea of absolute power" for the "oppressors."[141]

While Prestes recognized the "courage and audacity" of Marighela and Mário Alves de Sousa Vieira (who also died during a clash with the police), he insisted that their "political errors"—their "leftist adventurism and opportunism"—had been harmful to the Brazilian revolutionary movement.

Prestes censured the terrorists for not concerning themselves with "the role of the masses." Arguing that "a handful of heroes" was not going to "liberate the people," he called attention to the fact that for Marxist-Leninists the struggle is a class struggle.

"After 1964," Prestes was quoted as saying, "the only correct revolutionary attitude was to admit the defeat, draw back, and once more begin the patient work of propaganda on the level of the masses."[142]

NOTES

1. Interview with Leôncio Basbaum, São Paulo, Nov. 16, 1966.

2. The PCB's internal fight of 1956–57 is vividly described in Osvaldo Peralva, *O Retrato* (Pôrto Alegre: Editôra Globo, 1962).

3. *Tribuna Esportiva*, Feb. 7, 1963.

4. George W. Bemis, *From Crisis to Revolution, Monthly Case Studies* (University of Southern California, 1964), p. 228.

5. *O Estado de S. Paulo*, Jan. 4, 1964.

6. At the Fifth Congress, held in Rio de Janeiro in 1960, there was elected the PCB national directorship which was to govern during most of the years covered by this paper. The following (all of them making up the membership of the Central Committee) were elected: (1) members of the *Comissão Executiva Nacional:* Luís Carlos Prestes, Carlos Marighela, Giocondo Alves Dias, Ramiro Luchesi, Manoel Jover Teles, Mário Alves de Sousa Vieira, Orlando Bonfim Júnior, Ivan Ramos Ribeiro, Marco Antônio Coelho, Geraldo Rodrigues dos Santos, Elson Costa, and Sérgio Costa; members of the *Secretariado:* Luís Carlos Prestes, Antônio Ribeiro Granja, Mário Dinarco Reis, Giocondo Alves Dias, and Severino Teodoro de Melo; *Membros Efectivos* (of the Central Committee): Agostinho Dias de Oliveira, Jacob Gorender, Agliberto Vieira de Azevedo, Osvaldo Pacheco da Silva, Antônio Chamorro, Benedito de Carvalho, David Capistrano da Costa, Armênio Guedes, Zuleika Alambert, Renato de Oliveira Mota, Armando Ziller, Francisco Antônio Leivas Otero, Antônio Ribeiro Granja, Roberto Morena, Apolônio Pinto de Carvalho, Astrogildo Pereira, Adalberto Timóteo, Orestes Timbaúba Rodrigues, Luís Tenório de Lima, Lourival da Costa Vilar, Miguel Batista, Lourdes Benaim and Joaquim Câmara Ferreira.

7. The Goulart government, preparing to expropriate lands near federal railroads, highways, and irrigation works, drew up a decree affecting all properties exceeding 200 hectares; but at the request of the PCB, which did not want to alienate medium-size property owners from "popular fronts," the government modified its stand and issued its decree affecting properties only in excess of 500 hectares.

8. *Teses Para Discussão*, special supplement of *Novos Rumos*, March 27–April 2, 1964; see p. 14, col. 3.

9. Leonel Brizola, *Organização dos "Grupos de Onze Companheiros" ou "Comandos Nacionalistas,"* Rio de Janeiro, Nov. 29, 1963.

10. Interview with Colonel Osneli Martineli, Rio de Janeiro, Oct. 12, 1966.

11. Brizola's secret instructions, reproduced in *O Estado de S. Paulo*, July 16, 1964; also in Inquérito Political Militar 709, *O Comunismo no Brasil*, IV, pp. 396–408.

12. See "Reply to Khrushchov: Resolution of the Central Committee of the Communist Party of Brazil," *Peking Review*, Vol. 6 (Sept. 13, 1963). This article is made up of excerpts of the Resolution of the CC of the PC do B adopted on July 27, 1963 and published in *A Classe Operária* of Aug. 1–15, 1963. It explains the

establishment of the PC do B and attacks the PCB leadership and the CC of the Communist Party of the Soviet Union.

13. Diary of Wang-chin, revealed by Colonel Gustavo Borges in Rio de Janeiro on May 9, 1964; see *O Estado de S. Paulo*, May 10, 1964.

14. See Francisco Julião, *Que São as Ligas Camponesas?* (Rio de Janeiro: Editôra Civilização Brasileira, S.A., 1962).

15. Leda Barreto, *Julião, Nordeste, Revolução* (Rio de Janeiro: Editôra Civilização Brasileira, S.A., 1963), p. 83.

16. Interview with Márcio Moreira Alves, Rio de Janeiro, December 11, 1967. Interview with Padre Paulo Crespo, Recife, Oct. 16, 1968.

17. Document reproduced in *O Estado de S. Paulo*, Jan. 29, 1963. See also "Report from Cuban Agent Coincides with the Facts Gleaned by the Brazilian Military" (translated from *Correio da Manhã*, Feb. 1, 1963), given on pp. 99–101 in Testimony of Jules Dubois (Oct. 2, 1963) in *Hearing before the Subcommittee to Investigate the Administration of the Internal Security Act and Other Internal Security Laws of the Committee on the Judiciary, United States Senate, Eighty-eighth Congress, First Session. (Documentation of Communist Penetration in Latin America).* Lt.-Col. Nicolau José Seixas' report is given in Appendix II (pp. 389–91) of the same hearing.

18. Interview with Irineu de Macedo Soares, Rio de Janeiro, Nov. 1, 1966.

19. Legal denouncement of PORT, reproduced in *O Estado de S. Paulo*, April 30, 1965.

20. Interview with Arnaldo Sussekind, Rio de Janeiro, Oct. 26, 1965.

21. Interview with Gilberto Crockatt de Sá, Rio de Janeiro, Dec. 17, 1968.

22. J. V. Freitas Marcondes, *Radiografia da Linderança Sindical Paulista* (Instituto Cultural do Trabalho, São Paulo, 1964), p. 51.

23. For a report on communism and youth movements, see Escola Superior de Guerra, *O Comunismo e os Movimentos da Juventude*, Rio de Janeiro, 1965.

24. See Departamento de Ordem Política e Social, *Relatório: Inquérito Instaurado Contra Luiz Carlos Prestes e Outros por Ocasião da Revolução de Março de 1964* (São Paulo, 1964).

25. See Luiz Carlos Prestes, *Carta ao Dr. Sobral Pinto*, 1965.

26. See Carlos Marighela, *Por Que Resisti à Prisão* (Edições Contemporâneas, 1965).

27. In *Eu, Gregório Bezerra, Acuso!* 1967, Bezerra tells of his tribulations following his capture in 1964. By the end of 1967 Bezerra's total time spent in jail (around 16 years) was about to surpass that of Agliberto Vieira de Azevedo, another Communist who used his weapons in 1935. Agliberto Vieira de Azevedo, arrested in July, 1964, was freed on a habeas corpus appeal in Sept., 1966. See Agliberto Vieira de Azevedo, *Minha Vida de Revolucionário*, 1967.

28. See Márcio Moreira Alves, *Torturas e Torturados* (Rio de Janeiro, 1967).

29. The investigation resulted in the publication of the four-volume Inquérito Policial Military 709, *O Comunismo no Brasil* (Rio de Janeiro: Biblioteca do Exército, Editôra, 1966–67).

30. *Jornal do Brasil*, Nov. 24, 1966.

31. 5ª R.M. e 5ª D.I., *IPM sôbre Atividades Comunistas, Paraná e Santa Catarina* (Curitiba, 1967).

32. Interview with Ferdinando de Carvalho, Curitiba, Paraná, Nov. 10, 1967.

33. "Tese para Discussão" (mimeographed).

34. "Sôbre a 'Tese para Discussão'" (mimeographed).

35. Non-voting alternates are those who, nominated for CC posts, fail to be elected at the National Congress.

36. "Le Communisme au Brésil en 1965," *Est & Ouest*, No. 357 (Paris, France, Feb. 16–28, 1966).

37. "Los Grupos Revolucionarios del Brasil," *Este & Oeste*, IX, 142 (Caracas, Venezuela, Nov. 1970), p. 7.

38. Partido Comunista Brasileiro, "Trabalho Especial" (typewritten), 1966.

39. *Arma da Crítica*, No. 4, quoted in *O Guia* (Orgão dos comunistas da orla marítima), No. 26 (Rio de Janeiro, June, 1966).

40. *O Guia*, No. 26 (June, 1966).

41. "Teses, Aprovadas na Reunião do Comitê Central, Primeira Quinzena do Mês de Junho de 1966." See 6th (last) Section.

42. "Los Grupos Revolucionarios del Brasil," *Este & Oeste*, IX, 142 (Caracas, Venezuela, Nov., 1970), p. 8.

43. Ibid.

44. Ibid.

45. *O Isqueiro*, No. 24 (Aug., 1966), Guanabara.

46. Suplemento de Debates, No. 2 in *O Isqueiro*, No. 30 (April, 1967), Guanabara. See also *O Isqueiro*, No. 33 (July, 1967).

47. See "Carta + Denúncia, A tôdas as organizações e a todos os membros do PCB" (mimeographed), signed "Um velho militante comunista da GB." See also *O Isqueiro*, Nos. 29–33.

48. *Combater*, No. 31 (June, 1967, "Edição Extra"), Recife, Pernambuco. (By this time the PCB's national leadership had accepted much of the "Pernambuco thesis" of May, 1964.)

49. A VIIIª Conferência Estadual do PCB do Rio Grande do Sul, "Resolução Política da Conferência Estadual do Rio Grande do Sul" (mimeographed).

50. "Resolução" (typewritten) of Convenção Municipal de Curitiba do PCB (early 1967). The resolution of the Paraná State Convention was drawn up by the same individual who drew up the Curitiba resolution and reflected the same sentiments.

51. "Los Grupos Revolucionarios del Brasil," *Este & Oeste*, IX, 142 (Nov., 1970), p. 10.

52. Carlos Marighela, *For the Liberation of Brazil*, pp. 184 and 187; "O camarada Menezes" (Carlos Marighela), quoted in fourth section of *Pela Unidade do Partido* (*Resolução do Comitê Central do Partido Comunista Brasileiro*), Sept., 1967, which accompanied *Voz Operária* (No. 32), Oct., 1967. See also "Los Grupos Revolucionarios del Brasil," *Este & Oeste*, IX, 142, p. 9.

53. "Resoluções Aprovadas na XVIᵃ Reunião (Ordinária) do Comitê Central (V) do Partido Comunista Brasileiro," March, 1967.

54. "Los Grupos Revolucionarios del Brasil," *Este & Oeste*, IX, 142, p. 10.

55. *Documentos e Resoluções: São Paulo (Conferência Estadual)*, April, 1967, p. 1, quoting "o camarada Menezes" (Marighela).

56. "Unidade e Ação do Partido pela Revolução Brasileira—Resolução do Comitê Estadual de São Paulo do Partido Comunista Brasileiro" (typewritten), Sept., 1967, p. 1.

57. *Voz Operária* (No. 31), Sept., 1967, p. 2.

58. *O Globo*, Rio de Janeiro, Aug. 7, 1967.

59. Carlos Marighela, *For the Liberation of Brazil*, pp. 124–26.

60. *Voz Operária* (No. 32), Oct., 1967, p. 3.

61. *Voz Operária* (No. 35), Jan., 1968, p. 1.

62. VI Congresso do Partido Comunista Brasileiro, *Estatutos do Partido Comunista Brasileiro*, Dec., 1967, p. 1.

63. VI Congresso do Partido Comunista Brasileiro, *Resolução Política*, Dec., 1967, p. 5.

64. *Realidade*, Ano I, No. 10 (Jan., 1967—Edição Especial: A Mulher Hoje). See p. 23: See also Lloyd A. Free, *Some International Implications of the Political Psychology of Brazilians* (Sept., 1961; 2d ptg., Institute for International Social Research, 1961), pp. 46–47.

65. *Le Monde* (Paris, France), July 31, 1965 (p. 6).

66. "Resolução da Sexta Conferência do Partido Comunista do Brasil (Junho de 1966): União dos Brasileiros para Livrar o País de Crise, da Ditadura e da Ameaça Neocolonialista." (mimeographed). See Section IV, pp. 25–34.

67. IV Exército, Inquérito Policial Militar—questioning Francisco Julião (typewritten document, Sept. 14, 1964). See also Francisco Julião, *Até Quarta, Isabela!* (Rio de Janeiro: Editôra Civilização Brasileira, S.A., n.d.), p. 62.

68. *Frente Operária* (mimeographed periodical), Year XIV, No. 145 (Second half of March, 1966), pp. 11–15. According to *Este & Oeste* (IX, 142), Posadas feels that three great Communists have existed in the twentieth cenutry: Lenin, Trotsky, and himself.

69. "Escola de Delatores" (mimeographed publication), third edition, July, 1967.

70. "Declaração Política do 4⁰ Congresso da ORMPO" (mimeographed), Sept., 1967. Also "Organização Revolucionária Marxista—Política Operária: Programa Socialista para o Brasil (aprovado no IV Congresso Nacional, Setembro de 1967)."

71. "Los Grupos Revolucionarios del Brasil," *Este & Oeste*, IX, 142 (Nov., 1970), p. 12.

72. Interview with José Rota, São Paulo, Nov. 30, 1965.

73. Interview with Colonel Ferdinando de Carvalho, Rio de Janeiro, Oct. 11, 1966.

74. "Los Grupos Revolucionarios del Brasil," *Este & Oeste*, IX, 142 (Nov., 1970), p. 9.

75. Ibid.

76. Interview with Raimundo Moniz de Aragão, Rio de Janeiro, Oct. 11, 1966.

77. "Before 1964 the UNE was corrupted. However, now the movement has prestige. The state, by its performance, has made the movement popular." This observation, together with unfavorable comments about Brizola and other politicians who helped the pre-1964 UNE, was made in an interview given to the writer in São Paulo on Nov. 21, 1968, by jailed student leaders Vladimir Palmeira, Luís Travassos, José Dirceu de Oliveira e Silva, and Antônio Ribas.

78. Arthur José Poerner, *O Poder Jovem*, p. 305; George H. Dunne, "Happening in São Paulo," *America* (Sept. 23, 1967).

79. See Emanuel de Kadt, "Religion, the Church, and Social Change in Brasil," in *The Politics of Conformity in Latin America*, Claudio Véliz, ed. New York: Oxford University Press, 1967. See also Thomas G. Sanders, "Brazil's Catholic Left," *America* (Nov. 18, 1967).

80. Inquérito Policial Militar No. 709, *O Comunismo no Brasil*, III, 503–47.

81. See Márcio Moreira Alves, "Discurso Pronunciado a 27/11/67 na Câmara dos Deputados" (mimeographed).

82. Escola Superior de Guerra, *O Comunismo e os Movimentos da Juventude*, p. 44. Anselmo, speaking in Havana in Aug., 1967, attributed his escape in part to the "corruption" of the Brazilian police. A few days later Brazilian authorities gave the absent sailor an 18-year jail sentence, based largely on his activities in March, 1964.

83. Ação Popular's mimeographed releases in 1966 included "Textos para Militantes," "Estratégia Revolucionária," and "Ação Popular."

84. Ação Popular, "Resolução sôbre o Debate Teorético e Ideológico" (mimeographed), April, 1967. See also Ação Popular's National Committee, "Assuntos Gerais," May, 1967, containing plans (including election methods) for the Second National Congress.

85. *O Estado de S. Paulo*, Jan. 19, 1964.

86. Interview with Clodsmidt Riani, Juiz de Fora, Nov. 2, 1968. All the arrangements having to do with the rally were made by the CGT. CGT member Riani, head of the CNTI, "presided over the rally."

87. Leôncio Basbaum, in an interview published in 1969, estimated PCB membership at that time to be "around ten thousand." See Josué Machado, "PC Brasileiro Errou Tanto que Fêz Mais Mal a Si Mesmo do que ao Regime em Vigor," *Jornal do Brasil*, April 27, 1969.

88. The periodical *Política Operária*, once the organ of POLOP, became the central organ of the new Partido Operário Comunista. Issue 17 (May, 1968), of *Política Operária*, tells of the foundation of the Partido Operário Comunista to work for a general strike by factory workers and "to prepare armed forms of class struggle, beginning with guerrilla warfare, which will establish the alliance with the peasants." Additional information about the establishment of the PCBR and POC may be found in "La Situation du Communisme au Brésil," *Est & Ouest*, Nos. 419 and 420 (Feb. 1–15 and 16–28, 1969), Paris, France.

89. Carlos Marighela, *For the Liberation of Brazil*, p. 52.

90. Fay Haussman, letter, Jan. 23, 1971.

91. "O Líder Foragido e Sua Mulher," *Veja*, Sept. 25, 1968. This article is one of a series on the UNE which appeared in the weekly, *Veja*, between Sept. 11 and Nov. 12, 1968.

92. "A Palavra de Vladimir," *Veja*, Oct. 2, 1968.

93. *Jornal do Brasil*, July 16, 1968.

94. Fay Haussman, letter, Jan. 23, 1971.

95. Partido Comunista Brasileiro Revolucionário (PCBR), "Reencontro Histórico ou Simples Mistificação?" (typewritten), p. 1.

96. Ibid., p. 6.

97. Ibid., p. 8. See also "Resolução da Comissão Executiva Nacional do Partido Comunista Brasileiro Revolucionário (PCBR) sôbre Atividades Divisionistas no Comité Estadual da Guanabara" (typewritten), June, 1968.

98. Milovan Djilas, "There'll Be Many Different Communisms in 1984," *The New York Times Magazine*, March 23, 1969.

99. "Terror e Reação," *Veja*, Oct. 23, 1968.

100. Ibid.

101. Ibid.

102. Ibid.

103. Richard Gott, Introduction to Carlos Marighela, *For the Liberation of Brazil*. See p. 14.

104. Ninety-second Congress, First Session (May 4, 5, and 11, 1971), *Hearings before the Subcommittee on Western Hemisphere Affairs* (Frank Church, Chairman), p. 42.

105. Carlos Marighela, *For the Liberation of Brazil*, p. 122.

106. Ibid., p. 23.

107. Ibid., p. 100.

108. From ALN document dated Jan., 1969, quoted in "Los Grupos Revolucionarios del Brasil," *Este & Oeste*, IX, 142 (Nov., 1970), p. 14.

109. Carlos Marighela, *For the Liberation of Brazil*, p. 99.

110. "Los Grupos Revolucionarios del Brasil," *Este & Oeste*, IX, 142.

111. João Quartim, "Note to Readers of NLR," *New Left Review*, No. 59 (Jan.–Feb., 1970).

112. Ibid.

113. Ibid.

114. "Interview with a Brazilian Revolutionary," *LIBERATION News Service*, No. 225 (Jan. 14, 1970), pp. 10–11. This article says that Captain Lamarca brought 200 rifles. The *New York Times* (September 26, 1971) states that Captain Lamarca, a sergeant, and two enlisted men brought the terrorists 63 automatic rifles and sixteen submachine guns from their infantry regiment.

115. Ibid., p. 9.

116. Ibid., p. 12.

117. Carlos Marighela, *Handbook of Urban Guerrilla Warfare* in Carlos Marig-

hela, *For the Liberation of Brazil* (Penguin Books, 1971). Also Carlos Marighela *Manuel du Guérillero Urbain* in Carlos Marighela, *Pour la Libération du Brésil*, edited by Conrad Detrez (Paris, 1970).

118. Carlos Marighela, *For the Liberation of Brazil*, pp. 93–94.

119. Fay Haussman, letter, May 11, 1971.

120. Carlos Marighela, *Pour la Libération du Brésil*, p. 137.

121. Carlos Marighela, *For the Liberation of Brazil*, p. 87.

122. "Estratégia para Matar o Terror," *Veja*, No. 62 (Nov. 12, 1969), p. 30.

123. *Brazil Herald*, Sept. 5, 6, 7, 9, and 10, 1969.

124. Carlos Marighela, *For the Liberation of Brazil*, p. 27.

125. Ronald M. Schneider, *The Political System of Brazil*, p. 295.

126. "Estratégia para Matar o Terror," *Veja*, No. 62.

127. Carlos Marighela, *For the Liberation of Brazil*, pp. 28–29.

128. "Estratégia para Matar o Terror," *Veja*, No. 62. See also *Brazil Herald*, Nov. 8, 1969.

129. *Le Monde*, Paris, France, Nov. 20, 1970.

130. Ibid., based on information in *O São Paulo* (organ of the Catholic archdiocese of São Paulo), Nov. 29, 1969.

131. *Brazil Herald*, June 13, 1970.

132. Ronald M. Schneider, *The Political System of Brazil*, p. 317. The *New York Times*, Sept. 26, 1971.

133. *Brazil Herald*, June 17, 1970.

134. Ibid., June 18, 1970.

135. Ibid.

136. Ronald Schneider, *The Political System of Brazil*, p. 325.

137. *Brazil Herald*, Dec. 9, 1970.

138. Ibid., Dec. 24, 1970.

139. Ibid., Jan. 16, 1970.

140. Ibid.

141. *Correio da Manhã* and *O Estado de S. Paulo*, Dec. 29, 1970, based on Prestes' comments "num artigo de 7,500 palavvras, publicado, ontem, em Paris, pela *Nova Revista Internacional*, orgão teórico e de informações dos partidos comunistas ortodoxos."

142. Ibid. The year 1971 amply confirmed Prestes' view about the ineffectiveness of the Brazilian terrorists. Carlos Lamarca, the last important terrorist leader, was forced to flee from the Rio-São Paulo-Minas Gerais area and go into hiding in the backlands of Bahia. While some of his lieutenants were captured, others turned themselves over to the authorities with the explanation that "Lamarca was no longer a director of revolutionary ideas, but rather, a simple bandit." (See *Diário de Notícas*, Sept. 19, 1971.) In the middle of September, 1971, Lamarca and a companion were killed in a battle with the police in Bahia.

LOOKING AHEAD

Donald L. Herman

T IS POSSIBLE, AT THE CONCLUSION OF OUR STUDY, TO MAKE SEVERAL PROJEC-
tions into the future based on the two themes which have been developed.
One always takes a risk when he attempts to prognosticate about an area
as volatile and complex as Latin America. Nevertheless, several trends seem
to be clear based on our findings thus far.

As long as Russian nationalism extends into the area, we can expect the
Soviet Union to continue in the effort to further its interests as an important
part of the Communist movement.[1] We might have to add the element which
tries to further China's interests, but this will depend upon the development
of Chinese power in the future.

There may well be a decline of Soviet influence within the Latin-American
Communist movement, as exemplified in Brazil. But this does not mean that
Soviet influence in Latin America necessarily will decline. On the contrary,
Soviet relations with particular Latin-American governments may be
strengthened as Soviet ties with local Communist movements are loosened.
This can cause additional strains within the Latin-American Communist
movement, and we see Fidel Castro highly critical of certain Latin-American
governments with which the Soviet Union is developing trade agreements
and cultural exchanges.

Third, in the conflict which brings a major external force, the Soviet Union,
into opposition with a major internal force, the Jacobin Left, we see a continued weakening of the Latin-American Communist movement. Perhaps the
Jacobin Left will appear as some form of National Communism. Furthermore,
we may be able to observe the seeds of a major change in form through the
quarrels between the Havana-oriented Jacobin Left and the Peking-oriented
Communist groups. Peking is opposed to a guerrilla group not led by the
proletariat, i.e., the Communist party. Moscow would agree with Peking in
this regard. But if the Havana version of guerrilla warfare were successful
over the Moscow and Peking tactics, the framework could change with the
decline in importance of the Communist party within the Latin-American
Communist movement. Thus from a dispute over tactics in the 1930s—insurrection in Brazil vs. the Popular Front in Chile—the schism in the Latin-
American Communist movement in the 1970s involves tactics (violence *vs.*
non-violence), leadership of the Communist movement, and the form the
movement is to take.

We can expect the various elements of the Communist movement to continue to be opportunistic by taking advantage of the failures of the non-Communist revolutionary movements and the left wing democratic regimes. The problems are immense. As one author has indicated, a Marshall Plan with its emphasis on the reconstruction of Western Europe after World War II would be inadequate for Latin America, which must emphasize new industries and in fact new economies.[2] Elements of the middle class will continue in their attempt to alleviate the conditions of the mass of the people in their countries. And in this effort, some of them will gravitate toward the Communist movement and listen to the words emanating from Moscow, Peking, or Havana.

There probably will be setbacks, not only to the Communist movement but to political development in Latin America, as the more conservative elements of the military try to eliminate what they consider to be a Communist threat. Although the immediate threat may be eliminated by virtue of a military coup, what happens to the Communist movement when the military decides to stay in power over a period of time? Here we have an area for further research—the development of Communism under the rule of the military.

One specialist on Latin-American affairs believes the setback to the Communist movement because of direct military intervention in politics may be only temporary.[3] In fact, Víctor Alba maintains that the solidification of the power of the military regime offers "the next chance for Communism in Latin America." Thus, by overthrowing a government to lessen and if possible destroy the influence of Communism in a country, the military may sow the seeds of its own destruction.

According to Mr. Alba, the non-Communist revolutionary movements have failed because they have not provided the mass of people with economic and social liberty. "It is this failure (and not poverty, as many claim) that creates a fertile ground for Communist propaganda and also for the dictatorial paternalism of the experts, for the efficient dictatorship." The efficient experts accept the Marxist authoritarian methods to justify their actions, and they find themselves using Communist tactics to fight Communism. However, the rule of the efficient dictatorship leads to violence because the promises made to the masses are not fulfilled. It then becomes necessary for the government to turn to the Communists for help in keeping the situation under control.[4] This is the stage of Nasserism[5] in Latin America, a transition between two opposing forces—"We would say that Nasserism is the Fascism of the underdeveloped countries in the epoch of the struggle between democracy and totalitarianism."

If we take Mr. Alba's analysis and create a continuum, or perhaps a vicious circle might be more appropriate terminology, we can observe the stages of non-Communist and Communist political development in Latin America as one becomes an outgrowth of the other—left wing democratic reform movement—militarism—Communism. The failures of the reform movement lead to militarism which in turn, because of the "inefficiency of the efficient ones," leads to totalitarian Communism. The way to break the cycle, according to Mr. Alba, is to have the democratic reform movement succeed; "the political democracy must be transformed into economic and social democracy to avoid new dictatorships."

One can test Mr. Alba's analysis by applying it to current political developments in Latin America, particularly in the cases of Argentina and Brazil. The "efficient experts" of the respective countries have been in control of Brazil since 1964, now under the regime of General-President Emilio Garrastazu Médici, and in control of Argentina since 1966, now under the regime of Lt. General-President Alejandro A. Lanusse. After the initial overthrow of the democratic reform movements, have these dictatorships acted as catalysts in the development of Communism in their countries? Will the Communist movement continue to splinter in Brazil, or will the various factions follow the example of the non-Communist groups and unite in the common effort to oppose the military dictatorship? In this regard, we should consider also the 1969 land reform program of the Peruvian military junta as an indication of what may occur in other countries. If the Peruvian government truly becomes reform-oriented as many of its supporters say it will, then the setbacks to social and economic development which have accompanied militarism in the past may not necessarily hold true for all cases in the period ahead.

Thus we conclude with the observation made at the beginning of this study. Communism in Latin America is a dynamic process. And because of this, periodic scholarly treatment of the phenomenon is required. Old theories must be tested, new theories must be created, and the process must be understood within the context of the development of Latin America.

NOTES

1. It has been reported that United States Intelligence specialists are disturbed by what they regard as a steady increase in the number and quality of Soviet agents in Latin America (*New York Times*, December 7, 1970). Costa Rica and Venezuela have reestablished diplomatic relations with the Soviet Union. Guatemala has sent a trade mission to the Communist countries of Eastern Europe (*New York Times*, March 21, 1971).

DONALD L. HERMAN

2. Herbert K. May, *Problems and Prospects of the Alliance for Progress* (New York: Frederick A. Praeger, 1968).

3. Víctor Alba, "El Ascenso del Militarismo Tecnocrático," *Panoramas*, Número 6 de Noviembre–Diciembre, 1963.

4. The dictator often will aid the Communists to gain control of the labor movement. The Communists then show their gratitude by discouraging strikes and unrest.

5. After Gamal Abdel Nasser, late president of Egypt.

LIST OF ABBREVIATIONS

General

AAPSO	Afro-Asian Peoples Solidarity Organization
Amtorg	American Trading Corporation in New York
CI	Comintern
CIA	Central Intelligence Agency (United States)
CPSU	Communist Party of the Soviet Union
KGB	Russian Intelligence Agency
MOPR	International Relief Organization of Revolutionaries
OAS	Organization of American States
USSR	Union of Soviet Socialist Republics

Latin-American

CSLA	Confederación Sindical Latino Americano (Latin-American Confederation of Trade Unions)
CTAL	Confederación de Trabajadores de América Latina (Confederation of Workers of Latin America)
CUTAL	Central Única de Trabaljadores de América Latina (Single Center of Workers of Latin America—Communist-controlled Latin American labor organization)
Iuzhamtorg	South American Trading Corporation
LASO	Latin American Solidarity Organization
OLAS	Organización Latino Americana de Solidaridad (Latin-American Solidarity Organization)

Chapter I

CTM	Confederación de Trabajadores de México (Confederation of Workers of Mexico)
APRA	American Revolutionary Popular Alliance (Aprista Party of Peru)
AD	Acción Democrática (Venezuela)
COPEI	Comité de Organización Política Electoral Independiente (Social Christian or Christian Democratic Party—Venezuela)
FDP	Frente Democrática Popular (Venezuela)
MAS	Movimiento al Socialismo (Venezuela)
MEP	Movimiento Electoral del Pueblo (Venezuela)
PCV	Communist Party of Venezuela
URD	Unión Republicana Democrática (Venezuela)

Chapter II

AD	Acción Democrática (Venezuela)
COPEI	Christian Social Party (Venezuela)
CTE	Confederacion de Trabajadores del Ecuador
CTV	Confederación de Trabajadores de Venezuela
FAR	Fuerzas Armadas Rebeldes (Rebel Armed Forces, Guatemala)
FLN	Frente de Liberacion Nacional (Ecuador)
JC	Juventud Comunista (Young Communist League, Colombia)
MI	Movimiento de la Izquierda Revolucionaria (Fidelist, Chile)
MIR	Movimiento de la Izquierda Revolucionaria (Venezuela)
MPD	Movimiento Popular Dominicano (Dominican Republic)
MR-13	13th of November Movement (Guatemala)
PCB	Partido Comunista Brasileiro
PCC	Partido Comunista de Colombia
PCC	Partido Comunista de Cuba
PCM-L	Partido Comunista Marxista-Leninista (Colombia)
PCR	Partido Comunista Revolucionario (Revolutionary Communist Party—Pro-Chinese, Chile)
PGT	Partido Guatemalteco del Trabajo (Guatemala)
PR	Partido Revolucionario (Guatemala)
PRN	Partido Revolucionario Nationalista (Venezuela)
PSA	Partido Socialista Argentino (Argentina)
PSP	Partido Socialista del Peru
PSR	Partido Socialista Revolucionario (Colombia)
PSR	Partido Socialista Revolucionario (Ecuador)
PSRE	Partido Socialista Revolucionario Ecuadoriano
UA	Unión para Avanzar (Union to Advance, Venezuela)
UCR	Unión Comunista Rebelde (Chile)
UJC	Union de Jovenes Comunistas (Colombia)
VP	Vanguardia Popular (Costa Rican Communist Party)
VPN	Vanguardia Popular Nacionalista (Venezuela)

Chapter III

FALN	Fuerzas Armadas de Liberación Nacional (Venezuela)
FAR	Rebel Armed Forces (Guatemala)
FIDEL	Left Liberation Front (Uruguay)
FLN	(Venezuela)
FRAP	Popular Action Front (Chile)
	Mexican Communist Party
PCC	Communist Party of Cuba
PCV	Partido Comunista de Venezuela
PSP	Cuban Communist Party
PURS	United Party of the Socialist Revolution

Chapter IV

CGOCM	General Confederation of Workers and Peasants of Mexico
CPM	Communist Party of Mexico
CSUM	Unitary Trade Union Confederation of Mexico
CTM	Confederación de Trabajadores de México (Confederation of Workers of Mexico)
PNR	Partido Nacional Revolucionario (National Revolutionary Party)
PRM	Partido de la Revolución Mexicana (Party of the Mexican Revolution)

Chapter V

AC	Ação Católica (Catholic Action)
ALN	Ação Libertadora Nacional (National Liberating Action)
AP	Ação Popular (Popular Action)
CC	Comitê Central (Central Committee)
CGT	Comando Geral dos Trabalhadores (General Labor Command)
CNTC	Confederação Nacional dos Trabalhadores no Comércio (National Confederation of Workers in Commerce)
CNTI	Confederação Nacional dos Trabalhadores na Indústria (National Confederation of Industrial Workers)
COLINA	Comando de Libertação Nacional (National Liberation Command)
CONTAG	Confederação Nacional dos Trabalhadores na Agricultura (National Confederation of Workers in Agriculture)
CPOS	Comissão Permanente de Organizaçoes Sindicais (Permanent Commission of Syndical Organizations)
DOPS	Departamento de Ordem Política e Social (Department of Political and Social Order)
FLN	Frente de Libertação Nacional (National Liberation Front)
FSD	Forum Sindical de Debates (Syndrical Forum of Discussions) of Santos
JEC	Juventude Estudantil Católica (Catholic Student Youth)
JUC	Juventude Universitária Católica (Catholic University Youth)
MNR	Movimento Nacional Revolucionário (National Revolutionary Movement)
MR8	Movimento Revolucionário de 8 de Outubro (Revolutionary Movement of October 8), honoring Ché Guevara, killed Oct. 8, 1967.
PCB	Partido Comunista Brasileiro (Brazilian Communist Party), Moscow-oriented

PCBR	Partido Comunista Brasileiro Revolucionário (Revolutionary Brazilian Communist Party)
PC do B	Partido Comunista do Brasil (Communist Party of Brazil), Peking-oriented
POC	Partido Operário Comunista (Labor Communist Party)
POLOP	Política Operária (Labor Politics); also called ORMPO—Organização Revolucionária Marxista—Política Operária
PORT	Partido Operário Revolucionário Trotsquista, Secção Brasileira da IV Internacional (Trotskyite Labor Revolutionary Party —Brazilian Section of the IV International)
PSB	Partido Socialista Brasileiro (Brazilian Socialist Party)
PUA	Pacto de Unidade e Ação (Pact of Unity and Action)
UBES	União Brasileira dos Estudantes Secundários (Brazilian Union of Secondary School Students)
UEE	União Estadual dos Estudantes (State Union of Students)
ULTAB	União dos Lavradores e Trabalhadores Agrícolas do Brasil (Union of Farm Hands and Agricultural Workers of Brazil)
UNE	União Nacional dos Estudantes (National Union of Students)
UME	União Metropolitana dos Estudantes (Metropolitan Union of Students
UST	União Sindical dos Trabalhadores (Syndical Union of Workers)
VAR-Palmares	Vanguarda Armada Revolucionária–Palmares (Palmares Armed Revolutionary Vanguard); Palmares was a 17th Century "republic" of runaway slaves
VPR	Vanguarda Popular Revolucionária (Popular Revolutionary Vanguard)

INDEX

AAPSO. *See* Afro-Asian Peoples Solidarity Organization
AD. *See* Acción Democrática
ALN. *See* Ação Libertadora Nacional
AP. *See* Ação Popular
APRA. *See* Aprista Party
Ação Católica. *See* Catholic Action
Ação Liberatadora Nacional: formation of, 169; as terrorist group, 171, 174–75, 177
Ação Popular: and F. Julião, 141; and agricultural unions, 144; and Communism in Brazil, 146–47; and L. Brizola, 158–59; size of, compared to size of POLOP, 162; and the UNE, 165; effect of 1964 coup on, 166–67; First and Second National Congresses of, 166, 167; in Front of Popular Mobilization, 167–68; and PCB, 168; internal struggles of, 168; and L. Travassos, 169; death of, 169; and VAR-Palmares, 173
Acción Democrática: and MAS, 31; and Venezuelan Communist Party, 62–64; and violence, 64, 65; split of, 67
Acción Social: and CTM, 127–28; and the Mexican petroleum workers, 132
Acosta, Raul: 44
Afonso, Almino: 165
Africa: and Chinese Communism, 51; Cuba advocates violence in, 57–58; mention of, 75. *See also* Afro-Asian Peoples Solidarity Organization
Afro-Asian Peoples Solidarity Organization: 97–99
age: and violence, 41; and Venezuelan Communism, 64–65; *See also* youth
Agrarian movement: Pestkovsky on, 108 n 3; Soviet-oriented groups gain control of, 166
agrarian program: lack of, 15–16
agrarian reform: in Cuba, 23–24; in Peru, 32; in Venezuela, 64; in Mexico, 116, 119–20, 122, 130, 131–32; in Brazil, 135, 137–38, 167–68
agricultural organizations: strength of Communists in, in Mexico, 129–30
agriculture: Cuban, 56–57, 96, 105
Airforce Sergeant's Club, Recife, Brazil: 161–62
Aksenov, Nikolai: 80
Alagoas, Brazil: 141
Alambert, Zuleika: 179 n 6
Alba, Víctor: 187–88
Albanian Party of Labor: and Chile, 49–50

Alexander, Robert J.: 26
Algeria: training of Communists in, 23; "Long War" in, 66; Miguel Arrais in, 158; release of Brazilian terrorists to, 177
Allende, Salvador: as president of Chile, 30; effect of, on other countries, 30–31; and Eduardo Frei, 93; and Castro, 107
Alliance for Progress: decrease in U. S. funds for, 32; Miguel Arrais denounces, 137; UNE denounces, 147
Almeida, Antônio: as pseud. for Prestes, 154
Almeida, Neri Reis de. *See* Reis de Almeida, Neri
Almeyda, Clodomiro: 50–51
Althusser, Louis: 167
Amazonas, João: and the split of the Brazilian Communist Party, 139–40; cancellation of political rights of, 147; receives jail sentence, 148; and PC do B, 160, 170; and Ação Popular, 166–67; and Grabois, 170
American Revolutionary Popular Alliance. *See* Aprista Party
Amilpa, Fernando: 125
Amorim de Miranda, Jaime: 151–52
Anaconda Copper Company: 32
anarchists: form PCB, 35; and early Communist parties, 35, 37; and CTM, 126; and Roberto Morena, 148
Angarita, Isaias Medina: 19
Anselmo dos Santos, José: and Ação Popular, 166; imprisonment of, 183 n 82
anti-Americanism: USSR leads, 20; and utilization of the inexperienced, 22; and the Cuban Revolution, 24; in Peru under Juan Velasco, 45. *See also* United States
Anti-Imperialist League: and Comintern, 14; and education under Lázaro Cárdenas, 123
Aprista Party (Peru): and decline of Communist power among labor, 20–21; and Peruvian Communist Party, 45
Argentina: Comintern in, 11, 12, 83; and USSR, 20, 76, 77, 79, 85, 86; dual Communism in, 21; per capita income in, 23; coup of 1971 in, 30; Nelson Rockefeller in, 30; formation of Communist party in, 35; violence in, 40, 47; and Soviet-Uruguayan relations, 83, 84; and Eastern Europe, 86; effect of military rule on Communism in, 188
Argentine Communist Party: and Victorio

Codovilla, 13, 37, 41; and Paraguayan Communist Party, 48

Arma da Crítica: 153

army, the. *See* military, the

Amtorg (American Trading Corporation): 82

Arrais, Miguel: and violence, 135, 150; as a government official, 137–38; and Francisco Julião, 141; and Heráclito Fontoura Sobral Pinto, 147–48; accused of vacillating, 150–51; activity of, after release from prison, 158; and Leonel Brizola, 158; deprived of political rights, 161; sentenced to prison, 161; and Front of Popular Mobilization, 167–68

Asia: and lack of Soviet interest in Latin America, 12; Cuba advocates violence in, 57–58; mention of, 75

Atlantida, Uruguay: 159

Azevedo, Agliberto Vieira de: as member of PCB Central Committee, 179 n 6; imprisonment of, 180 n 27

Bahia (city), Brazil: guerrilla training centers near, 142

Bahia (state), Brazil: and Carlos Lamarca, 185 n 142

Bahia Group: 139–40

Banco do Estado de São Paulo: 171

Bandeira, Luís Alberto Moniz: 162–63

Bank of the Republic (Uruguay): 86

Barata, Agildo: 168

Barras, Ademar de: 171–72

Bâsbaum, Leoncio: 135

Bastos, Paulo de Melo: 145–46

Batista, Fulgencio: and the Popular Front, 17; Communists support, 19; U. S. supports, 24; compared to Pérez Jiménez, 64; Miguel Arrais compares Brazil to Cuba under; 158

Batista, Miguel: 157, 179 n 6

Bay of Pigs invasion: 91

Becerra, Longimo: 108

beef: 86

Belgrade, Yugoslavia: 81

Belo Horizonte, Brazil: and UNE, 165, 170

Benaim, Lourdes: 179 n 6

Benítez, Graciano G.: 127–28

Berger, Harry: 162

Berlin, Germany: 77

Betancourt, Rómulo: and Communism, 63, 65, 131; and youth, 64; and urban terrorism, 65

Bezerra, Gregório: and prison, 149, 161, 180 n 27; freed by terrorists, 175

Blanco party (Uruguay): 30; (Blancos) and Soviet-Uruguayan relations, 86

Bolivia: Revolution of 1952 in, 9–10, 23, 28; dual Communism in, 21; and Ché Guevara, 25; coup of 1970 in, 30; and violence, 32,

71; split of Communist party in, 48; and USSR, 76, 108; and Charles Chandler, 177

Bolshevik Revolution: 10th Anniversary of, 13; attractiveness of, to Latin America, 35; 50th Anniversary of, 62, 71, 105; and Stanislov S. Pestkovsky, 77

Bonfim Júnior, Orlando: and PCB, 151–52, 179 n 6

Borodin, Michael: in Mexico, 12, 36; in China, 36

Borges da Silveira, Maurina: 176

bourgeoisie. *See* middle class

Branco, Castelo: and PCB, 43; cancellation of political rights by, 147, 152; and L. Brizola, 158–59; and labor, 164; and students, 164–65; and the U. S., 165; and Communist unity, 168

Bravo, Douglas: 102

Brazil: one party system in, 10; Comintern in, 11, 83; Manuilsky's insurrection in, 16, 17; and USSR, 20; labor in, joins CTAL, 21; compared to Mexico, 28; democratic left and Communism in, 28; coup of 1964 in, 29, 134–35; Nelson Rockefeller in, 30; restricts political freedom, 30; relations between USSR and, 76, 79, 85, 108; and Boris Kraevsky, 83; and Soviet-Uruguayan relations, 84, 85; USSR supports Carlos Prestes' revolt in, 84, 109 n 24; East Europe and, 86; and Fidel Castro, 93; overthrow of Goulart and Soviet policy, 93; pro-Soviet faction from, at Havana Conference, 94; Rebellion of 1935 in, 136; Navy Minister in, 145–46; invasion of, from Uruguay, 159; and the dispute over violence, 186; decline of Soviet influence in, 186; effect of military rule on Communism in, 188

Brazil, Military Region of the Northeast: sentences Gregório Bezerra, 149

Brazil, Secretaryship of Public of Security. *See* Departamento de Ordem Política e Social

Brazilia, Brazil: 142–43

Brazilian Communist Party. *See* PCB; PC do B

Brazilian Constitution: attitude of Brazilian leftists toward, 135

Brazilian elections. *See* elections, Brazilian

Brazilian government: and leftists, 135; Communists in, 136; and Leonel Brizola, 138, 159; PCB on, 153–54

Brazilian Labor Party: 138

Brest-Litovsk treaty: 77

Brezhnex, Leonid: and Latin America, 22, 76

Britain. *See* United Kingdom

Brizola, Leonel: as a leftist leader, 138–39; and UNE, 147; and Miguel Arrais, 158; in Uruguay, 158–60; blamed for invasion of Brazil, 159; aids guerrilla camps in Brazil,

159–60; and PORT, 161; deprived of political rights, 161; Julião on, 161; informed
against by POLOP, 162; Juan Posadas on,
162; and Front of Popular Mobilization,
167–68; student leaders on, 183 n 77. *See
also* Groups of Eleven
Broad Front: in Uruguay, 30; PCB supports,
155; formation of, 168
Browder, Earl: 133
Bucher, Biovanni Enrico: 176, 177–78
Buenos Aires, Argentina: South American
Bureau of the Comintern in, 13, 83; Communist congress in, 14; Iuzhamtorg in, 84
Bukharin, Nikolai: 13
businessmen: and the Popular Front, 16, 17;
as Communists in Paraná, 149–50

CGOCM: 125
CGT: and Communist strength in Brazil-
ian labor, 144–45; elimination of, 163; and
Front of Popular Mobilization, 167–68
CIA: and Brazilian terrorists, 172
CNTC: 145
CNTI: and Communist strength in Brazil,
144–46; and Benedito Cerqueira, 145–46;
and Pelacani, 145–46; and Clodsmidt
Riani, 145–46, 183 n 86; military interven-
tion in, 163
COLINA: 173
CONTAG: 163
COPEI: and violence, 64, 65
CPOS: leaders of, 145–46; elimination of,
163
CSLA: established, 13, 14; and "dual union-
ism," 15; dissolved, 18
CSUM: 125
CTAL: creation of, 18; and Vicente Lom-
bardo Toledano, 18, 19; Communists gain
control of, 19; decline of, 21
CTM: and Vicente Lombardo Toledano, 18;
Communists in, 118, 119, 121, 125, 128,
129–39; and Cárdenas, 119, 125; and the
Popular Front, 119, 128–29; and Comin-
tern, 124–25, 133; formation of, 126–27;
and the PNR, 127; growth of, 127–28; and
the Workers University, 128; supports
crushing or revolts, 128; opposes Franco,
129; and petroleum workers' strike, 132;
split of, 133
CUTAL: 145–46
Cairo, Egypt: and AAPSO, 97; and Tricon-
tinent Conference, 98
Caldera, Rafael: and violence, 65; recognizes
PCV, 68
Cali, Colombia: 19
Calles, Plutarco Elías: and Pestkovsky, 78;
and Lázaro Cárdenas, 126
Câmara, Diógenes de Arruda: and split of
PCB, 139–40; as Communist leader, 139–

40; cancellation of political rights of, 147
Campa, Valentín: 125
Caparáo Mountains, Brazil: 159–60
Capistrano da Costa, David: issues "Thesis
for Discussion," 150; sentenced to prison,
161; as member of PCB Central Committee, 179 n 6
capitalism: Luis G. Monzón on, 123–24; and
Christianity, 166
Cárdenas, Lázaro: and Communism, 28,
119–20, 129–30; and the military, 28–29;
and the belief that liberal movements offer
strong resistance to Communism, 116–17;
as President of Mexico, 116–17; destroys
the Popular Front, 118; opposes Fascism,
119; and land reform, 119–20; and Saturnino Cedillo, 120; nationalizes industry,
120; and labor, 121; and Six Year Plan,
122; and education, 122–25; and CTM,
126–27, 128
Cardim de Alencar Osório, Jeffersion: and
PCB Central Committee, 151; invasion of
Brazil by, 159
Cardonnel, Thomas: 165
Carupano, Venezuela: 65
Carvalho, Apolônio Pinto de: expelled from
PCB, 157; and urban terrorists, 177; as
member of PCB Central Committee,
179 n 6
Carvalho, Benedito de: 179 n 6
Carvalho, Ferdinando de: Supreme Military
Tribunal on, 149; investigations of Communists by, 149–50; and Communist labor
leaders, 164
Casals, José: 67
Castro, Fidel: and U. S., 10, 104–105; and
political freedom, 24; and violence, 24–
25, 69, 95, 99, 102, 142–43; rivals to the
example of, 32; and the Jacobin Left, 51,
52; and USSR, 51, 71–72; and PCV, 62,
100, 102; and Venezuela, 64, 68; and the
Sino-Soviet split, 72; and Mao Tsetung, 90;
turns to Communism, 90–91; compromise
of, with Khrushchev, 92–93; and Brazil,
93; and Chile, 93; and Mexico, 93; and
Nuclear Test Ban Treaty, 93; and United
Party of the Socialist Revolution, 93;
awarded Lenin Peace Prize, 93; and Ché
Guevara, 95–96; and Regis Debray, 100;
and FALN, 100, 102; on East Europe,
105; and Allende, 107; and North Korea,
107; and Vietnam, 107; and Brazilian Communists, 134, 161, 168; and Tiradentes
Radical Movement, 141; and Francisco
Julião, 141, 161; UNE favors, 147; Carlos
Marighella on, 156; Juan Posadas on, 162;
and Communism in Latin America, 186,
187. *See also* Cuba; Cuban Revolution
Castro, Raul: 95
Castro, Tarzan de: trains guerrillas, 142, 160;

Wolf, 78; and Boris Kraevsky, 83; and Carlos Prestes, 84; debate over Soviet relation to, 84; and Soviet-Uruguayan relations, 85; and United Front, 124; and CTM, 124–25, 133; and Earl Browder, 133

Comintern Fifth Congress: 13, 78

Comintern First Congress: 35

Comintern Second Congress: 11

Comintern Seventh Congress: and Fascism, 16; revival of themes of, 96–97; tactics decided upon during, 117; and Popular Front, 117; on trade union unity, 125; and CTM, 126–27

Comintern Sixth Congress (1928): 83

Comintern Latin-American Bureau: 36, 37

Comintern, South American Bureau of the: establishment of, 13; activities of, 13–14, 83; at Congress of Latin-American Communist parties, 14; membership of, 37

Comité Nacional de Defensa Proletaria: 125

commerce: USSR turns from revolution to, 26–27; and U. S. and Latin-American relations, 31–32; and Cuban-Chinese relations, 60; and CPSU Twentieth Congress, 76; and Uruguayan economy, 83–84

commercial relations: Castro criticizes USSR about, 62; between USSR and Uruguay, 75, 76, 77, 82–89; between USSR and Mexico, 75, 76, 77, 85; between USSR and Argentina, 76, 77, 79, 85; between USSR and Brazil, 76, 79, 85, 108; between USSR and Chile, 76, 85; between Germany and USSR, 77; between USSR and Panama, 77; between USSR and Venezuela, 77, 85; between USSR and Paraguay, 85; between Cuba and the USSR, 85, 89–108 *passim;* between USSR and Latin America, and Castro, 105; USSR seeks, 107; of USSR, 108

communal farms. *See* ejidos

"Communism in one country." *See* "Socialism in one country"

Communist Congress of 1969: disunity at, 33

Communist Information Bureau. *See* Cominform

Communist International. *See* Comintern

Communist International Union of Students: 147

Communist Manifesto: and Socialist education, 124

Communist parties (Latin America): creation of, 11, 12; and Nazi-Soviet Non-aggression Treaty, 19

Communist Party of Brazil. *See* PCB; PC do B

Communist Party of Chile: and Eudosio Ravines, 37; Soviet opinion of attitude of, toward violence, 55; and Havana Conference, 95

Communist Party of China: on violence, 40; and Peruvian Communist Party, 45; and Chile, 49–50; and Castro, 161

Communist Party of Colombia: and violence, 41, 46–48

Communist Party of Costa Rica: 39–40

Communist Party of Cuba: and Popular Front, 17; and political freedom, 24; and Jacobin Left, 51; and Armando Hart, 57; and Sino-Soviet split, 72; and Soviet-Cuban relations, 90; and Fidel Castro, 90–91; and Tricontinent Conference, 98. *See also* Castroism; *Granma;* PURS

Communist Party of India: 12

Communist Party of Italy: and Havana Conference of 1964, 95

Communist Party of Japan: 12

Communist Party of Mexico: formation of, 36; Victorio Codovilla and purges of, 37; subversive activity by, 77; and Bertram D. Wolf, 78; and Soviet-Mexican relations, 78, 80; and Party of the Mexican Revolution, 117; supports Cárdenas, 119–20; opposition to the nationalism of industries by, 120; Seventh Congress of, 121; and Miguel Aroche Parra, 122; and Lombardo Toledano, 125–26

Communist Party of the Dominican Republic: at the Moscow Congress of 1969, 33

Communist Party of the Soviet Union: and call for Bolshevization, 13; and Raul Acosta, 44; and Armando Hart at 23rd Congress of, 57–58; and subversive activity, 75; and Latin America, 76, 79; and Uruguayan-Soviet relations, 87–88; and Soviet-Cuban relations, 90; and PCB, 152, 157. *See also Kommunist*

Communist Party of the Soviet Union Central Committee: and Latin America, 22; and Sharaf R. Rashidov, 88

Communist Party of the United States: at Congress of Latin-American Communist Parties, 14; and Earl Browder, 133

Communist Party of Uruguay: 18

Communist Party of Venezuela. *See* PCV

Communists: number of, in 1923, 11

Communist Youth International: 14

"Concentration Camps in Peru": 45

Confederação National dos Trabalhadores na Agricultura: 163

Confederação Nacional dos Trabalhadores na Indústria. *See* CNTI

Confederación de Trabajadores de América Latina. *See* CTAL

Confederación de Trabajadores del Ecuador: and Jacobin Left, 45

Confederación de Trabajadores de México. *See* CTM

Confederación de Trabajadores de Venezuela: 63

Confederación Sindical Latino Americano. *See* CSLA

Confederation of Workers of Latin America. *See* CTAL

Confederation of Workers of Mexico. *See* CTM

Conference of Communist parties (1929): and Peru, 36

Conference of Peaceful Coexistence: 58

"Congress Against Fascism and War": 119

Congresso Camponês: 135

Congress of the Latin-American Communist Parties: 14

cooperatives: 122

Copacabana Fort, Brazil: Osneli Martineli in, 158

Corvalan, Luis: 50

Costa, David Capistrano da. *See* Capistrano da Costa, David

Costa, Elson: 179 n 6

Costa e Silva, Artur da: and L. Brizola, 158–59; would-be killers of, freed, 175

Costa, Sérgio: 179 n 6

Costa Rica: Communism illegal in, 40; violence and labor in, 40; Jacobin Left in, 52; and USSR, 188 n 1

Council of Nationalities: 77

Creydt, Oscar: 48

Crispim, José Maria: as Trotskyite, 143; rights of, cancelled, 147

Crockatt de Sá, Gilberto: 145–46

Cuba: urban nature of, 23

Cuba (Communist): and violence, 10, 32; and Sino-Soviet dispute, 23; per capita income in, 23; and USSR, 23, 26–27, 87, 108; training of Communists in, 23, 142; political freedom in, 24; and U. S., 24, 76; and China, 26, 98; as example to revolutionaries, 39; economic policy of, 56–57; and Venezuela, 64; and Ricardo Ramírez de Léon, 69; OAS sanctions against, and Mexico, 81; and Secretariat of Tricontinent organization, 99; and Comecon, 105; and Leonel Brizola, 138; and Francisco Julião, 141, 142; and Clodomir dos Santos Morais, 142; and Brazil, 142, 158, 159–60; and Miguel Arrais, 158; Dirceu in, 170; Marighella on, 173; kidnappers of Charles Burke Elbrick in, 175; mention of, 78, 82. *See also* Castro, Fidel

Cuba (non-Communist): and Comintern, 11, 12; and Popular Front, 17; Communists support Batista in, 19; and dual Communism, 21; utilization of the inexperienced in, 22; and USSR, 76, 85

Cuban agent: on guerrilla training in Brazil, 142

Cuban citizens: and training of Brazilian guerrillas, 142

Cuban military: and Cuba's break with China, 60–61

Cuban missile crisis: and Soviet-Cuban relations, 27, 89, 91–92; and Jacobin Left, 52; and export of revolution, 106

Cuban Revolution: and U. S., 10; and Castro, 23–24; result of, for Cuba, 23–24; and International Communism, 24–25, 35; and Soviet-Cuban relations, 90–91; and China, 91; and Ché Guevara, 95; Regis Debray on, 102; export of, 106; mention of, 95

Cuba Socialista: 58

Cultural Revolution: and Latin America, 41

Cultural Soviética: 81

Curitiba, Paraná, Brazil: 149–50

Czechoslovakia: Soviet invasion of, 31, 71, 169; and Ricardo Ramírez de Léon, 69

Dager, Jorge: 31

Dantas, Francisco San Tiago: 137–38

Debray, Regis: Chilean Revolutionary Communist Party on, 70; on urban terrorism, 90; and Castro, 100–103; Rodolfo Ghioldi on, 103

Decree Law 477 (Brazil): 174

Democratic Party (Chile): 16

Detalles de la Educación Socialista Implantables en México: 123–25

Devlin, Kevin: 99

Día, El: 88

Dianópolis, Goiás, Brazil: 142–43

Dias, Giocondo Alves: as Communist leader, 139–40; receives jail sentence, 148; and PCB, 151–52; 157, 179 n 6

Dimitrov, Georgi: 16–17

Dinerstein, Herbert: on Sino-Soviet split, 38–39, 54–56; on Paraguayan Communist Party, 48; on Guatemalan violence, 69

diplomatic relations: USSR turns from revolution to, 26–27; Castro criticizes USSR about, 62, 105; between Mexico and the USSR, 75, 77–87; between USSR and Uruguay, 75, 82–89; between USSR and Latin-American countries, 76, 77, 86; between Germany and USSR, 77; between Cuba and USSR, 89–108 *passim*; USSR seeks, 107

Dirceu, José: and UNE, 169–70; freed by terrorists, 175

Director General of Social Welfare Funds: Dante Pelacani removed as, 145

Djilas, Milovan: 171

doctors. *See* professional people

Documentos Políticos: 47

Dominican Communist Party: 33

Dominican Republic: and dual Communism, 21; Jacobin Left in, 52; invaded by U. S., 96

Draper, Theodore: on Castroism, 90–91, 100

Dual Communism: 21–22

"dual unionism": 15
Dulles, John W. F.: on Brazil, 29
Dutra, Eurico Gaspar: 144

economic development: and Mexican Revolution, 131–32
economic nationalism: and Cárdenas, 122; and Socialism, 123
economic relations. *See* commercial relations
Ecuador: confiscation of Chinese funds in, 45; coup of 1966 in, 45; split of Communist party in, 45; Jacobin Left in, 52; and USSR, 108
education: in Mexico, 122–25, 129–30; Luis G. Monzón on, 123–25; and Socialism, 124; Soviet, 124; in Brazil, 149, 157–58
Eisenhower, Milton: 32
ejidos: emphasized by Cárdenas, 116; Communists in leadership of, 122
Elbrick, Charles Burke: kidnapping of, 174–75; freeing of kidnappers of, 176–77
elections: Costa Rican, 39; Peruvian, 44–45; Ecuadorian, 46; Colombian, 48; during the Popular Front era, 117
elections (Brazil): Communists elected during, 136; and PCB, 143–44, 151, 152, 157, 166–67; Trotskyites on, 162; students in, 165; and Ação Popular, 166–67
elections (Venezuela): and Communists, 63, 68, 103; and violence, 65; and Soviet policy, 93
El Porto, Colombia: 47
Engels: and Peruvian Communist Party, 44; Brizola on, 139
England. *See* United Kingdom
Escalante, Anibal: 105–106
Escobar, Federico: 48
Espalter, José: 84
"España-Mexico" School: 123
Espírito Santo, Brazil: 169
Estenssoro, Víctor Paz: 28
Europe: López Mateos in, 81; mention of, 75
Europe, Eastern: USSR promotes Latin-American trade with, 20; and Argentina, 86; and Brazil, 86; and Cuba, 93, 105; Pestkovsky on, 109 n 3; blamed for invasion of Brazil, 159; and Guatemala, 188 n 1; mention of, 38
Europe, Western: trade of, with Uruguay, 87; and Soviet-Cuban relations, 105
Europeans, East: in Comintern South American Bureau, 37
Excelsior: 80

FALN: as urban terrorist group, 65; and rural violence, 66; and Tricontinent Conference, 98; and PCV, 98, 100; and Castro, 98, 99, 100, 102, 161
FAR: activity of, 69; and Castro, 95; and Tricontinent Conference, 98

FDP: 31
FIDEL: 98
FLN: and Tricontinent Conference, 98
FRAP: 98
FSD: as a Communist labor organization, 144; elimination of, 163
Falcon, Venezuela: 66
Farías, Jesús: 64, 67
fascism: and Comintern, 15; and Popular Front, 17, 117, 119; and Communist strength, 21; and Mexico, 118, 119, 122; Monzón on, 124; Nasserism as, 187. *See also* Germany
Feasible Details of Socialist Education in Mexico: 123–25
Federación Obrera de Chile: 11
Federal District (Mexico): 120
Federation of Peasant Leagues, Paraíba, Brazil: and PCB, 141; receive guns, 142–43
Federation of Workers of the State of Oaxaca: 127–28
Federations of Workers at the Service of the State: 122
Federations of Workers of the CTM: 122
Fernando de Noronha Island, Brazil: 158
Ferreira, Joaquim Câmara: and PCB Central Committee, 157, 179 n 6; and Carlos Marighella, 169; in Labor Communist Party, 169; as urban terrorist, 174, 175
Fidelistas. *See* Castroism
First Conference of Solidarity of the Peoples of Africa, Asia, and Latin America. *See* Tricontinent Congress
Foreign Trade Bank of Mexico: 76
Forum Sindical de Debates. *See* FSD
Fourth International, Montevideo headquarters of: and PORT, 162
France: and lack of Soviet interest in Latin America, 12; Popular Front in, compared to Popular Front in Mexico, 118
Franco, Francisco: opposition to, 117, 119, 129
Frei Montalva, Eduardo: 93
French Resistance: and Apolônio Pinto de Carvalho, 169, 177
Frente Amplio. *See* Broad Front
Frente da Juventude Democrática: 147
Frente de Liberacion Nacional: and United Front, 46
Frente de Libertação Nacional: and Brizola, 138, 158–59
Frente de Mobilização Popular. *See* Front of Popular Mobilization
Frente Democrática Popular: 31
Frente Operária: 143
Front of Popular Mobilization: and Leonel Brizola, 138; and Goulart, 167–68
Frugoni, Emilio: 86

Fuerzas Armadas de Liberación Nacional. *See* FALN

Fuerzas Armadas Rebeldes. *See* FAR

Fuerzas Armadas Revolucionaries Colombianas: 46

Gall, Norman: 66

General Confederation of Workers and Peasants of Mexico: 125

General Labor Command. *See* CGT

Germany: and CTAL, 19; and USSR, 19, 75–76, 77; and Popular Front, 117. *See also* Nazi-Soviet Non-Aggression Treaty; World War II

Ghioldi, Rodolfo: 103

Giraldo, Ignacio Torres: 37

Goiás, Brazil; and Tarzan de Castro, 142; guerrillas in, 142, 159–160; and F. Julião, 161

Gómez, Eugenio: 18

Gorender, Jacob: as Brazilian Communist leader, 139–40, 151, 154, 156, 157, 179 n 6; political rights of, cancelled, 147; receives jail sentence, 148; and Prestes, 151; and violence, 151; and PCBR, 169

Gott, Richard: 48

Goulart, João: and Communism, 28, 150; overthrow of, 29, 43, 93; and PCB, 43, 151, 153–54; and labor, 134–35, 144; and Prestes, 136; and Brizola, 138; and Arrais, 138; and Chinese Communists, 140; and UST, 145; and CGT, 145–46; and Ferdinando de Carvalho, 149; masses not prepared to support, by violence, 150; in Uruguay, 159; deprived of political rights, 161; Julião on, 161; Juan Posadas on, 162; and CONTAG, 163; and Front of Popular Mobilization, 167–68; expropriation of private property by, 167–68, 179 n 7; joins Broad Front, 168

Grabois, Maurício: and split of PCB, 43, 139–40; cancellation of political rights of, 147; found not guilty, 148; and PC do B, 160, 170; and Ação Popular, 166–67; and Amazonas, 170

Granja, Antônio Ribeiro: 179 n 6

Granma: and Cuba's break with China, 62; Regis Rebray in, 102

Griffith, William E.: 40

Groups of Eleven: and Leonel Brizola, 138–39; investigated, 149, 158; blamed for invasion of Brazil, 159

"Groups of Five": 162

Grupos de Onze Companheiros. *See* Groups of Eleven

Guanabara, Brazil: Communist strength in, 137; Leonel Brizola as congressman from, 138; CPOS in, 144, 145–46; and Negrão de Lima, 152; and PCB, 152, 155; government refuses to allow Communist Labor

officials in, 164; students in 1966 election in, 165; death of Ação Popular in, 169

Guanabara Metalworkers Union: and Benedito Cerqueira, 164

Guani, Alberto: 85

Guatemala: and CTAL, 21; utilization of the inexperienced in, 22; violence in, 24–25, 71, 95; U. S. in, and the Cuban Revolution, 91; and Eastern Europe, 188 n 1

Guedes, Armênio: 179 n 6

guerrillas. *See* violence

Guevara, Ché: death of, 25; and violence, 29, 100–104, 176; in Bolivia, 48; and the Jacobin Left, 52; Chilean Revolutionary Communist Party on, 70; and Soviet policy, 89; and Castro, 95–96, 100–104; and MR8, 174

"Guevarists": and Soviet-Cuban relations, 92

Guild Socialism: in Mexico, 120

Guimarães, Juarez: 177

Guralsky, A.: 13

Haiti: and dual Communism, 21; invasion of, 25; Havana Conference (1964) on violence in, 95

Halperin, Ernst: on Sino-Soviet split, 38; on Chilean Communism, 49, 50–51

Hart, Armando: 57–58

Havana, Cuba: meeting of pro-Soviet parties in, 55–56; Tricontinental Congress in, 60, 88, 97–99, 152; OLAS Conference in, 68, 156; propaganda from, for Brazilian guerrillas, 142–43; Anselmo in, 183 n 82

Havana compromise: and Castro, 97, 100

Havana Conference of 1964: events of, 94–95; and Soviet–Latin-American relations, 96, 105; and Sino-Soviet split, 97; and Regis Debray, 102

Havana Congress (1967): and the independent Cuban line, 59

History of Mexican Revolutions, A: 109 n 3

Ho Chi Minh: as honorary president of PCB 6th National Congress, 157

Holleben, Ehrenfried von: 176, 177

Honduras: Havana Conference (1964) discusses violence in, 95

Hora, A: 151

"How to Destroy the Capitalist State": 78

Hull, Cordell: 85

Humbert-Droz, Jules: and Latin-American Communism, 12, 13

Iguaçá River, Brazil: 159

illiteracy: decline of, 29, 116; and Communism, 157–58

illiterates: enfranchisement of, called for, 135

Indians: in Peru, 36; in Mexico, 131–32

Indonesia: 51

industrialization: Cuba attempts, 56–57, 89, 96; and Venezuela, 64

industries: nationalization of, 116, 120, 130, 135, 138
Institute for the Study of Latin-American Relations: 22–23
Institutional Act Number Two: 152
Instituto Superior de Estudos Brasileiros: 149
insurrection. *See* violence
intellectuals: as early Communists, 11; and the failure of labor to lead the Communist movement, 16; in Chile, 16, 50; in Brazil, 35, 143, 154, 166; in Mexico, 117–18, 125, 129–30
Intercambio Cultural: 8
Internationale, The: 124
International Monetary Fund: 136–37
International Red Aid: 14
International Relief Organization of Revolutionaries: 109 n 3
International Union of Students, Prague: 167
Isqueiro, O: 154–55
Italian Communist Party: 95
Italian Socialist Party: 35
Italy, Fascist: Mexico votes for sanctions against, 119
Iuzhamtorg: 82–84, 85
Izvestiia: on Soviet–Latin-American relations, 82–83, 84–85

JEC: 146–47
JUC: and Communism in Brazil, 146–47; and Ação Popular, 165
Jacobin Left: and USSR, 26; and violence, 41, 45, 72; and youth, 42; defined, 51; and Castro, 52; at Tricontinent Congress, 59; and Communism in Latin America, 186
James, Daniel: 22–23
Japan: invades China, 15; and CTAL, 19
Japanese Consul General in São Paulo: kidnapping of, 176
Jiménez, Pérez: and Venezuelan Communist Party, 62–64
José de Sousa, Herbert: and Ação Popular, 166, 167
Julião, Francisco: as a Marxist leader in Brazil, 140–41; and Brazilian guerrillas, 142; and Tarzan de Castro, 160; after 1964 coup, 161; and Castro, 161; deprived of political rights, 161; imprisonment of, 161
Juventude Comunista: 46, 47–48
Juventude Estudantil Católica: 146–47
Juventude Universitária Católica. See JUC

KGB: 82
Katayama, Sen: 12
Kennedy, John F.: Latin-American policy of, 32, 64
Kollontai, Alexandra M.: 78–79
Kolosovsky, Igor: 88, 89
Kommunist: 54–55
Kommunista: 93–94

Kosygin, Alexis: and Latin America, 22, 76
Kraevsky, Boris: 82–83
Khrushchev, Nikita S.: and Mexico, 80; and Soviet-Uruguayan relations, 87–88; and Soviet-Cuban relations, 91, 92–93; and Prestes, 136; and Brazilian Communist Party, 139–40, 160–61; Julião on, 161; mention of, 136–37
Kubitschek, Juscelino: and labor, 144; and Ferdinando de Carvalho, 149; and Broad Front, 155, 168
Kuusinen, Otto: 22
Kuznetsov, Sviatoslav F.: 82

LASO. *See* OLAS
labor: and Communism, 11, 13, 14, 15, 20–21, 28, 29–30, 186, 189 n 4; and Comintern, 11, 15; and Socialism, 13; congress of unions of, in Motevideo, 14; and dual unionism, 15, 17–18; failure to assume leadership of Communist movement, 16; and Popular Front, 17, 124; and Nazi-Soviet Non-Aggression Treaty, 19; and World War II, 19–20; and USSR, 19–20, 29–30; and dual Communism, 22; and the democratic left, 28; and violence, 39, 40–41; and youth, 41; Mikhailov on, 87; and Regis Debray, 101, 103; and Rodolfo Ghioldi, 103; and Luis G. Monzón, 123–24; and the military, 189 n 4
labor (Argentina): and violence, 40
labor (Bolivia): and Communist split, 48
labor (Brazil): Communist strength in, 15, 28, 136, 143–46; and 1964 coup, 29–30, 150, 163–64; and Goulart, 134–35; and Brizola, 138; and Julião, 141; and Trotskyites, 143; leaders of, listed 144–45; and Crockatt de Sá, 145–46; and PCB, 152–53; and PORT, 162; and Ação Popular, 166; and UNE, 170
labor (Chile): and the Popular Front, 17; and violence, 40
labor (Colombia): and violence, 40; and Communists, 47
labor (Costa Rica): and violence, 40
labor (Ecuador): Communist control of, 15; and Pedro Saad, 45
labor (Mexico): and Communism, 15, 118, 119, 121, 122, 129–30; and Bertram D. Wolf, 78; and Pestkovsky, 78, 109 n 3; agitation among, 80; and Cárdenas, 116, 121, 122; abolition of Communist unions of, 117; and Popular Front, 117, 128–29; in the Party of the Mexican Revolution, 117–18; direct control of industries by, 120; and Spanish refugees, 129; opposed Franco, 129
labor (Peru): and violence, 40
labor (Uruguay): Communist Congress on, 14; Communist control of, 15; and vio-

lence, 40; and Uruguayan-Soviet relations, 83, 88; agitation among, 88
labor (Venezuela): and Communism, 62–63, 64
Labor Communist Party. *See* POC
Laborde, Hernán: on Cárdenas, 119; withdraws as candidate, 120; on Communist Party of Mexico, 121; and trade union unity, 125; advocated Popular Front, 129
labor laws: Brazilian, 144
labor party (Brazil): 137
labor unionists: invited to USSR, 13; from PCB, 35
Lacerda, Carlos: opposition of, to Negrão de Lima, 149; and Broad Front, 155, 168
Lacerda, Suplici de: 164–65
Lack, Joseph: 36
Lamarca, Carlos: and terrorists, 173, 177, 184 n 114, 185 n 142
landowners: and the Popular Front, 17; and PCB, 153–54
land reform. *See* agrarian reform
Lanusse, Alejandro A.: 188
Larrazábal, Wolfgang: 63
Latin-American Confederation of Trade Unions. *See* CSLA
Latin American Solidarity Organization. *See* OLAS
Latin American Worker, The. See Trabajador Latino Americano, El
lawyers. *See* professional people
League of Nations: and Soviet-Uruguayan relations, 85; Mexico votes for sanctions against Italy in, 119
Leagues of Agrarian Communities and Peasant Syndicates: 122
Leftist National Liberation Party: 52
Left Liberation Front: 98
left, the: and Communist strength among labor, 20–21; democratic, 26, 27–28, 116, 130–31, 187, 188
left (Brazil): advocates violence, 29; and military, 29; policies on which they agree, 135; and United Front, 137; and Brizola, 138–39; and UNE, 147; and PCB, 154
left (Ecuador): 46
left (Mexico): and Popular Front, 118
Lei Suplici: 164–65
Lenin: forms Comintern, 11; on peaceful revolution, 40; and Peruvian Communist Party, 44; and New Economic Policy, 77; and Pestkovsky, 77; and Khrushchev, 87; and education under Cárdenas, 123; and Ação Popular, 167, 168; Posadas on, 182 n 68
Lenin Peace Prize: awarded to Fidel Castro, 93
Lenin's Birth, 100th Anniversary of: Cuban treatment of, 71
Léon, Ricardo Ramírez de: 69

Leoni, Raúl: election of, 65; and Communism, 131
Liga Feminina Nacionalista: 167–68
"Lighter, The" (*O lsqueira*): 154–55
Lima, Francisco Negrão de. *See* Negrão de Lima, Francisco
Lima, Luís Tenório de. *See* Tenório de Lima, Luís
Lima, Pedro Mota: and guerrillas, 142–43
Litvinoff, Maxim: 85
"Long War tactics": 66
López, Carlos: on violence, 65, 66
López Mateos, Adolfo: 81
Lorenzio, Juan A.: 87
Losovsky, Alexander: and CSLA, 13; and Lombardo Toledano, 127
lower class: and Jacobin Left, 51
Luchesi, Ramiro: 179 n 6

MAS: 31
MEP: 30
MI (Chile): 52
MIR: and Castro, 64; formation of, 64; and violence, 64, 65, 66–67; Betancourt suspends recognition of, 65; and Domingo Alberto Rangel, 67; split of, 67; and China, 70
MNR (Bolivia): 28
MNR (Brazil): 172
MOPR: 109 n 3
MR8: 174–75
Maack, Tomás: 143
Machado brothers: 64
Machéte, El: 78
Makar, A.: 79
Malina, Salómão: 152–53
Mancisidor, José: 123
Manet, Alberto: 84
Manual do Guerrilheiro Urbano: 174
Manuelita plantation, La, Colombia: 47
Manuilsky, Dimitri: 16, 17
Maoism: Rodolfo Ghioldo on, 103; and OLAS Conference, 104; and Brazilian coup of 1964, 134
Mao Tse-Tung: and Peruvian Communist Party, 44; and Chile, 50; and Venezuelan guerrillas, 66; and Castro, 90; Brizola on, 139; Julião on, 141, 161; and Ação Popular, 166–67
Maranhão, Brazil: 142
Marighella, Carlos: as Communist leader, 139–40; cancellation of political rights of, 147; receives jail sentence, 148; wounding of, 148; and PCB, 151–52, 155, 156, 157, 179 n 6; and violence, 155, 171–77 *passim*; and São Paulo State Committee, 155–56; and Luís Carlos Prestes, 155–56, 178; as example to imprisoned Communists, 162; forms ALN, 169; and Joaquim Câmara Ferreira, 169, 175; death of, 175–76

Marques dos Santos, Sidnei Fix: 143
Marquetalia, Colombia: 47
Marshall Plan: 187
Martineli, Osneli: 158
Martineli, Rafael: 145–46
Marx, Karl: on peaceful revolution, 40; and Peruvian Communist Party, 44; writings of, and education under Cárdenas, 123; Brizola on, 139; and Ação Popular, 167, 168
Massachusetts Institute of Technology: 40
Mater et Magistra: 141
Mato Grosso, Brazil: 142
Médici, Emílio Garrastazá: bans freed terrorists, 178; and Communism, 188
Melo, Severino Teodoro de: 179 n 6
Merida, Simón Saez: 65
Mexican Agrarian Problem, The: 109 n 3
Mexican Confederation of Workers: 125
Mexican Constitution: and Cárdenas, 122–23
Mexican Economic Commission: 81
Mexican Embassy (Brazil): and José Anselmo dos Santos, 166
Mexican government: Communist influence in, 119, 121; mention of, 120
Mexican independence, 150th Anniversary of: and Khrushchev, 80
Mexican Revolution: and hostility of U. S., 9; and Comintern, 12; Cuban Revolution compared to, 23; and Cárdenas, 116; interpretations of Socialism during, 123; as true social revolution, 131–32
Mexican-Russian Institute of Cultural Exchange: 81
Mexico: one party system in, 10; and Comintern, 11, 12, 36; CTAL splits in, 21; dual Communism in, 21; and USSR, 26–27, 75, 85, 108; Communism in, and the democratic left, 28; compared to Brazil, 28; violence in, 32; Michael Borodin in, 36; split of Communist party in, 48; Tito in, 81; and Cuba, 81, 93; votes for sanctions against Italy in the League of Nations, 119; exile of Julião in, 161; and Francisco Lage Pessoa, 166; Dirceu in, 170. *See also* Cárdenas, Lázaro
Mexico City, Mexico: release of Brazilian terrorists to, 175, 176
middle class: and Communism, 11, 29–30, 187; and Cuban Revolution, 23; and violence, 41; Communists to cooperate with, 117, 152; as danger to PCB, 154; and UNE, 170
Middle East: and USSR in Latin America, 12, 106; mention of, 75
Mikhailov, Sergei S.: 87–88
Mikoyan, Anastas I.: and Soviet-Mexican relations, 79; and Soviet-Uruguayan relations, 86
military, the: and violence, 10; and political

development, 29; and Communism in Latin America, 187–88; and Communist control of labor, 189 n 4
military (Brazil): and political development, 29; João Goulart favors labor over, 134–35; and the United Front, 137; and rise of radical left, 139; rebellions among, 140; and Trotskyites, 143; trying of Communists by, 147–49; investigations of Communists by, 149–50; and guerrillas, 159–60; and PORT, 161–62; and MNR, 172
military (Cuba): and Soviet-Cuban relations, 90
military (Mexico): and Communist development, 28–29; in the Party of the Mexican Revolution, 117–18; and Popular Front, 118
military (Peru): non-violent revolution by, 32
military (Venezuela): and Communist party, 63
Minas Gerais, Brazil: and coup of 1964, 134–35; guerrilla groups in, 159–60; Francisco Lage Pessoa in, 166; and Ação Popular, 169; and Carlos Lamarca, 185 n 142
Minkin, Alexander: and Iuzhamtorg, 83, 85; and Prestes, 84
missile crisis. *See* Cuban missile crisis
Montalva, Eduardo Frei: and Communism, 28, 32
Montenegro, Julio César Méndez: 70
Montero, Marco Arturo: 123
Montevideo, University Law School: and Brizola, 159
Montevideo, Uruguay: Comintern in, 13, 36, 37, 83; and *El Trabajador Latino Americano,* 14; Communist Congress in, 14; Iuzhamtorg in, 82; and Prestes, 84; Radovitsky in, 85; and Soviet-Uruguayan relations, 86; Mikhailov in, 87; Trotskyites in, 143; and Frente de Libertação Nacional, 158–59; meeting of violence-oriented Communists in, 161
Monzón, Luis G.: writings of, 123–25
Morais, Clodomir dos Santos: 142
Morena, Roberto: and CPOS, 144; and labor, 144–46, 164; and PCB, 145, 179 n 6; in Soviet Union, 145–46; on CUTAL, 145–46; early life of, 148; flees to Paris, 148; receives jail sentence, 148
Moscow, USSR: Comintern congresses in, 11, 16, 78, 117; Comintern headquarters in, 12, 13, 37; trade unionists invited to, 13; training of Latin Americans in, 22; Congress of 1969 in, 33; Jesús Ferías in, 67; Lenin's centenary celebration in, 71; director of Foreign Trade Bank of Mexico in, 76; and Soviet-Uruguayan relations, 86; Juan A. Lorenzi in, 87; USSR Academy of Sciences Latin-American Institute in, 87;

50th Anniversary of Bolshevik Revolution in, 105
Mota, Renato de Oliveira: 179 n 6
Mounier, Emmanuel: 165
Movimiento al Socialismo: 31
Movimiento de Izquierda Revolucionaria (Chile): 52
Movimiento de la Izquierda Revolucionario (Venezuela). *See* MIR
Movimiento Electoral del Pueblo: 30
Movimiento Nacionalista Revolucionario (Bolivia): 28
Movimiento Nacional Revolucionário (Brazil): 172
Movimiento Popular Dominicano: 52
Movimiento Revolucionário de 8 de Octubro: 174–75

Nación, La: 77
Nardone, Benito: 88
Nasserism: 187
Natal: Giocondo Alves Dias in, 157
Nation, The: on Bolivia, 48
National Committee of Proletarian Defense: 125
National Confederation of Industrial Workers. *See* CNTI
National Confederation of Workers in Agriculture: 163
National Confederation of Workers in Commerce: 145
National Federation of Railway Workers: 163
Nationalist and Democratic United Front: 137
National Law School (Brazil): 153
National Liberation Command: 173
National Union of Students. *See* UNE
National Workers' and Peasants' Congress: 125
Nazi-Soviet Non-Aggression Treaty: and Latin-American Communism, 18–19, 129; and the tactic of neutrality, 20; and Popular Front era, 117
Needler, Martin C.: 30
Negrão de Lima, Francisco: and Ferdinando de Carvalho, 149; and PCB, 152
Neuva Fuerza: in Venezuela, 30–31
New Economic Policy: of Lenin, 77
New Force: 30–31
New Leader: 66
New York, New York: Latin American information for *Tass* and, 12; and Amtorg, 82
New York Times: on Soviet-South American trade, 83
Nicaragua: and dual Communism, 21; Castro, and revolution in, 24–25
Nixon, Richard: sends Nelson Rockefeller to Latin America, 30; and U. S. economic policy, 31

North America. *See* United States
North Korea: training of Latin Americans in, 23; on Secretariat of Tricontinent organization, 99; and Castro, 107
North Vietnam. *See* Vietnam
Novos Rumos: 151
nuclear tests: and Soviet-Uruguayan relations, 88

OAS: and invasion of Haiti, 25; and U. S. policy toward Latin America, 32; sanctions of, against Cuba, 81; and Tricontinent Conference, 99
OLAS: formation of, 59; violence in Venezuela, 68; and Tricontinent Congress, 104; and Soviet-Cuban relations, 104–105; and Marighella, 156; supported by ALN, 175
ORMPO. *See* POLOP
Odria Union (Peru): 45
Oest, Lincoln Cordeiro: and the split of the Brazilian Communist Party, 140, 160
Oliveira, Agostinho Dias de: 179 n 6
Operação Joaquim Câmara Ferreira: 177
Organização Revolucionária Marxista-Política Operária. *See* POLOP
Organización Latino Americana de Solidaridad. *See* OLAS
Organization of American States. *See* OAS
Oswald, J. G.: on Soviet-Uruguayan relations, 27; mention of, 26
Otero, Francisco Antônio Leivas: 179 n 6
Oumansky, Konstantin A.: 79

PCB: and USSR, 20, 86; and Osvaldo Peralva, 37; and Prestes, 37, 147–48; split of, 42–43, 139, 160; and Uruguay, 86; expected to control Brazil, 134; policies supported by, 135; problem of legalization of, 135, 136, 147–48; size of, 136, 143–45, 154, 162, 169, 183 n 87; Party Congresses of, 137, 153–58 *passim*, 179 n 6; Brizola on, 139; and Julião, 141; and Pedro Mota Lima, 142–43; and José Maria Crispim, 143; and labor, 143–45; and agricultural unions, 144; and Osvaldo Pacheco, 144; and students, 146–47; and Luís Tenório de Lima, 148–49; and 1964 coup, 150, 154; and CPSU Congress, 152; and Tricontinent Congress, 152; Special Work of, 152–53; and violence, 153, 174–75, 176; and *Frente Ampla*, 155; and Latin-American Solidarity Organization Conference, 156; Marighella expelled from, 156; and Manoel Jover Teles, 156, 170; and Julião, 161; and POLOP, 162; and military intervention in the São Paulo Metallurgical Workers Union, 163–64; and UNE, 165; and Ação Popular, 166–67, 168; and Agildo Barata, 168; internal struggles of, 168; expulsion of Marxists from, 169; and VAR-Palmares, 173; and Charles Burke Elbrick, 174–75;

and Goulart's expropriation of land, 179 n 7; mention of, 160. *See also Novos Rumos;* PC do B; POC; União dos Lavradores e Trabalhadores Agrícolas do Brasil
PCB Central Committee: and Castelo Branco, 43; members of, 145, 179 n 6; meetings of, 151–54 *passim;* and labor, 153; denounced preceding 6th National Congress, 155; and Marighella, 155, 156; and Jacob Gorender, 156; and Manoel Jover Teles, 156; censures state organizations, 156; supports Soviet invasion of Czechoslovakia, 169
PCB Convenção Municipal de Curitiba do: 181 n 50
PCB Guanabara State Committee: leaders of, removed, 156
PCB leadership: structure of, 139–40; hides in Brazil, 150; unpopularity of, 152, 153, 155; and Marighella, 155
PCB National Executive Commission: and 1964 coup, 151; membership of, 151–52, 155, 179 n 6; and labor, 153; mention of, 160
PCB Pernambuco State Committee: and 6th National Congress of PCB, 155
PCB Secretariat: members of, 151–152, 179 n 6
PCBR: and AP, 169; formation of, 169, 170; and PC do B, 170–71; and Apolônio Pinto de Carvalho, 177
PCBR Guanabara State Committee: and Manoel Jover Teles, 170
PCC. *See* Communist Party of Cuba
PC do B (Chinese-oriented): and violence, 43; formation of, 43, 139–40; and Brizola, 139, 158–59; strength of, compared to strength of PCB, 143; sentencing of leaders of, 148; Central Committee meeting of, 160; Sixth National Conference of, 160; and the "Union of Brazilians to Free the the Nation from the Crisis, the Dictatorship, and the Neocolonialist Threat," 160; and 1964 coup, 160–61; on Soviet-oriented Communists, 160–61; and military intervention in São Paulo Metalurgical workers union, 163–64; and Ação Popular, 166–67; and PCBR, 170–71; and VAR-Palmares, 173
PCML: 46
PCV: and New Force, 31; split of, 31; and Sino-Soviet split, 48–49; and Havana Congress (1967), 59; and violence, 62–68, 102–103; Betancourt suspends recognition of, 65; recognized by Rafael Caldera, 68; and Castro, 68, 98, 100, 102; and FALN, 68, 98, 100, 102; and revival of Popular Front, 97; and Tricontinent Conference, 98, 100; and elections, 103; and OLAS Conference, 104
PNR: dissolution of, 118; and the CTM, 127

POC: formation of, 169; and Joaquim Camara Ferreira, 174; and *Política Operária,* 183 n 88
POLOP: and students, 146–47; and Brizola, 158–59; and 1964 coup, 162–63; Fourth National Congress of, 163; internal struggles in, 163, 168; and UNE, 167; and Labor Communist Party, 169; and VPR, 172; and VAR-Palmares, 173; and *Política Operária,* 183 n 88
PORT: strength of, compared to strength of PCB, 143; and Brizola, 158–59; Cláudio Vasconcelos Cavalcanti and *Bureau Político* of, 161; and 1964 coup, 161–62
PRM: and the Popular Front, 117–20 *passim,* 128
PSP. *See* Communist Party of Cuba
PUA: as a Communist labor group, 144; and Osvaldo Pacheco, 145–46; elimination of, 163
PURS: creation of, 93; changed to PCC (Communist Party of Cuba), 98
Pacheco, César Batlle: and Soviet-Uruguayan relations, 88
Pacheco da Silva, Osvaldo: and PUA, 144; as labor leader, 144, 145–46; and PCB, 145, 179 n 6; in Soviet Union, 145–46; and UNE, 147; flees to Uruguay, 148; and Goulart, 168
Pact of Unity and Action. *See* PUA
Palmeira, Vladimir: 169–70; 175
Panama: invasion of, 25; 1968 coup in, 30; and USSR, 77
Paraguay: one party system in, 10; and dual Communism, 21; Nelson Rockefeller in, 30; and Comintern, 83; and USSR, 85; Havana Conference (1964) on violence in, 95
Paraguayan Communist Party: and violence, 39; split of, 48
Paraíba, Brazil: 161–62
Páramo, Manrique: 128
Paraná, Brazil: Ferdinando de Carvalho on Communism in, 149–50; PCB leaders in, denounce Party leadership, 155; invaders from Uruguay in, 159
Paredes, Saturnino: 44
Paris, France: and Roberto Morena, 148, 164
Parra, Miguel Aroche: 122
Partido Comunista Brasileiro. *See* PCB
Partido Comunista Brasileiro Revolucionária. *See* PCBR
Partido Comunista de Colombia. *See* Communist Party of Colombia
Partido Comunista de Cuba. *See* Communist Party of Cuba
Partido Comunista do Brasil. *See* PC do B
Partido Comunista Marxista-Leninista (PCM-L): 46
Partido Comunista Revolucionario (Chile): 50

Partido de la Revolución Mexicana. *See* PRM
Partido Guatemalteco del Trabajo: 69–70
Partido Nacional Revolucionario. *See* PNR
Partido Operário Comunista. *See* POC
Partido Operário Revolucionário Trotsquista. *See* PORT
Partido Revolucionario: 70
Partido Revolucionario Nacionalista: 67
Partido Socialista Argentino: 35
Partido Socialista del Peru: and Conference of 1929, 36; split of, 36
Partido Socialista del Uruguay: 35
Partido Socialista International: 35
Partido Socialista Obrero de Chile: 35
Partido Socialista Revolucionario: joins Comintern, 36; and Jacobin Left, 52
Partido Socialista Revolucionario Ecuadoriano: 45, 46
Party of the Mexican Revolution. *See* PRM
Peace Congresses: as a tactic, 20
peaceful coexistence: Tricontinental Congress on, 58–59
peaceful evolution. *See* violence
Peasant Congress: 135
peasant federations: of Ação Popular conflict with, of PCB, 166
peasants: and early Communism, 11; and lack of agrarian program, 15–16; Regis Debray on, 101
peasants (Brazil): and Miguel Arrais, 137–38; and Brizola, 138; and Julião, 14–41; and violence, 142–43, 150; and Trotskyites, 143; and 1964 coup, 150; and Ação Popular, 166
peasants (Cuba): small number of, 23; and Cuban Revolution, 23–24
peasants (Mexico): and land reform, 116, 120; in Party of the Mexican Revolution, 117–18; Luis G. Monzón on, 124; and Popular Front, 124, 128–29; and the CTM, 124–25
peasants (Venezuela): and Communism, 62–63
Peking, China: Manoel Jover Teles in, 170
Peking Review: and Peruvian Communist Party, 45; and Communist Party of Colombia, 46; claims ten pro-Chinese parties, 48; on Chile, 50; and Cuba's break with China, 61
Pekin Informa: and Cuba's break with China, 61
Pelacani, Dante: as labor leader, 144–46; and Communist strength in Brazil, 145; as pro-Chinese, 145–46; in Chile, 145–46
People's Friendship University: and Mexico, 81
People's Front. *See* Popular Front
Peoples Vanguard Party: 39–40
Peralva, Osvaldo: 37
Pereira, Astrogildo: death of, 148; and PCB, 179 n 6

Pérez, Roberto Reyes: 123
Permanent Commission of Syndical Organizations. *See* CPOS
Pernambuco, Brazil: Julião in, 140–41; and Clodomir dos Santos Morais, 142; party leaders in, issue "Thesis for Discussion," 150; peasants in, not prepared for revolution, 150–51; PORT in, 161–62; mention of, 135, 158
Peru: and U. S., 9; coup of 1968 in, 9, 30; labor in, 20–21, 40; dual Communism in, 21; and Nelson Rockefeller, 30; agrarian reform in, 32; Conference of 1929 regarding, 36; Communism illegal in, 40; violence in, 40, 71; youth in, 42; Jacobin Left in, 52; and USSR, 76, 108; pro-Soviet faction from, at Havana Conference of 1964, 94; military rule and Communism in, 188
Peruvian Communist Party: and Eudosio Ravines, 37; split of, 43–45; Fourth National Conference of, 44
Pessoa, Francisco Lage: 166
Pestkovsky, Stanislav S.: early activities of, 77; in Mexico, 77–78; later life of, 109 n 3
Petrobrás: and Brazilian Communism, 135; and UNE, 147
petroleum: USSR opposes exploitation of, 20; and Soviet-Uruguayan relations, 86; and Soviet-Cuban relations, 91, 105
petroleum industry: nationalized, 120, 167–68
petroleum workers, Mexican: strike of, and CTM, 132
Petty Bourgeois Line in the Chilean Revolution, A: 70
Pechincha (Quito), Ecuador: and split of Communist party, 45
Pinheiro, Humberto Menezes: 145–46
Pinto, Heráclito Fontoura Sobral: and Prestes, 147–48; defense of Communists by, 147–48
Pinto de Carvalho, Apolônio: and PCBR, 168
plebiscites: called for in Brazil, 135
Pokrovsky, M. N.: 109 n 3
Poland: López Mateos in, 81; Pestkovsky on, 109 n 3
political parties: and the one party system, 10
political parties (Brazil): and United Front, 137; dissolved by Institutional Act Number Two, 152
Política Operária. See POLOP
Pomar, Pedro: 139–40
Pope John XXIII: and Catholic peasant organizations in Brazil, 141; quoted by defense lawyers, 147–48
Pope Paul VI: quoted by Prestes, 147–48
Poppino, Rollie: 83
Popular, El: 128
Popular Action Front: 98
Popular Committees (Venezuela): 30, 31
Popular Front: and Communist unions, 15;

and Fascism, 16; and Dimitrov, 16–17; importance of, 18; and utilization of the inexperienced, 22; and USSR, 76; revival of, 96–97; Regis Debray on, 101–102; and United Fronts, 177; dates of era of, 117; and Comintern, 124

Popular Front (Chile): in Chile, 16–18; and Eudosio Ravines, 37; and the dispute over tactics, 186

Popular Front (Mexico): and the democratic left, 28; failure of, 118–19; and trade union unity, 125; and CTM, 126–27, 128–29; and El Popular, 128; PRM as, 128; attempts to organize, 128–29; and Communist strength, 130

Popular Front (Venezuela): 30–31

Posadas, Juan: and PORT, 162; on great Communists, 182 n 68

poverty: and Communism in Brazil, 157–58

Prague, Czechoslovakia: training of Latin Americans in, 22–23; Pedro Mota Lima in, 142–43; Communist International Union of Students in, 147, 167; Benedito Cerqueira in, 164

Pravda: and Peruvian Communist Party, 44; and Soviet-Cuban relations, 90; Rodolfo Ghioldi on Regis Debray in, 103

Prestes, Luis Carlos: imprisonment of, 17; and USSR, 20, 86, 139–40; and Comintern, 37, 84; and split of PCB, 43, 139–40; and violence, 84, 109 n 24, 136–37, 138, 150, 178, 185 n 142; and Uruguay, 86; and Goulart, 136–37; and leader of Brazilian Communists, 136–37, 151–52, 154, 155, 157, 169, 179 n 6; in Recife, Brazil, 137; Brizola on, 139; and labor, 144–45; finding of journals of, 147; and Sobral Pinto, 147–48; receives jail sentence, 148; and 1964 coup, 150; hides in Brazil, 150; and PC do B, 160–61, 170–71; deprived of political rights, 161; and Ação Popular, 166–67; mention of 160

professional people: and Popular Front, 16, 17; and Jacobin Left, 51; as Communists, 149–50

professions (Venezuela): and Communists, 63

Profintern: and early Communists, 11; and Alexander Losovsky, 13; in Chile, 14; in Colombia, 14; and "dual unionism," 15

proletariat. See labor

propaganda, Communist: and Mexico, 80, 81; and academic analysis, 87

Proposal Concerning the General Line of the International Communist Movement: 40

Pueblo, El: 46

Peurto Cabello, Venezuela: 65

Quadros, Jânio: and Miguel Arrais, 137–38; deprived of political rights, 161

Quintero, Rodolfo: 64

Radical Republicans (Chile): and Popular Front, 16

Radical Socialists (Chile): 16

Rádio Mayrink Veiga: 138, 139

Radovitsky, Simon: 85

railroads. See industries

Rangel, Domingo Alberto: 67

Rapallo, Treaty of: 77

Rashidov, Shasaf: 88, 89

Ravines, Eudocio: and Popular Front, 16; as Comintern agent, 37

Realidade: poll on Communism by, 157–58

Rebel Armed Forces. See FAR

rebellions. See violence

Recife, Pernambuco, Brazil: Communist strength in, 137; as headquarters of Federation of Peasant Leagues, 142–43; imprisonment of Gregório Bezerra in, 149; military tribunal in, 161

Red International of Labor Unions. See Profintern

Reis, Hércules Correia dos: as leader of CPOS, 144; as labor leader, 145–46

Reis, Mário Dinarco: receives jail sentence, 148; as PCB leader, 151–52, 179 n 6

Reis de Almeida, Neri: and violence, 151; gives information to police, 157

religious groups: and Popular Front, 16. See also Catholic Church

Remisov, Nikolai M.: 80

Remmin Ribao: and Cuba's break with China, 61

revolution. See violence

Revolutionary Committee of Kirghizia: and Pestkovsky, 77

Revolutionary Communist Party: 70

Revolution in the Revolution: 90; and Castroism, 100

Riani, Clodsmidt: as labor leader, 144–46; as head of CNTI, 183 n 86

Ribeirão Prêto, São Paulo State, Brazil: and terrorists, 176

Ribeiro, Darci: 159

Ribeiro, Evan Ramos: and Tricontinent Congress, 152; and PCB Central Committee, 179 n 6

rice: and Cuban-Chinese relations, 60, 98

Riff, Raul: 140

"Right Opposition": and internal Comintern strife, 13

Riochiquito, Colombia 47

Rio de Janeiro, Brazil: Alberto Guani in, 85; and Brizola, 138; guerrilla training centers near, 142; as headquarters of CNTI, 145–46; and Astrogildo Pereira, 148; and Marighella, 148; and PCB, 153; National Law School in, 153; and Miguel Arrais, 158; and Osneli Martineli, 158; meeting of Front of Popular Mobilization in, 167–68; Vladimir Palmeira in, 169–70; and Charles

Tricontinent Congress: and violence, 58–59; and Cuban-Chinese relations, 60; and Soviet-Uruguayan relations, 88; and Soviet-Cuban relations, 97–100, 105; and PCV, 100; and Régis Debray, 102; and OLAS, 104; and PCB, 152

Trotsky, Leon: and Popular Front, 118; assassination of, and decline of Communist strength in Mexico, 129; Posadas on, 182 n 68

Trotskyism: and CTAL, 19; in Venezuela, 31; Régis Debray on, 102; and Brazilian coup of 1964, 134

Trotskyites: on Castro and Ché Guevara, 96; Rodolfo Ghioldi on, 103; and OLAS Conference, 104; mention of, 25, 161. *See also* POLOP; PORT

Trotskyites (Brazil): and violence, 29; activities of, 143; in *Política Operária*, 146–47; PC do B on, 161; and Communist infighting, 168

Trotskyites (Chile): and Communist split, 49, 50

Trotskyites (Guatemala): and violence, 69

Trujillo, Venezuela: guerrillas in, 66

26 de Septiembre, Colombia: 47

26th of July Movement: and Jacobin Left, 52; and Soviet-Cuban relations, 95

Tupamaros: in Broad Front, 30

UBES. *See* União Brasileira dos Estudantes Secundários

UEE: 169

ULTAB: 136

UNE: and Communism, 146–47, 162, 163; on Castro, and on Alliance for Progress, 147; former leader of, blamed for invasion of Brazil, 159; and 1964 coup, 165; and PCB, 165; and Ação Popular, 165, 166, National Congresses of, 165, 167, 170, 175; and Herbert José de Sousa, 166; in Front of Popular Mobilization, 167–68; and Luís Travassos, 169; and terrorists, 175; student leaders on, 183 n 77

URD: 30

USSR: and Communism in Latin America, 9, 18–22, 31, 37–38, 71, 169, 186, 187, 188 n 1; and violence, 10, 76, 84, 109 n 24, 138, 158; and Latin America, 12, 20, 22–23, 75–76, 83, 108; and World War II, 15, 19, 75–76, 129; and Popular Front, 18, 76, 119; and Cold War, 21; and dual Communism, 21–22; and Cuba, 23, 26–27, 51, 71–72, 76, 85, 87, 108; and Jacobin Left, 16; and Uruguay, 26–27, 75, 76, 77, 82, 108; and Mexico, 26–27, 75, 76, 85, 108, 119, 129; and formation of Communist parties, 36; visits to, by Latin Americans, 37, 38, 145–46; and Communist Party of Ecuador, 46; subversive activity of, 75;

and the U.N., 75–76; and Catholic Church, 76; and urban working class, 76; and Argentina, 76, 77, 79, 85, 86; trade between Venezuela and, 76, 77, 85, 107, 188 n 1; and Brazil, 76, 79, 84, 85, 86, 108, 109 n 24, 138, 145–46, 158; and Chile, 76, 85, 86, 108; and Colombia, 76, 107; and Bolivia, 76, 108; and Peru, 76, 108; early diplomatic activity of, 76–77; and Panama, 77; and World War I, 77; and Comintern, 84; and Luis Carlos Prestes, 84, 86, 109 n 24; and Paraguay, 85; and Uruguay, 85; and Tricontinent Congress, 88; and Ecuador, 108; Pestkovsky on, 109 n 3; Lombardo Toledano in, 127; Brizola on, 139; PC do B on, 160–61; Marighella on, 173; and Costa Rica, 188 n 1; mention of, 26, 120. *See also* Cuban missile crisis; Nazi-Soviet Non-Aggression Treaty

USSR Academy of Sciences Latin-American Institute: and Sergei Mikhailov, 87; and Victor V. Vol'sky, 88

UST: 145

¿Una Linea Pequeño Burgesa en la Revolucion Chilena?: 70

União Brasileira dos Estudantes Secundários: 167–68

União dos Lavradores e Trabalhadores Agrícolas do Brasil: 136

União Estadual dos Estudantes: 169

União Metropolitana dos Estudantes: 169–70

União Sindical dos Trabalhadores: 145

Unidad: 44–45

Unión Comunista Rebelde: 50

unionism, dual: defined, 15; movement away from, 17–18

Union de Jovenes Comunistas: 46

"Union of Brazilians to Free the Nation from the Crisis, the Dictatorship, and the Neocolonialist Threat": 160

Unión para Avanzar: 68

Unión Republicana Democrática: 30

unions. *See* labor

Union to Advance: 68

Unitary Trade Union Confederation of Mexico: 125

United Front. *See* Nationalist and Democratic United Front; Popular Front

United Kingdom: and Soviet interest in Latin America, 12; trade of, with Uruguay, 87

United Nations: and USSR, 75–76; and Soviet-Uruguayan relations, 85–86; Castro on nuclear weapons in, 93; and Castro and guerrillas, 97; and Tricontinent Conference, 99

United Party of the Socialist Revolution. *See* Communist Party of Cuba; PURS

United States: Communism in ghettos of, 9; hostility to, 9–10; and Soviet–Latin-American relations, 12, 85, 92, 107, 188 n 1;

and Cuba, 23, 24, 53, 76; Latin-American policy of, 31–32, 116, 137–38; and Jacobin Left, 53; and Sino-Soviet split, 54; and Castro, 54, 61, 104–105; and China, 61; and Soviet Union during World War II, 75–76; and CPSU, 76; and Konstantin A. Oumansky, 79; and Soviet-Uruguayan relations, 86, 87; Mikhailov on, 87; and Soviet-Cuban relations, 90–91, 92; and Havana Conference of 1964, 95; invades Dominican Republic, 96; and revival of Popular Front, 97; and OLAS Conference, 104–105; and Pestkovsky, 108 n 3; and Brazil, 135, 150, 158, 160, 165, 166; and Miguel Arrais, 137–38, 158; and Brizola, 138; and Castelo Branco, 165; Ação Popular on, 166; ALN on kidnapping and, 175. *See also* anti-Americanism; Cuban missile crisis

United States citizens: Luis G. Monzón on, 124; and Brazilian terrorists, 172
United States Embassy (Mexico): size of, compared to size of Soviet embassy, 80
United States Navy: and Castro's attempts to export revolution, 24–25
Universidad Obrera. *See* Workers University
University of Minas Gerais: and Ação Popular, 165
upper class: and violence, 41
urban areas (Brazil): importance of, 29–30
urbanization: in Cuba, 23
urban-oriented Communists (Brazil): oppose rural guerrillas, 28
urban working class: and USSR, 76
Uruguay: and Comintern, 11, 12; CTAL split in, 21; and USSR, 26–27, 75, 76, 77, 82, 108; Broad Front in, 30; and violence, 40, 159–60; and Brazilian Communist Party, 86; and Prestes, 86; and Western Europe, 87; and Osvaldo Pacheco, 148; and Brizola, 158–60; Goulart in, 159; training of Brazilian guerrillas in, 159–60
Uruguayan Communist Party: and Nazi-Soviet Non-Aggression Treaty, 18
Uruguayan Embassy (Brazil): and PC do B, 160
Uzbekistan Communist Party Central Committee: and Sharaf R. Rashidov, 88

VAR-Palmares: 173
VPR: as terrorist group, 172, 177–78
Van der Weig, Jean-Marc: 170
Vanguardia Armada Revolucionária-Palmares: 173
Vanguardia Popular: and violence, 39–40
Vanguardia Popular Nacionalista: and violence, 67
Vanguardia Popular Revolucionária. *See* VPR
Vargas, Getúlio: and Prestes, 64; Arrais on death of, 137–38
Vargas, O.: on violence, 39–40

Varig Airlines: and Brazilian terrorists, 177
Vaz, Henrique de Lima: and youth, 165; and Ação Popular, 167
Vela, Gonzalo Vásquez: 123
Velasco, Juan: 45
Velázquez, Fidel: and CTM, 126–27; on petroleum workers' strike, 132
Venezuela: and U. S., 9; and Isaias Medina Angarita, 19; and USSR, 20, 76, 77, 85, 93, 94, 107, 188 n 1; dual Communism in, 21; Christian Democrats in, 23; Democratic Action Party in, 23; per capita income in, 23; result of revolution in, 26; and Nelson Rockefeller, 30; New Force in, 30–31; youth in, 42; Jacobin Left in, 52; and violence, 66, 72, 94, 95; and Havana Conference, 95; and Castro, 100; government resistance to Communism in, 131
Venezuelan Communist Party. *See* PCV
Venezuelan government: Communists in, 63, 64, 65, 68; and violence, 68
Venezuelan leftists. *See* FALN
Vera Cruz, Mexico: Alexandra M. Kollontai in, 78
"Viaje Por Suscripción Popular": 132
Videla, Gabriel Gonzales: 16
Vieira, Gilberto: 48
Vieira, Mário Alves de Sousa: as Communist leader, 139–40; receives jail sentence, 148; and violence, 151; and PCB, 151–52, 154, 157, 179 n 6; and PCBR, 169; death of, 178; Luís Carlos Prestes on, 178
Vietnam: training of Latin Americans in, 23; and Sino-Soviet split, 53–54; and Castro, 53–54, 107; "Long War" in, 66; and Secretariat of Tricontinent organization, 99; Régis Debray on, 100; and Charles Chandler, 172, 177
Vigevânia, Tulo: 143
Vilar, Lourival de Costa: 179 n 6
Villegas, Cruz: 64
violence: and China, 10; and the military, 10; and Cuba, 10, 25, 57–59; and USSR, 10, 26–27, 55, 76, 87–89, 90, 94, 106–107; and early Communists, 11; and Manuilsky, 16, 17; debate over, 19, 32; training areas for, 23; and Castro, 24–25, 29, 53, 54, 55, 72, 89–107 *passim*; rural versus urban, 25; and Cuban missile crisis, 27; and democratic left, 28; and Sino-Soviet split, 38–51 *passim*; and South African Communist Party, 39; and Paraguayan Communist Party, 39, 48; and Communism, 40–41, 186; and urban labor, 41; and Peruvian Communist Party, 44–45; and Communist Party of Ecuador, 45, 46; and Colombian Communists, 46–48; and Bolivian Communist Party, 48; and Venezuelan Communist Party, 48–49; and Jacobin Left, 53, 72; and Chilean Communist Party, 55; and Salvadorean Communist Party, 55; and

Armando Hart, 57–58; Chilean Revolutionary Communist Party on, 70; failure of, 71–72; and youth, 72; and Castro, 89–107 *passim;* and Régis Debray, 90, 100–104; and Havana Conference of 1964; 95, 96; Rodolfo Ghioldi on, 103; and OLAS, 104; and Popular Front, 117; and Marighella, 156, 176; POLOP and, 163; and Ação Popular, 166. *See also* subversive activity

violence (Brazil): disagreements over, 28, 29, 186; failure of, 29; and PC do B, 43; and leftists, 135; and Prestes, 136–37, 147–48; and land reform, 137; and Miguel Arrais, 138, 158; and Brizola, 138, 158–60; and Julião, 140–41; training for, 142–43, 159–60; and PCB, 149–57 *passim,* 169; and 1964 coup, 150; and Marighella, 155; expelled PCB leaders debate, 157; and China, 160; and "Union of Brazilians to Free the Nation from the Crisis, the Dictatorship, and the Neocolonialist Threat," 160; and POLOP, 163; and Ação Popular, 166; rural versus urban, 172

violence (Chile): advocated by Socialists, 30

violence (Colombia): support for, 46–47, 55, 95; and Tricontinent Congress, 58

violence (Cuba): and Acción Democrática, 64; and Christian Social (COPEI) Party, 64; and Movimiento de la Izquierda Revolucionaria, 64; and Venezuelan youth, 64; and Castro, 89–107 *passim;* and Soviet-Cuban relations, 92

violence (Guatemala): Havana meeting supports, 55; Tricontinent Congress, 58; and youth, 69; and Partido Guatemalteco del Trabajo, 69–70; switches from rural to urban, 69–70

violence (Haiti): Havana meeting supports, 55

violence (Honduras): Havana meeting calls for support, 55

violence (Mexico): and Pestkovsky, 78; and Mexican-Soviet relations, 78, 79, 80; opposition to, 128

violence (Paraguay): Havana meeting supports, 55

violence (Peru): and Tricontinent Congress, 58; and Castro, 69

violence (Uruguay): and Broad Front, 30

violence (Venezuela): and destruction of Communist movement, 26; and the New Force, 31; and Castro, 52, 68, 69, 100, 102–103; Havana meeting supports, 55; and Tricontinent Congress, 58; and USSR, 59, 94; and MIR, 64, 66–67; increase in, 65, 95; and PCV, 65–68 *passim,* 102–103; Norman Gall on, 66; rural versus urban, 66–67, 68; Domingo Alberto Rangel on, 67; Jesús Farías on, 67; and students, 68

Visko, Georgii S.: 82

Vol'sky, Victor V.: 88, 89

Voz Operária: and 1964 coup, 150; and 6th National Congress of PCB, 154

Voz Proletaria: on violence, 41; and Colombian Communists, 47–48

wages: and Miguel Arrais, 137–38; and urban terrorism, 173

war: Luis G. Monzón on, 123–24. *See also* violence; World War I; World War II

Warsaw Pact: and Cuba, 92–93

Washington, D. C.: and Soviet-Mexican Relations, 77; and Soviet-Uruguayan relations, 85

Wolf, Bertram D.: 78

women: in the Party of the Mexican Revolution, 117–18; organizations of, in Mexico, 122; as terrorists, 173, 177; in death of Marighella, 176

wool: and Soviet-Uruguayan relations, 86

workers. *See* labor

Workers' and Peasants' United Front of the Third International: 124

Workers University: establishment of, 128; Spanish refugees in, 129

World Federation of Trade Unions: and Benedito Cerqueira, 164

World Marxist Review: Vargas in, 39–40; on violence, 39–40, 65, 68, 96; on Bolivia, 48; and Venezuela, 65, 68; on invasion of Dominican Republic, 96; and PCV-Castro split, 102–103; Longino Becerra in, on USSR and Latin America, 108

World War I: and formation of Communist parties, 35; and USSR, 77

World War II: and USSR, 18–19, 75–76; and Soviet–Latin-American relations, 18–19, 85; and Latin-American Communism, 20; and Uruguay, 85; and decline of Communist strength in Mexico, 129

Wspomnienia Rewolucjonisty: 109 n 3

Young Communist League: and violence, 46, 47–48

youth: and violence, 41, 72; and Castroism, 42; as pro-Chinese, 42; and Jacobin Left, 51. *See also* age; students

youth (Colombia): and Communism, 42

youth (Ecuador): and control of Communist party, 45

youth (Guatemala): and violence, 69

youth (Mexico): in the Party of the Mexican Revolution, 117–18; Communists in leadership of, 122

youth (Peru): and Communism, 42

youth (Venezuela): and Communism, 42, 63–64; and Betancourt, 64; and violence, 64–65

Yugoslavia: and Mexico, 81

Zevada, Ricardo: 81

Ziller, Armando: 179 n 6

NOTES ON CONTRIBUTORS

ROBERT J. ALEXANDER is Professor of Economics at Rutgers University. He has published several hundred articles and some fourteen books, among them, *The Perón Era, The Bolivian National Revolution, Communism in Latin America*, and *Today's Latin America*. Through annual trips to the area, he has remained active in political and inter-American labor affairs.

JOHN W. F. DULLES is University Professor of Latin-American Studies at the University of Texas at Austin, and Professor of History at the University of Arizona (where he spends spring semesters). Professor Dulles is the author of *Yesterday in Mexico, Vargas of Brazil*, and *Unrest in Brazil*. His most recent book, *Brazilian Anarchists and Communists, 1900–1935*, will soon be published by the University of Texas Press. Mr. Dulles is now writing a history of the Hanna Mining Company in Brazil.

DONALD L. HERMAN, the editor, is Associate Professor of Political Science at Grand Valley State College, Allendale, Michigan, and director of the college's Latin-American Studies program. His publications have appeared in *The Western Political Quarterly, The Hispanic American Historical Review, Michigan Academician*, and *Problemas del Comunismo*. He is the author of *The Comintern in Mexico*.

MARTIN C. NEEDLER, Professor of Political Science at the University of New Mexico, is director of the university's Inter-American Studies program. He has traveled throughout Latin America and is the author of articles in various professional journals. His books include: *Latin American Politics in Perspective, Political Systems of Latin America*, and *Political Development in Latin America*.

J. GREGORY OSWALD is currently Professor of History at the University of Arizona. He is consultant to the Hispanic Foundation of the Library of Congress, and Compiler-translator of *The Soviet Image of Contemporary Latin America: A Documentary History, 1960–68* (University of Texas Press), Austin-London, 1970. He is also Co-editor of *The Soviet Union and Latin America* (Praeger Press), New York, 1970, and some of his publications have appeared in *Hispanic American Historical Review, Historia Mexicana, Latin American Research Review, Slavic Review*.